MASTER YOUR CAREER

Navigating the 12 Stages of Your Career for a Fulfilling Work Life

Gugu Khazi

TALENT INTEL PUBLISHING

Paperback ISBN: 978-1-0370-0981-5
Ebook ISBN: 978-1-0370-0982-2

Published by Talent Intel Publishing
www.thetalentintel.com/master-your-career

Contents

Foreword

I met Gugu Khazi twenty years ago when she was working in the training department at Airports Company South Africa, one of my first clients. Since then, Gugu's journey has taken her from training and development to roles at Coca-Cola as a talent and development specialist, and later as Director of Talent for EMEA at Kimberly Clark. Her passion for career development has only deepened along the way. Recently, we reconnected over dinner in Amsterdam, where she asked me to write this foreword to her new book—a pleasure and a privilege. The next day, she sent me a copy of *Master Your Career*, and I had ten uninterrupted hours to read it on my flight home.

If I had to describe this book in one word, it would be "thoughtful." Gugu introduces readers to twelve stages—or what might be considered twelve disciplines—that serve as continuous practices to shape a purposeful career. The first is defining your career identity, an essential yet often overlooked question in building a fulfilling career. Most of us approach our careers with a sense of urgency—"I need to find a job, so let's see what's out there"—and often end up falling into a role by default rather than by design.

There's a well-known saying by Lao Tzu that "the journey of a thousand miles begins with a single step," but an equally important truth lies in a lesser-known extension: A step in the wrong direction can lead to a journey of 10,000 miles. This is why that first step — understanding who you are and who you want to become — is so vital. The discipline of defining your career identity, asking yourself not just what job you want but what kind of professional you aim to be, is one of the most valuable practices you can adopt. By grounding your career in a clear sense of identity, you create a compass to guide each step forward, helping you avoid paths that may lead you away from your true goals.

A compelling metaphor Gugu uses throughout *Master Your Career* is that of a theater production. She invites us to envision our careers as a continuous unfolding play, with each decision, each role, and each chapter acting as scenes in a broader narrative. This analogy brings an intriguing perspective to the choices we make: every position, project, and conversation becomes a scene we set with intention.

In this production, we are not merely actors following a script. We are the playwright, the director, and the protagonist all at once. It encourages us to think about the arc of our career story: What's the overarching narrative? What challenges are we trying to overcome, and how do we envision the story unfolding? Each scene becomes an opportunity to shape not only the present moment but the future as well. How do we want this scene to conclude, and how will it set the stage for the next act?

What makes *Master Your Career* especially timely is Gugu's focus on career agility. In previous generations, people might make five or six significant transitions, often staying within one or two related industries. Today, we are likely to experience up to twenty significant career moves, spanning multiple industries as entire sectors evolve almost overnight. This demands adaptability and resilience, and Gugu equips readers with questions and mental models to navigate career shocks and thrive through transitions.

This book is thoughtful not only because it's filled with insights but because it actively encourages you to pause and reflect. It challenges you to ask yourself questions you may not have considered in years — or, in my case, decades. After thirty-five years in my career, I found myself wondering why I hadn't consciously developed the twelve disciplines Gugu lays out so clearly.

Master Your Career is thought-provoking in the best way possible; it prompts you to revisit your own journey with fresh eyes. Returning to Gugu's theater analogy, the book allows you to step back and watch your own career play from different vantage points, as if from various seats in the audience. It makes you wonder: if I were to rewrite parts of my story, what choices might I have made differently?

I don't regret my own career journey by any means, but there's no question that had I been more deliberate, had I paused to ask myself the questions Gugu raises here, I might have found a shorter path to where I am today. This book is a gift of perspective, and its thoughtful guidance will undoubtedly help others craft a career story with intention and clarity.

Martin Sutherland
Director: Strategy and Innovation Peopletree Group

Introduction

Congratulations! You have enormous talent to bring to this world!

I have always believed that each one of us has a set of unique talents and passions that we bring to this world. This means that all of us possess certain intrinsic potentials and capabilities. We have a yearning to express these talents and become our true selves. We achieve this through the process of individuation, self-realisation, and self-actualisation.

I also believe that we each have a primordial knowledge or preconception of our true nature, our destiny, our abilities, and our calling in life. Not only do we have a particular path to follow, but on some instinctive level, we know what that path is. Our fulfilment, happiness, and well-being are dependent on discovering this pattern and cooperating with its self-actualisation.[1]

Your career journey is one way of expressing or realising your passions, talents, and potentialities. Employment or working provides us with a stage to express our talents and passions. It is a platform where we get to share our talents with the world and fulfil our potentialities. You have your talents, passions, and strengths to bring with you. Your biggest career challenge is to connect with these talents, passions, and strengths and continuously develop, grow, and discover new ones. Your second biggest career challenge is finding a platform to express your talents; that platform is your profession, your employer, and your career.

The Changing Psychological Contract

Although employers provide a platform for us to express our talents, the psychological contract has shifted over the years. Employers now place more responsibility on us to manage our own careers, although they still recognise their role in providing resources and opportunities for growth and development. This shift is often referred to as the knowledge-based economy, where we as employees can no longer rely on employers to set the rules and provide structured career paths.[2]

Each person is now responsible for their own market value and making sound career decisions based on their personal criteria. The responsibility for managing your career has, therefore, completely shifted to you. The problem, however, is that not much has been done to equip you to take ownership of your career. While the responsibility for career management has been handed to us, many of us do not know what that involves.

We've been told to "own our careers," but we do not know how to do it. We've been empowered to take charge without being trained or equipped to navigate this complex, often overwhelming task. It's like being handed the keys to a car without being taught how to drive. This is where the disconnect happens—we understand the psychological contract has changed, and we know that we are now responsible for managing our career growth, but we don't fully understand what needs to be managed or how to manage it.

This disconnect inspired me to write this book. It stems from my observations of countless employees grappling with these challenges. I've seen people struggle with the concept of taking ownership of their careers—not because they don't want to, but because they don't fully understand what it means or how to go about it. I see it repeatedly in my coaching sessions, where frustration and disappointment arise from a perceived lack of career development opportunities.

This frustration is also evident in the common reason cited for leaving employers: a "lack of career growth." A 2022 McKinsey study found that a lack of career development and advancement was the most frequently given reason for quitting a job.[3] You can also see this in the low engagement ratings in response to questions related to career progression. The Gallup engagement survey reports that 62% of employees are disengaged at work, falling into the category of "quiet quitting," while 15% are actively disengaged, known as "loud quitting."[4] These figures highlight the gap between employers saying they provide career development opportunities and employees assuming a lack of them.

This gap is the reason I wrote *Master Your Career*—to bridge the divide between employers' calls for us to "take ownership of our careers" and the reality that many of us do not know how to manage our career journey. My goal is simple: to provide a framework that will help you identify the key areas of your career that you need to actively manage. If an employer is providing a stage for your career to unfold, what is the script you are performing on that stage? What areas of the stage do you need to manage, and what character do you play through the different acts?

Master Your Career is about taking control of your career script. Think of your career as a story, where you are the lead character and the world of work is your stage. Whether you're just starting out or have been in your career for years, you own the power to shape and direct your career narrative. This book will guide you through the stages where you write, edit, and refine your career narrative, making purposeful choices that align with your goals and aspirations.

It's also about helping you navigate the different stages of your career. Just like a play or performance has distinct acts, your career unfolds in different stages—from early stages of career identity and building your career capital to later stages of building your legacy. Each stage requires different strategies; this book will provide you with the tools to identify where you are on your journey and success strategies that will help you move forward confidently.

Master Your Career is about understanding the role you play in managing your career. If your career is a script and you are a character in it, you need to be aware of what character you are playing: are you playing a leading character or a supporting one? This book will help you identify the common character you tend to adopt when navigating your career and how it impacts your progress.

Ultimately, *Master Your Career* is about building the competencies you need to take full ownership of your career. There are specific behaviours and skills you must master to effectively manage your career. You will also have the opportunity to assess yourself against these competencies, allowing you to identify areas for improvement and focus on developing the skills you need to succeed.

Through this book, I hope you will develop the mindset, skillset, and practices you need to feel empowered in your career—much like an actor preparing for a role on stage. You'll learn to approach your career with the same strength and confidence that a lead performer brings to the spotlight, equipped with the tools not only to manage where you are today but to shape the next act of your career journey. This transformation begins when you step into the role of taking ownership of your career, as you navigate your journey in the ever-changing world of work.

The Changing World of Work

The world of work is constantly evolving, and these changes significantly impact the nature and shape of our careers and career journeys. To effectively manage our careers, it's important to understand the shifts taking place in the workplace. The main change is about *who does the work (the workforce)*. Organisations now have a broad continuum of options for finding workers, from hiring traditional full-time employees to using managed services and outsourcing, independent contractors, gig workers, and crowdsourcing.

On the positive side, this shift in the composition of the workforce offers newfound flexibility and opportunities. Non-traditional arrangements like gig work and independent contracting allow for greater autonomy and the ability to choose projects and tasks that align with our personal interests and strengths. Additionally, the availability of diverse work arrangements facilitates a better work-life balance, enabling individuals to tailor their careers to their specific needs and priorities. The expanding gig economy opens doors for entrepreneurial endeavours, enabling us to build our personal brand, explore multiple professional paths, and cultivate a versatile skill set.

However, the changing workforce landscape also brings potential challenges. The fragmentation of employment relationships can lead to a lack of stability and security for workers. Gig workers and independent contractors often face a more unpredictable income stream and limited access to benefits and the protections typically associated with traditional employment. The absence of a stable career trajectory within a single organisation has made long-term career planning and progression more complex. Competition for gig work and independent contracting opportunities may intensify as more individuals embrace non-traditional work arrangements, potentially leading to heightened pressure to secure projects and clients. Proactively managing one's career becomes paramount in this dynamic landscape.

Another major change is *how work gets done (automation)*. This transformation holds profound implications for our careers, as it introduces a multitude of new avenues for completing tasks, including the utilisation of bots and artificial intelligence. We are continually reminded that today's jobs may not exist in the future. Overall, the World Economic Forum analysis estimates that sixty-nine million jobs will be created and eighty–three million destroyed by automation. This will lead to a contraction of global labour markets of fourteen million jobs over the next five years.[5]

On the positive side, automation opens new possibilities and efficiencies in the workplace. Repetitive and mundane tasks can be automated, liberating employees to focus on higher-value and intellectually stimulating work. This shift can enhance job satisfaction and provide opportunities for skill development in areas that require creativity, critical thinking, and emotional intelligence. It will also improve productivity, streamline processes, and enhance overall organisational performance, potentially leading to increased opportunities for career growth and advancement.

However, the adoption of automation also presents challenges and potential negative consequences for workers. Jobs that can be easily automated may be at risk of becoming obsolete, displacing individuals from their current roles. For example artificial intelligence (AI) has already displaced jobs, particularly in sectors where tasks are repetitive and easily automated. For instance, manufacturing and data processing industries have seen significant reductions in human labour as machines and AI systems take over assembly line work and routine data analysis.

A study by McKinsey Global Institute found that by 2030, as many as 800 million jobs could be automated globally, with roles in transportation, customer service, and even legal work being affected.[6] These developments are reshaping the world of work by reducing the need for human intervention in tasks that can be handled more efficiently and at a lower cost by AI systems.

Looking to the future, AI is expected to further erode job opportunities in areas that require complex decision making, but not creativity or emotional intelligence. In their seminal study on the future of employment, Frey and Osborne estimate that 47 percent of total U.S. employment is at risk of automation over the next few decades, with AI taking over not only low-skill tasks but also roles in healthcare, finance, and even creative industries.[7]

However, these changes are expected to create new jobs that focus on managing and collaborating with AI, suggesting that while AI may take away certain jobs, it will also give rise to new opportunities that leverage human creativity, emotional intelligence, and the ability to adapt to technological shifts.

Another significant area of change in the world of work lies in *where work gets done—(the physical workplace itself)*. The options available for work locations are diversifying, ranging from fully-collocated offices to entirely distributed worksites. Employers face an ongoing challenge of justifying the necessity for employees to work in traditional office settings versus embracing remote work or hybrid models. This evolving landscape continues to unfold, with further changes on the horizon. Examining the positive and negative impacts of this change is essential for employees so that they can manage their careers.

On the positive side, the flexibility in work locations offers newfound autonomy and convenience for employees. Remote work or distributed work models eliminate the need for commuting, providing time and cost savings while promoting a better work-life balance. Such flexibility can enhance job satisfaction, increase productivity, and improve overall well-being. Additionally, remote work allows individuals to tap into a global talent pool, opening up opportunities for collaboration with diverse professionals worldwide.

Several studies have found that people who work from home tend to be happier and more motivated. This increase in job satisfaction often comes from spending more time at home, which helps balance work and personal life. Additionally, when colleagues offer strong support during teleworking, it can make employees feel better about their work environment.[8]

Remote working has also been linked to better job performance. When people are happier with their lives, they tend to be more productive. This means that the positive effects of working from home, like higher job satisfaction, also contribute to better work outcomes.

In short, working from home can lead to a happier, more engaged, and productive work experience. Good experiences can broaden skillsets, expand networks, and facilitate professional growth. A study conducted by Stanford University found that remote workers reported increased job satisfaction, attributing it to better work-life balance and reduced commuting stress.[9]

Additionally, remote work can lead to a sense of autonomy and flexibility, allowing employees to tailor their environments for maximum productivity. Nicholas Bloom, a leading economist at Stanford, highlights that companies adopting remote and hybrid models have seen improvements in employee retention and performance due to flexibility.

However, there are also potential negative impacts associated with this shift in workplace location. For some employees, the lack of a physical office may lead to feelings of isolation or reduced social interaction, potentially affecting their sense of belonging and team cohesion. Maintaining work-life boundaries can become more challenging, as the lines between personal and professional life blur when working from home.

Additionally, the absence of face-to-face interactions may hinder certain aspects of communication, such as non-verbal cues and spontaneous brainstorming sessions, which can impact teamwork and innovation.

The impact of the change in the physical workplace on careers is significant, reinforcing the need for individuals to adapt and proactively manage their career journey. It requires employees to develop skills related to remote collaboration, virtual communication, and self-discipline. Flexibility and adaptability become critical as individuals navigate different work environments and embrace new ways of collaboration.

Career advancement may require a shift in mindset, as traditional markers of success tied to physical office presence may need to be re-evaluated in favour of outcome-based evaluations and remote performance metrics.

Another area of change is work time reduction which has to do with *when work gets done (working hours)*. For the longest time, the familiar rhythm of a five day workweek and nine-to-five jobs has dictated our professional lives. However, the idea of a four-day workweek is gradually gaining acceptance and becoming an intriguing prospect for the future. The four-day work week gained traction as companies began exploring how to optimise employee output without overburdening workers.

Studies grounded in Frederick Herzberg's motivation-hygiene theory have demonstrated that improving quality of life through flexible work schedules can increase job satisfaction and productivity, which explains the growing popularity of the four-day week as a strategy to enhance both business outcomes and employee well-being.[10]

The potential developments in this area hold implications for employees, such as double-digit productivity and work output increase, reduced sick days and turnover of employees, higher customer satisfaction, and a marked decrease of employee stress and burnout.[11]

The idea of reducing the workweek is driven by the pursuit of improved work-life balance, enhanced employee well-being, and increased productivity during the remaining workdays. Shorter workweeks should provide individuals with additional time for personal pursuits, family commitments, and self-care, leading to a more harmonious integration of work and life.

This change holds the potential to contribute positively to the overall satisfaction and happiness of employees, allowing them to lead more fulfilling lives beyond the confines of their professional obligations.

It could also lead to shifts in how careers are structured. Employers might need to reassess workloads, distribute responsibilities more efficiently, and encourage flexible work arrangements. This could pave the way for job-sharing initiatives, where multiple employees share the duties of a single position, thus accommodating the reduced working hours while maintaining the necessary level of productivity.

Such restructuring could create opportunities for greater specialisation and collaboration within teams, allowing individuals to focus on their core strengths and contribute more effectively to organisational goals.

On the negative side, concerns may emerge regarding reduced income for employees, as working fewer hours could lead to lower overall earnings. The redistribution of workloads and responsibilities may require careful planning and effective management to ensure that employees do not face excessive work demands within compressed timeframes.

Furthermore, this might influence career progression and professional growth. A compressed workweek structure could potentially slow down the trajectory of career advancement, as reduced working hours may limit the opportunities for exposure, skill development, and networking. Employees may need to explore alternative strategies for continuous learning, staying relevant in their fields, and expanding their professional networks outside of traditional work hours.

Balancing the benefits of a shorter workweek with the need for career progression will be a vital consideration for individuals navigating the evolving world of work.

As the concept of work hours continues to evolve, it is imperative to adapt and prepare proactively for potential changes in our careers as the concept of work hours continues to develop. Embracing a shorter workweek requires individuals to cultivate a growth mindset, seeking out opportunities for personal development, honing their skills, and leveraging their strengths.

Exploring flexible work arrangements, engaging in lifelong learning, and building strong professional networks will become increasingly crucial in maintaining career momentum and seizing emerging opportunities.

All these changes bring insecurity, anxiety, and the need for workers to adapt to new skills and roles in order to remain relevant in the changing job market. The impact on careers reinforces the importance of taking ownership and actively managing our career journey.

As the nature of work evolves, we must proactively identify opportunities to upskill, reskill, and adapt to the changing demands of the job market. Embracing lifelong learning, staying abreast of technological advancements, and developing a growth mindset become imperative to remain competitive and agile in the face of automation.

Amidst these ongoing changes, the demand for new skills becomes paramount. The expectation from employers is that we must continuously improve ourselves by acquiring fresh competencies. Merely possessing qualifications and feeling competent in a specific field is no longer sufficient; it only serves as a foundation.

What holds greater importance now is *learnability*—the capacity to consistently acquire novel skills to remain pertinent to your chosen profession. While the world of work undergoes constant and unpredictable changes, it is essential to recognise that as employees, we have limited control over these transformations.

However, we possess a significant degree of control over our own careers. In fact, it has become more crucial than ever to seize the reins of our careers, adopting an intentional and deliberate approach to managing our careers.

Author's personal story

For over two decades, I've had the privilege of observing and guiding professionals across various industries and countries navigate career changes in this changing world of work. My roles as a Career Coach and HR leader have afforded me unique insights into the patterns and stages that define every career journey. I've seen firsthand how different individuals, when faced with the same career challenges, can either thrive or struggle based on the strategies they employ.

In this book, I bring insights shaped by years of hands-on experience working across diverse industries, from manufacturing and consumer goods to services and corporate sectors. Having worked within both local and international markets, I've gained first hand exposure to a wide range of career dynamics.

These experiences have allowed me to understand the complexities professionals face in different environments and industries, giving me the knowledge to help people from all walks of life manage and master their career trajectories. My background also means I've been in the trenches, working with people at various stages of their careers and guiding them through challenges similar to those you may be facing today.

Beyond my corporate background, I've spent years coaching individuals on how to build careers that align with their passions and long-term goals. My role as a business and career coach enables me to offer actionable insights that go beyond theory. I've lived through many of the career transitions, challenges, and opportunities that I now teach.

I've also shared my knowledge in my previous book *Passion to Careers*. With *Master Your Career*, I'm equipping you with practical strategies to take charge of your professional journey, blending my coaching expertise with my own personal experience navigating the evolving world of work.

Key to the lessons I have learnt is that the world of work unfolds on a grand stage, and you—the employee—are both actor and director of your career. In the world of work, you have a career script. This *script* could be one that you are actively writing, or it could be one being written for you by external forces like your employer, your environment, or even your circumstances.

You take on a character in your script. Some of us play a leading *character* in their career stories, taking bold steps to shape your career, while some take on a supporting character, allowing others to direct their career story. What character are you playing?

In every successful production, actors do not just arrive and wait for their moment to shine. They rehearse, refine their lines, and actively develop their characters. Likewise, to effectively manage your career, you need to acquire specific *career competencies* that will enable you to take ownership of your career journey.

Ultimately, this book will guide you not only to recognise the stage your career is playing on. You will learn to identify the role you tend to adopt when navigating your career. You'll learn the competencies you need to take charge and manage different stages of your career.

What sets this book apart is that it is not just an assemblage of abstract theories. While my writing draws from a thorough desktop review of existing career management theories, it is deeply rooted in the practical, real-world experience I've accumulated over the years. **The Twelve Stages** serve as a roadmap, representing different "stages" through which your career plays out from setting and navigating career identity challenges to mastering self-actualisation. These stages parallel the twelve houses in astrological psychology, where each stage is a key episode in your personal and professional growth.

The **Career archetype**s help you identify the role you tend to play in your career. By understanding these archetypes, you can recognise the patterns that either propel or hinder your progress. Lastly, the **Career Competencies** provide you with practical skills and knowledge you need to manage your career successfully. These competencies ensure that you're equipped to take ownership and thrive in a constantly evolving work environment. Together, these components offer a holistic approach to mastering your career.

What Readers Will Learn from This Book

The idea of this book came after observing a large number of employees' career journeys and observing challenges that my career coaching clients often present without being aware of the patterns and the roles they tend to play when dealing with these challenges. They might go through different experiences; however, the *challenges*, the *lessons*, and the *career practices* we discussed were similar.

I realised that the role I played in the coaching sessions was to help them become aware of what was happening in their career, the role they played in what was happening.

This sets the stage for what I now refer to as the twelve stages of career growth. Upon realising that we were each actors in this journey, I had to find an easy way to articulate the roles we each play in our career journeys, and the idea of using the archetype was the best option I could think of. This should help us know that we each play a certain role in managing our career, which results in a particular career trajectory.

Once the twelve stages were defined and the career archetypes were clear in my mind, I went about testing it through coaching over sixty individuals over a period of a year. Throughout this period, as I coached my clients, I helped them identify their career stages and the roles they are playing in each stage. I played a key role in helping them "unstick" themselves at each stage and transition to the next stage of their career.

This book is, therefore, a platform I use to share the key insights and wisdom collected over the years I have worked as a senior Human Resources Leader, all the while observing and helping people deal with career challenges. It emanates from over a thousand hours of coaching I have been doing over the years as well as the deliberate research I conducted after discovering the twelve stages of a career.

In the book, you will first learn that your career unfolds in twelve stages that are common to all of us. The stages have common characteristics: challenges we all go through. You will also learn that what makes your experiences unique is the active role you assume at the various stages of your career. You will eventually learn that the role you assume at each one shapes the progression and development of your career.

Being aware of the stage of your career and the roles you play at each one is key to building a successful career. Whether or not you are aware of it, your career is playing out in one of the twelve stages, and you are assuming a particular role at each stage. It's better to know what stage your career is at and become aware of what role you play. This is how you take ownership of your career.

It is my personal mission to cultivate that awareness and guide you in making a success of each stage.

How the Book is Structured

Master Your Career is structured to guide you through the evolving stages of your professional journey, offering practical insights at each step.

In **Section One**, we explore the **twelve stages of a career**, helping you identify which stage your career is currently in and what challenges or opportunities it presents. This understanding provides a foundation for navigating transitions and making intentional, informed decisions as your career progresses.

Section Two focuses on **career archetypes** that either support or hinder your progress. By recognising these archetypes in yourself and others, you can better understand how behaviours, mindsets, and attitudes shape your career development.

In **Section Three**, we dive into the **career competencies** you need to successfully take ownership of your career. These key skills and behaviours will empower you to manage your professional growth, overcome obstacles, and seize opportunities.

Throughout the book, I share real-world examples drawn from my experience coaching clients. To protect their privacy, names and details have been changed. These examples serve to illustrate the concepts and show how they apply in real-life scenarios, helping you relate the lessons to your own career journey.

How to Use This Book

Master Your Career is a highly interactive book. Throughout the book, you are meant to reflect, immerse yourself in the different stages, draw insights from the stories, and reflect on your personal experience, using the tools provided online. You will come to identify how the different stages have impacted your life and gain awareness of the common roles or archetypes you assume in dealing with different challenges at each of the twelve stages.

This book is not meant to be read; it is meant to be experienced. It would help to have a dedicated notebook to record your reflections and insights as you read.

At the end of each chapter, I will ask you to reflect on your personal experiences and draw some insights from your experiences and commit to an action. I ask that you connect and use your intuition throughout the book. Trust the thoughts, instincts, and insights that arise as you go through the book.

Make note of them and avoid questioning or doubting yourself. Believe that deep down, you know yourself better than others, and the book is helping you connect with what you know about yourself and your experiences.

To enhance your journey through *Master Your Career*, I invite you to explore the array of tools available on the dedicated web page on my website. These resources are designed to complement the insights shared in the book and support your career development.

Access them at *Master Your Career* website for additional guidance and practical applications: www.thetalentintel.com/master-your-career-tools.

SECTION ONE
THE TWELVE STAGES

Introduction to the Twelve Stages of Your Career Journey

Imagine your career as a theatrical production where your career script is developing and being acted in various episodes as it unfolds. In this theatre production, you take on both the director role and the actor. The workplace serves as your stage with each job, promotion, change, setback, and success contributing to your career narrative.

Much like actors navigating multiple acts and scenes, your career follows a similar trajectory. The twelve stages outlined in this book form the acts that structure your career journey, guiding you through pivotal moments of growth, challenge, and opportunity. With every stage, the backdrop shifts, reflecting the evolution of your career story, but it is up to you to take charge of the script and direct the action as it unfolds.

These twelve stages aren't simply steps to check off; they're disciplines—areas that demand thoughtful, intentional practice to truly master. Much like an actor who invests time and dedication to refine their performance, you're invited to approach each stage of your career journey with purpose and commitment. Mastering these disciplines is not about following a linear path; it's about building the skills, mindset, and resilience needed to make the most of every career experience. By treating each stage as a discipline, you empower yourself to navigate your career with a structured, focused, and committed approach, ensuring that you extract maximum growth and fulfilment along the way.

These twelve stages are based on my belief that each of us possesses unique talents, strengths, and passions. The workplace provides a platform to bring our career stories to life, similar to the stage upon which actors perform. As you experience changes and challenges at work you make decisions and take action that either progress or derail your career story.

While we may all go through the same twelve stages, your career journey and how you experience the twelve stages will be unique to you. If you consider your career journey as a continuously developing narrative, the stages represent settings where each career experience unfolds. As William Shakespeare said, *"All the world's a stage, and all the men and women are merely players; they have their exits and their entrances and one man in his lifetime plays many parts."* [12]

The different stages illustrate the progression, the challenges, and the lessons to be learnt throughout your career journey. Each stage has assignments you are meant to master where significant decisions and actions are required. The pace at which you move through these stages differs from person to person. As you progress through this book, you may find yourself reflecting on the stages you have already experienced and the challenges you have encountered. You may also identify the stage you are currently navigating.

It is essential to note that the stages are not tied to seniority. A junior person goes through the same stages as a manager might go through. This is because the stages are aligned to the universal human evolution as outlined by astrological psychology's *twelve astrological houses*. These twelve areas highlighted by each stage are the battlefield on which we fight, prove ourselves, struggle, and work. The twelve astrological houses have been used by some of the most respected thinkers in psychology and spirituality, such as Carl Jung and Caroline Myss. Jung explored the idea of archetypes and the unconscious mind through the lens of astrology, recognising the symbolic significance of the twelve houses in understanding human behaviour and personal development.[13] Similarly, Caroline Myss utilised the twelve houses in her work on the archetypal wheel to map out the spiritual journey of individuals.[14]

A common question I'm often asked is whether we go through these stages in a linear way, and the answer is no. Your career progression through these stages hinges on your background, your personality, and the persona you tend to adopt when navigating your career. The stages don't follow a strictly linear progression, but rather a continuous process of growth and unfoldment that you may go through a number of times should you struggle with mastery of each stage.[15]

In the following chapters, I detail the *characteristics of each of the stages*, and you will discover key *tasks* to focus on. Potential *challenges and common derailers* that might impede your progress are also highlighted. You will learn *effective practices* that you can adopt to navigate each of the stages successfully.

In summary, the Twelve Stages outline a structured framework designed to help you navigate the different stages your career unfolds in. It emphasises that careers are not linear but rather involve a series of interconnected stages, each with its own challenges and opportunities. I encourage you to self-reflect on personal experiences as you read through each stage.

Stage One – Your Career Identity

"I am Doctor Ntombi, call me Dr Ntombi!" insisted my two-year-old niece, her tiny voice ringing with conviction and certainty, much to everyone's amusement. We were gathered in the living room of my sister's home. The room was filled with laughter and chatter as we watched this little girl, with her oversized stethoscope and makeshift doctor's coat, confidently assert her chosen title.

What prompted this bold declaration from a toddler who was just beginning to explore the world around her? Perhaps it was the influence of watching adults in her life—those who were established in their careers—exuding confidence in their professional identities. Or maybe, even at such a tender age, she was connecting with a part of herself that was eager to define who she wanted to be. Either way, her proclamation sparked a thought in me, reminding me of how our career identities often take shape in ways we might not even realise at first.

This seemingly innocent moment ties directly to the first stage of our career journeys. The first stage is where our first career identities begins, and it begins at a very early age. In the cycle of life, this is the stage where you are defining who you are.

Overview of the Career Identity Stage

Your initial perceptions about the world of work are formulated: Stage One shapes how we see and experience the world. Because we view things in a certain way, we naturally act and make decisions based on that perception; it then plays a big role in how our career unfolds. How we perceive the world of work (our lens) will influence both the way we relate to it and what is fed back to us.

By unconsciously or consciously choosing certain interpretations of situations or people's action and behaviour (while disregarding other ways of assessing the same circumstances), we organise our experience of life according to what we have elected to see. This will colour our view of our working life; if we have on red glasses, the world of work looks red, and we will act accordingly.

Your concept of the world of work is formulated: we dream the world of work according to our initial career experiences, and then we act on that dream. For example, for those who interpret the world of work as a place where you learn and grow, their actions will be based on that notion—continuously seeking and taking advantage of opportunities to learn and grow. Similarly, for those who interpret the world of work as a place where we get used and underpaid, their actions will reflect it—trying to avoid being used at all times.

The Career Identity Stage defines our entry style to all other stages: This stage also defines the manner in which we will enter different stages of our career. Any time we experience something new in our careers, each time we embrace a new area or experience, the qualities of our first stage are evoked. Each beginning resonates with qualities experienced earlier, with new beginnings reawakening similar issues. For example, if you entered your first stage in a culture that was welcoming and caring, your expectation at each entry will be the same. However, if your entry at Stage One was characterised by fear, doubt, and concern, then your new beginnings will evoke such feelings.

Our experience in Stage One profoundly shapes the way we approach various stages of our career journey. Every time we step into a new role or venture, the echoes of our initial stage resurface, influencing our reactions and behaviours.

For instance, when transitioning to a new job, the fears and uncertainties tied to our first-stage experiences may resurface. These early-stage qualities play a significant role in shaping how we navigate and respond to the challenges and opportunities that come with each new career endeavour.

This will forever affect the way you deal with the beginnings in your career: Given the profound impact of the first stage on how you approach our careers and engage with the world of work, the characteristics of this initial stage will manifest and shape your overall professional demeanour throughout your career trajectory.

Stage One serves as a blueprint, outlining the way we step into various stages and aspects of our professional journey. It provides a framework for how we define ourselves within our chosen vocations. Much like a first impression, the qualities and attributes we cultivate during this inaugural stage continue to reverberate throughout our careers.

The characteristics of our entry into the professional realm wield a profound influence on how we engage with life itself. Our experiences in Stage One leave an indelible mark, a subtle but enduring presence, on our overall career identity. It's a foundational layer that we carry with us, shaping our approach, decisions, and interactions in the world of work.

You develop your career identity during this stage: your career identity is made up of your unique dispositions, such as attributes, beliefs, values, motives, and experiences.[16] It is developed in stages, achieving stability over time.[17] You can look at it as a structure of meanings in which you, as an individual, link your own motivation, interests, and competencies with acceptable career roles.[18]

Rather than believing that career identity is something we all have, I subscribe to the idea that you co-create your career identity within a social setting as you interact with your immediate environment. In the process of building your career and crafting your career story, your career identity emerges. Your career identity is therefore a practice ('doing identity rather than having one') of articulating, performing and negotiating identity positions as you navigate your career experiences.

The role played by your career stories in developing your career identity: The process of crafting your career identity never ends. As you continue with your career journey, you are continuously crafting your identity. You do this through the narratives and the stories you tell yourself and others about events in your world of work, the role you choose to play, and the roles you allow others to play. As human beings, we tell ourselves stories that emphasise some parts and de-emphasise other aspects to create a particular meaning and identity.[19]

Your career story helps you define who you are and how you should act within a career context. It does so by creating and providing meaning and direction and by constructing a sense of causality and continuity about your career journey.[20]

Your career identity takes the shape of the stories you tell, expressing your life themes and the way you identify yourself based on those emerging throughout your career journey. In these career stories, you are telling how the self of yesterday became the self of today and will become the self of tomorrow.[21]

The outcome is the public image you present to the world, encompassing how you portray yourself to the world, how others perceive you, and the initial impressions you leave. It involves the comprehensive manifestation of your self-perception and how that translates into your professional identity, influencing how you and your professional persona are perceived within your career.

This stage serves as a fundamental cornerstone for your career and your overall professional image, forming the basis for presenting yourself to the world, shaping others' perceptions of you, and establishing the "first" impressions you make during career transitions.[22]

The key to the development of your career identity is known as a "boundary experience" (i.e., life-altering situation or event), your response to it, the inherent challenge to your identity, and the subsequent need to develop a new career story. Imagine working in your role for several years, steadily climbing the corporate ladder; unexpectedly, you're passed over for a promotion you were certain to get. The person who got the promotion is someone younger, with a different skillset; it makes you question your entire approach to your career. This is a "boundary experience"—a life-altering event that shakes your identity to its core.

At this moment, your career identity is challenged. You're forced to reassess your strengths, weaknesses, and perhaps even your core values. You may realise that the skills you've been focusing on are no longer as relevant, or that your industry is changing in ways you hadn't anticipated. The emotional impact of this event can be profound, leading you to question your place in the company, your career path, or even your professional worth.

To move forward, you must create a new career story. This might involve learning new skills, shifting your focus, or even changing industries. At the heart of Stage One lies the inception of your career, the prospect of transforming it, or the daring shift into uncharted professional territory. It's the platform where your career and its unique identity take shape. What's distinctive about Stage One is that it's a recurring episode in your career story, revisited time and again. It's the compass you consult when grappling with questions like, "Who am I? What will I become? What are my talents?"

Every career decision, especially when things are uncertain, questions about who we are professionally arise. During these crucial moments, Stage One's career identity significance becomes clear. This initial stage not only shapes our professional journey but also influences how we handle different aspects of our careers.

Positives of the Career Identity Stage

In each stage, there are both positive and negative characteristics. This section will highlight the positive traits that guide you through navigating the stage successfully. The first and most important characteristic is *defining your career story*—what emerges from your career choices is your career story, what story you are building about yourself and your career journey? What story do you want to tell about your career today and what story do you want to tell in future? What character do you play in your story? Who are the major characters in this story? Who do you allow as characters in your stage? Where is your career story going?

Another characteristic is about *defining your career brand*: you are defining your *career image / personal brand,* who you are in the world of work, how we want to be perceived. You try to have a certain image, make good impressions, and manipulate your image and appearance.

Navigating this stage requires making key decisions about who you are, how you want others to perceive you, who you are at work, what job you can get, and where you can get yourself working. For some, this process happens on its own without any guidance. It can also be influenced by perceived available choices and options.

You might have to take any job available to survive, and that gets to define your career identity to some extent. For others, this stage can be as illustrious as involving career counsellors, completing assessments to help you gain clarity on what your talents are and receiving guidance on what careers align well with your talents and passions.

Another key characteristic of this stage is *crafting your career identity*; we revisit this stage often when experiencing change in our career journey. Every change you go through affects your career identity. This means that at each point your career identity is impacted, you revisit this stage. The process of formulating your career identity can happen consciously; it can also happen subconsciously.

This can happen at the beginning of a new career where you are still learning the ropes and how things are done. It can also be after joining a new company and learning how things are done. It can also be learning a new industry because you have decided to change and move to a new field. It is also learning to be at a new level, having transitioned from a lower level of your career to a higher level. All these elements will impact how you define or perceive your career.

Navigating the Career Identity Stage requires *exploring*. Exploring is about trying out and confirming if you are cut out for this specific job or career, at a deep personal level, it is about exploring your connection and aligning with your career identity. Have you heard someone introduce themselves and tell you, "I'm currently doing this job but I'm working towards another"?

This is normally an indicator of dissatisfaction a person has with their current career identity. I'm currently a nurse BUT doing my degree towards becoming a doctor, said one of my coachees. The BUT is always the first indicator that you are still on your journey to career self-discovery.

The discovery process *happens* when you have arrived where you wanted to take your career; you are going through the discovery of whether it is what you thought it would be. You might find yourself saying, "I thought I might like being a doctor, but I'm not sure right now." During this stage, you are trying out a job and discovering if you are invested—if it aligns with your career identity, your career brand, and your overall career aspirations.

Potential Derailers of the Career Identity Stage

The Career Identity Stage carries potential pitfalls that, if not navigated wisely, can derail your career journey. These negative traits may hinder your professional growth and should be approached with awareness and caution.

Limited self-knowledge is a prevalent negative characteristic in Stage One that can significantly impede your career progress. It involves a lack of self-awareness, where you may struggle to identify your strengths, passions, and capabilities. Without a clear self-understanding, formulating a positive and healthy professional image becomes challenging. This limited self-knowledge and self-awareness will significantly impact your career identity, leading to confusion and the formation of negative narratives about your career journey. For instance, statements like "I have had no luck in my career" or "I don't think I'm cut out for that job" reflect the consequences of poor self-knowledge, contributing to a muddled career identity.

Career confusion is also a common derailer during this stage. This involves being unable to make a career decision that sticks or continuously being on a job search. Have you heard of someone who is always going on job interviews? Once hired, they begin looking for another job they perceive to be better. This indicates someone who is trying to learn about themselves through others or the external environment.

You are learning who you are through a process of elimination. You will try every job you are given so you can confirm whether you like it or not. It can also be an indication of a continued *career identity crisis.*

Another derailer in Stage One is *the tendency to wait.* Think of someone who is permanently waiting for something before their career can take off. This is normally someone with great potential, but they are immobilised because they are waiting for something they consider significant before launching their career journey.

The wait can be about anything such as "waiting to have enough money to study something." It can also be about waiting to obtain a certain qualification. At times, it is about waiting to be ready to start something when certain conditions are in place, for example, waiting for the new leader to start before showing interest in a particular job. Once those conditions have been met, there will be another reason to wait. At the core of the waiting is the fear of committing to something in case it doesn't work out.

Key Challenges of the Career Identity Stage

Challenges that you go through during this stage have to do with your *career identity crisis:* how you want to be known in your career. You will meet up with challenges where you question whether you are geared for the career journey you are on. As a career coach, I meet up with these challenges all the time.

It all has to do with *lack of self-knowledge*: not knowing who you are, not living according to who you want to be, and building your career identity in line with your expectations of yourself. The biggest career dissatisfaction arises when there is a difference between the stories you tell about your career and how it is actually penning out. This results from the misalignment between your ideal story and actual reality.

One of the issues I have come across in career coaching is someone who had acquired a number of qualifications and was still struggling with their career story and career identity.

Their key question was, "I have all these qualifications, so how do I bring everything together into the work that I want to do." As a result, they remained unhappy in their job while having no clue what other careers or jobs to pursue. They were trying to reach their career identity through acquiring multiple qualifications; however, the result was more confusion because the qualifications were diverse and pulled the person in different directions. From this, we can learn that defining your career identity must not depend on what you can gain from outside; it must be based on your inherent strengths and talents.

Success Strategies for the Career Identity Stage

Navigating the complexities of this stage requires adopting specific practices that empowers you to overcome challenges and set a solid foundation for your professional identity. The practices outlined here enhance self-awareness, promote intentional exploration, and foster resilience in the face of uncertainties.

Cultivating self-awareness is a critical practice you need to navigate this stage *successfully*. Navigating Stage One of your career with self-awareness is akin to embarking on a journey with a detailed map of your inner landscape. Understanding your strengths, values, and passions is important to making informed decisions that resonate with your authentic self. It serves as a compass, guiding you through the myriad choices and opportunities that characterise the early stages of your career. Self-awareness acts as the foundation upon which you build your professional identity, ensuring alignment between your aspirations and the unfolding reality of your career journey.

You can cultivate self-awareness by engaging in regular mindfulness meditation. Studies, such as those conducted by Tang and his colleagues, suggest that mindfulness practices enhance self-awareness by promoting focused attention on the present moment. Meditation allows you to observe your thoughts and emotions without judgement, fostering a deeper understanding of your inner experiences and thought patterns.[23]

Keeping a reflective journal can also help enhance self-awareness. This has been proven by research conducted by Pennebaker and Chung where they show that expressive writing can lead to increased self-awareness and improved emotional well-being. By jotting down your thoughts, feelings, and experiences, you will gain insights into your values, priorities, and triggers. Regular journaling can uncover patterns in your behaviour, assisting you to develop a clearer self-concept.[24]

Last, seek feedback from various sources to gain a holistic view of yourself helpful in cultivating self-awareness. Research by Atwater and Yammarino. supports the effectiveness of 360-degree feedback in enhancing self-awareness.[25] Requesting for feedback from peers, subordinates, and supervisors provides diverse perspectives on your strengths and areas for improvement. This multi-source approach contributes to a more accurate self-perception, helping you in your professional and personal development.

Personal Mastery, coupled with a self-aware mindset, helps you connect with who you are; who you want to be; what you want with your life' and clarify your personal purpose, your vision, as well as your goals. *Personal Mastery* is the process of living and working purposefully towards a vision, in alignment with one's values and in a state of constant learning about oneself and the reality in which one exists. It is not something you do once; it is a journey that continues with you. Your career identity unfolds as you continue on your personal mastery journey.

Mastering your career story is another important practice during the Career Identity Stage. Defining and reflecting on the stories you tell about your career. Through this practice, you reflect on what stories you tell yourself about your career. What self-image does those stories project? You also discover what stories you tell others about your career and what role or character you are consistently playing in your career.

Think of the interview question, *Tell us about yourself?* This is where your story often comes out. It should not be the first time you tell your story in an interview setup. It is important to define your story outside of an interview setting. What stories are you telling about your career?

Another useful practice during this stage is nurturing *your career identity.* Your identity is continuously evolving based on your career stories you tell. Nurturing your identity means that once you have some idea of what career identity you want, you need to start working towards making it a reality. In other words, take charge in becoming who you want to be in the world of work.

In summary, the career identify stage is like the opening act of a grand theatre production. It's where the foundations of your career identity are laid, shaping how you will interact with the world of work from this point forward. Much like an actor first stepping onto a stage, your initial experiences and perceptions determine how you see yourself and how others see you. At this stage, you begin to formulate your view of the world of work, and this view acts as a lens through which you interpret every opportunity, challenge, and interaction.

A key positive of this stage is that it enables you to develop a strong sense of self-awareness and clarity about your core values, talents, and ambitions. It is a moment where your career identity takes shape, providing a roadmap for how you wish to navigate future opportunities and challenges. As you become more aware of your strengths and what motivates you, you can more effectively align your career path with those elements, creating a solid foundation for long-term growth and success.

However, this stage also has potential derailers. Your initial perceptions can become limiting if they are too narrow or overly influenced by external factors. If your early experiences lead you to adopt a negative view of the workplace—such as seeing it as hostile or full of obstacles—you may carry those limiting beliefs into future stages. This could result in a more reactive approach to your career, where fear or uncertainty overshadows your ability to seize new opportunities. Much like wearing red glasses, the colour of your perception can either enhance or obscure the reality of the world around you.

The practices to navigate this stage include cultivating a flexible mindset, being open to feedback, and remaining intentional about nurturing your career identity as you gain more experience. By continuously reassessing your perceptions and adjusting your approach, you can ensure that your career identity evolves in alignment with your goals. This stage is not a one-time occurrence; it will reappear throughout your career, especially during times of transition. It is vital to return to this foundational understanding of yourself to ensure you're making deliberate, informed choices.

Stage One Coaching Questions

What does your ultimate career identity look like—one that reflects the essence of who you truly are? Assess how closely your current path aligns with that vision. Now, what daring actions will you commit to fully embody and realise that identity?

Stage Two – Building Your Career Capital

The second stage is like a continued journey of self-discovery and personal growth. It's all about finding out what you have, both in terms of tangible stuff and the things that can't be touched. Imagine this stage as a chance to build a strong and everlasting foundation using the materials life hands you.

Here, your unique qualities start to take shape. It's not just about possessions like money and things; it's about all the resources that make you who you are. This stage helps you elaborate on your identity, strengthening that sense of "I".

Think of it as the part of your career story where you elaborate on who you are, constructing a stronger sense of "I" or your personal ego. In a world that often feels standardised, this stage helps us stand out as unique individuals. We start realising the valuable possessions critical for success in our work life, focusing on what makes us feel safe, secure, and worthwhile. Building your career capital is essentially a chapter that details what we currently have and aspire to gain on our professional journey.

The Building Your Career Capital Stage is about building your career foundation, massing all you have into career resources. These can be tangible and intangible possessions that you can use in your career lifetime. The main components of your career foundation are your personal key resources which include *who you are*:

- Your passion
- Your skills
- Your interests: the things that excite you. They may well be your most precious resource because interests drive career satisfaction.[26]

It includes *what you have* which can be knowledge, experience, personal and professional contacts. For an example, if you enjoy an extensive network of professional contacts that forms part of your career capital. Similarly, you might list deep industry experience, strong professional reputation, thought leadership in a specific field, or any publications or other intellectual property to your credit.

Overview of the Building Your Career Capital Stage

This stage is about the approach you take to amass your career capital. Your career capital brings together a range of non-financial resources that you bring to work.[27] Through the course of your career, you build and use your career capital to create positional improvements within organisations and labour markets.[28]

Other intangible resources that make up your career capital include your *self-esteem and self-worth*. Self-esteem stands as a cornerstone within the realm of intangible career capital, playing a pivotal role in shaping your professional journey. It encompasses the inherent belief in your own worth and abilities, influencing how you perceive and navigate your career. A healthy level of self-esteem provides the confidence needed to take on challenges, pursue opportunities, and assert oneself in the workplace. It acts as a guiding force, enabling you to set and achieve meaningful career goals.

Self-esteem establishes a resilient foundation in the face of setbacks and adversities, bolstering the capacity to bounce back and persevere in the pursuit of long-term career success.

Your *personal values and those of others you have observed as role models* are a foundational component of your career capital, wielding a profound influence on the direction and fulfilment of your career journey. These deeply held beliefs and principles serve as a compass—guiding decision making, shaping priorities, and influencing the choices made in the workplace. When aligned with the values of an organisation or industry, they can lead to a sense of purpose and fulfilment in your career.

Having a clear understanding of your personal values empowers you to seek out opportunities and environments that resonate with your core beliefs. Knowing what truly matters helps you find jobs and workplaces that feel right for you. When your work aligns with your values, you feel more genuine and true to yourself, which makes work more enjoyable and fulfilling. This connection between your values and work not only boosts job satisfaction but also adds meaning to your career.

Conversely, a misalignment between your personal values and the culture or practices of your employers can lead to dissatisfaction and a sense of disconnect. This misfit may hinder your professional growth and limit the potential for long-term success and fulfilment in your career.

Personal values play a crucial role when making decisions, they tend to influence choices related to career transitions, projects undertaken, and ethical dilemmas you encounter in the workplace. They serve as a moral compass, guiding you towards choices that are in harmony with your deeply held beliefs. In essence, personal values are a vital and often overlooked aspect of career capital.

Recognising and honouring your values not only contributes to a more enriching and authentic professional life, but it also plays a pivotal role in shaping the journey of your career towards greater purpose and fulfilment.

Personal attributes constitute a significant and often underestimated facet of your career capital. This includes your unique personality traits and innate characteristics, which collectively shape your professional identity. These attributes, though intangible, have immense influence over how you interact within the workplace, how we handle challenges, and cultivate relationships with colleagues and superiors.

Your unique personal attributes serve as a distinctive currency you can use on your professional journey, to set you apart and enhance your chances of success. Recognising and using the power of these attributes is key in cultivating a robust and thriving career capital.

Family background and reputation bring a substantial impact on your career capital, exerting a profound influence on your career journey. This aspect encompasses a range of intangible assets that can significantly shape opportunities and outcomes in the workplace.

For example, a distinguished family background can provide a solid foundation, offering access to valuable resources, networks, and knowledge that may not be readily available to others. This advantage can serve as a springboard for career advancement.

A family's reputation can bring a certain level of credibility and trustworthiness. A respected family name can open doors, garner respect, and establish a positive initial impression in professional settings. This can be especially beneficial in industries where trust and reputation hold paramount importance, such as law, finance, or politics.

Conversely, a well-known family name can be overwhelming; imagine if everywhere you go, you are judged based on the standards of your overly successful parents. Such overexposure can dent your confidence to try new things because of the fears of being judged against your high profile family standards.

During the second stage when you are building your career capital, the emphasis shifts *to honing and refining your skillset,* a process crucial for establishing a robust professional foundation. This stage serves as the bedrock upon which your capabilities are identified and solidified. It provides a platform for identifying the precise skills you aim to cultivate, marking a critical step in your journey to career success.

It is within this stage that comprehensive plans are devised not only to nurture existing strengths but also to expand and diversify your skill repertoire, ensuring well-rounded and adaptable skillsets that can navigate the dynamic demands of your career landscape.

It is a stage *marked by deliberate choices aimed at bolstering your position within your chosen field.* As you accumulate and develop these assets, you not only strengthen your immediate career prospects but also position yourself for long-term success, ensuring a steadfast and secure foundation towards achieving your professional aspirations.

The pivotal focus of the second stage lies in evaluating both tangible and intangible assets within your possession, laying the critical foundation for your career journey. This stage underscores the significance of your collective habits directed at amassing valuable resources that will fuel your journey toward career advancement.

Positives of the Building Your Career Capital Stage

A lot of good happens during this stage, which provides key enablers that will play a pivotal role in shaping our career successes:

1. *Elaboration of individual work identity*: this encourages a deep dive into understanding who we are as workers. It continues the introspection and self-awareness journey that began in Stage One, allowing us to identify our strengths, weaknesses, and unique qualities that set us apart in the professional sphere.

2. *Defining and developing abilities and self-worth:* this is where you not only acknowledge your abilities but actively work towards your development. This is instrumental in establishing your sense of self-worth, as you recognise the value you bring to the table.

3. *Connecting with personal contribution*: what do you have that you bring to the workplace? This stage fosters a deeper connection with your individual contributions in the workplace. It encourages you to identify the specific ways in which you can make meaningful impacts and add value to our chosen field.

4. *Clarifying career values:* you reflect on your career values, determining what truly matters to you in the professional realm. This clarity informs your decision-making process and guides you towards opportunities that align with our core beliefs.

5. *Defining career valuation and growth plans*: here, you articulate how you envision your career being valued and strategize on what you need to acquire or cultivate to enhance your professional offering. This forward-thinking approach lays the groundwork for future growth and success.

6. *Determining what we hope to gain from our career*: this prompts you to identify your aspirations and what you hope to achieve in your working life. It helps set clear goals and objectives that serve as guiding principles in your career journey.

7. *Recognising your unique identity*: through introspection, you come to realise your own distinct shape and boundaries that differentiate you from others in your career journey. Such awareness is instrumental in leveraging your individuality for success.

The career capital stage places a strong emphasis on setting a foundation for personal growth, skill acquisition, and resource accumulation. It underscores the importance of aligning our values and abilities with our chosen career path, ultimately shaping how we perceive our own worth and value in the professional world. It plays a crucial role in defining our professional worth and setting the stage for future success. However, there are potential derailers that can affect your career should this stage not be managed proactively.

Potential Derailers of Building Your Career Capital Stage

The challenges you will experience during this stage are those that force you to connect with your values, what is important to you and get you to reevaluate what is important to you at work. Most career challenges you will experience emanate from this stage. Have you ever felt unhappy at work or with your job?

Most times, you will not be able to identify a specific reason or you might not pinpoint what is causing the dissatisfaction. Sometimes the cause of such dissatisfaction and unhappiness is a compromise you are making on your important values.

If you have not reflected on your important work values, you might not be aware which value you are compromising, but you will be aware of situations or people that are the source of this unhappiness. You will then find yourself blaming others for your unhappiness.

this experience of encounter with challenges helps you learn more about what is important to you. Through this experience, you go through lessons on how you define what is important to you.

For example, over emphasis of money in your career. This creates a situation where your career is defined by how much you earn such as salary, and earnings; resulting in a pattern where you are consistently looking for and being lured by the highest paying employer. You don't get to define your career or to fulfil your personal purpose, but your career journey gets defined and follows the highest bidder. At worst, you diminish your career contribution and your talents in the quest of increasing your salary.

Another challenge that arises in this stage is the inclination to accumulate qualifications without a clear understanding of their practical application. One of my coaching clients found herself grappling with this very challenge: A qualified psychometrist, with qualification in graphic design and working toward her MBA.

Her belief was the more qualifications she acquired the better chance she will have over her colleagues for a promotion. She realised that this was not true when one of colleague was promoted over her for the job she also wanted. This often stems from a desire for the prestige associated with qualifications and certifications, rather than a genuine intention to leverage the knowledge gained.

It's imperative for us to introspect and discern how each qualification aligns with their career goals. Over emphasis on acquiring certifications can lead to a misguided pursuit of credentials over meaningful professional growth.

Another common stumbling block is the tendency to measure your career worth by comparing your achievements or qualifications with others. This external benchmarking can diminish your sense of self-worth. It's important to recognise and appreciate your own journey, rather than seeking validation through external standards set by others.

One of my coaching clients did a great job that provided her with all the experience she needed. The company she worked for was small, which meant there were not a lot of people. She had to do most of the projects on her own, which provided wonderful opportunities to learn and manage varied projects. She was unhappy, however, because she was not working for one of the blue-chip companies. The unhappiness was based on expectations from her social circle: with all the qualifications and experience she possessed, she should be working in large blue-chip companies.

Another common challenge is to downplay what you're worth. Think of someone who has good qualifications, great experience, and skills, but in a job that is lesser than what they bring. They are constantly complaining about how they are not being remunerated according to what offer. In situations like these, it is often the inability to define and articulate your worth and the value you bring that becomes the source of unhappiness.

These challenges can be a source of some of your career derailers; at the same time they serve as opportunities for growth and self-discovery. They force you to confront your values and priorities in the workplace, leading to a deeper understanding of what truly matters to you. By adopting the right career practices, you can learn to define the worth of your contributions, gaining valuable insights on what value you bring and what it is worth. Addressing challenges encountered on the second stage of your career journey paves the way for a more authentic, purpose-driven, and ultimately fulfilling professional journey.

Success Strategies for the Stage of the Building Your Career Capital

Values prioritisation: one crucial practice for navigating challenges in Stage Two is the regular review and prioritisation of your personal work values. As you progress in your career, the significance of different values may shift, making it imperative to periodically reevaluate what matters most to you in your professional life.

This practice entails not only identifying your core work values but also taking the time to reflect on how well you are currently honouring them. It's equally important to acknowledge where you may be falling short of upholding these values. Once these are identified, committing to specific actions to rectify these discrepancies is important.

This proactive approach not only fosters self-awareness but also empowers you to align your career choices with your evolving values, ultimately leading to a more fulfilling and purpose-driven professional journey. It was only after she had finished reviewing her top five work values that Mbali realised that while career growth that came in the form of a promotion to head up the integrated data analytics team, the most important value of quality time with her family was being compromised. This led to an immediate commitment to do something about it. A compromised value does not add anything to your career capital; instead, it depreciates it.

A *career capital review* is another important practice in dealing with challenges and decisions in Stage Two. This practice involves a thorough assessment of the skills, knowledge, and experience you have accumulated over the course of your career. It also entails assigning a value to these assets based on your own professional perspective.

This assessment forms the basis for determining your perceived market worth. It helps clarify what you have and what you bring to any work environment and how valuable you want it to be. To support you with this practice, I have created an easy to use career capital assessment tool. This is available online on the *Master Your Career* website (www.thetalentintel.com/master-your-career-tools).

Adopting a lifelong learning approach to your career is an easy way of continuously enhancing your career capital. This involves proactively seeking new skills and knowledge, staying adaptable and relevant in any of your chosen fields.

For example, a software developer who regularly updates their programming skills in line with emerging technologies enhances their expertise and problem-solving abilities. This continuous learning not only makes them more adept and innovative but also increases their marketability and the value of their career capital.

In summary, the Building Your Career Capital Stage is like preparing the stage for a grand theatre performance; it's where you lay the foundation for everything that comes next in your career. This phase is about actively accumulating the resources—skills, experiences, knowledge, and networks—that will propel you forward.

The key benefit of this stage is that it equips you with the tools and assets necessary to seize future opportunities and successfully tackle challenges. By investing in your career capital, you build the expertise and relationships that form the backbone of your professional journey, ensuring you're well-positioned for long-term growth and success.

However, there are potential derailers to be aware of during this stage. Focusing too narrowly on skill acquisition without considering alignment with your personal values or broader career goals can lead to dissatisfaction or burnout. Similarly, neglecting to update and refine your career capital regularly might leave you unprepared for changes in your industry or professional landscape.

In some cases, an over-reliance on a particular set of skills or experiences can prevent you from embracing new learning opportunities or adapting to shifts along your career path.

One of the key challenges of this stage is staying proactive and continuously learning. It can be easy to get comfortable with your existing skillset and career trajectory, but the most successful individuals are those who remain adaptable and open to growth. Regularly reflecting on the state of your career capital, seeking feedback, and staying aligned with your core values will help you navigate this stage effectively.

To successfully build your career capital, adopt the practice of lifelong learning and self-assessment. Regularly evaluate the skills and experiences you possess, and identify areas where you can improve or expand. Embrace new opportunities to learn, whether through formal education, on-the-job experiences, or mentorship. Stay connected with your network and actively seek out experiences that align with your long-term career vision.

In conclusion, building your career capital is an ongoing and essential process that sets the stage for your future career success. Like any great performance, the work you put in behind the scenes determines how well you'll perform when the spotlight is on you. By continuously cultivating your skills, knowledge, and connections, and aligning them with your values, you ensure that when new opportunities arise, you're fully prepared to step into the role and shine.

Stage Two Coaching Questions

What have you built as your career capital so far, and how are you actively investing in and leveraging it to create new opportunities and propel your career to the next level? What gaps do you need to address to fully align your strengths, skills, and network with your long-term career vision?

Stage Three – Managing Background Effects on Your Career

Let me introduce you to Candice and Ronald, two individuals with vastly different backgrounds that have shaped their career journeys in unique ways.

Candice was born into a family of lawyers, with her parents meeting at an Ivy League law school. Growing up in affluent neighbourhoods with excellent schools and resources, she enjoyed the benefits of her parents' education and financial stability.

Candice's smooth path through posh private schools equipped her with impeccable English and access to powerful networks her parents had cultivated over the years. This privileged background paved the way for her to secure graduate opportunities with prestigious companies, thanks to her education from top-notch schools and universities. Make no mistake; Candice still had to work hard to achieve good marks to be able to remain in her top-notch schools.

On the flip side, Ronald, was the first in his family to earn a degree. His journey was marked by hard work and determination.

Attending government schools, he had to excel academically to secure scholarships that were afforded to children from disadvantaged backgrounds. While at university, he had to balance part-time jobs to support his younger siblings and cover some of her expenses, such as buying books. Ronald gained valuable work experience from his part-time customer service roles and learnt very early to be autonomous and independent in his career.

He knew that if he were to achieve anything with his career, it was all up to him. Ronalds' English carried hints of being a second language learner; this together with his confidence often impacted how he showed up in interviews. He managed to land a good job after university by demonstrating that he already had relevant work experience gained from his part-time work while studying. His concern was how to build strong networks that would help him advance his career as an investment banker.

As both Candice and Ronald step into the world of work, their backgrounds play a significant impact on the jobs they will secure; if they do not manage these effects, they may even impact their future career progression. Candice's family connections and elite education opened doors, and her early career benefited from this. Yet as her career grows, she now faces challenges of being able to progress, based on merit.

In contrast, Ronald's journey instilled self-reliance and a strong work ethic, but he grapples with potential communication barriers, confidence and having good networks that can support his career. Managing background effects is about navigating the influence of background effects like these in your career. Background effects can serve as an advantage and disadvantage in Stage Three; you will learn how to be deliberate in managing these effects.

This stage focuses on the influence and impact our different backgrounds and our surroundings have on your career journey. It represents all the factors that your growing personality finds in your environment and the type of judgement you pass on them.[29] It also represents the adjustment or lack of adjustments you make as an individual to fit into the collective factors you encounter in the immediate work environment.

To investigate the impact of background effects on our career, researchers Hornstra and Ineke conducted a study on how our family backgrounds may impact our career journeys.[30] They used data from the German Socio-economic Panel survey, which has been collected annually since 1984.

Using this data, they tracked families and siblings across several life stages and throughout their career journeys. They assessed the extent to which siblings are similar with respect to occupational status as opposed to individuals to which they are not related. This allowed them to estimate the impact of family and community effects on their career journey.

From their findings, they concluded that the total impact of our broad measure of—direct and indirect—*family effects* in status attainment goes beyond early career stages. In fact, it only starts declining after workers have been active on the labour market for a while. This means that our *social origin* affects our career success beyond labour market entry, increasing the impact of early differences in family resources across individual lives.[31]

The research found that individuals with more *parental resources* continue to profit from those in terms of occupation as they get to later life stages, with this effect mainly via the child's education.[32] Nevertheless, the benefit of occupational success turns after the child's position on the labour market stabilises. After that, the effect of family resources stabilises in importance, and employers increasingly select, based on more direct signals, such as worker productivity or employment records, which are—at least partly—unrelated to the family of origin.[33]

This study and other studies done prior have led to a belief that our careers are influenced by aspects of our background: the resources emanating from our parents and family backgrounds.

Overview of the Managing Your Background Effects Stage

Parental resources effect on your career background

There is an argument that parents help their children throughout their careers via financial and cultural resources or social capital. The notion of accumulative advantage suggests that those with more parental capital continue to profit as they get to the later stages in life, increasing their advantage over others.

This would mean Candice with well-known highly educated parents will have an advantage over Ronald when competing for jobs throughout their careers.

This theoretical argument states that parents help their children throughout their careers by providing parental resources. Consequently, this reinforces social inequalities, as parental resources are often unequally distributed over a population, with people occupying more privileged positions having access to more desirable resources.[34]

To begin, a child's choice of a career is impacted by personal resource—abilities or characteristics that are largely inherited from parents, such as talents or strengths. From a theoretical viewpoint, such features are often perceived as appropriate within schools or the labour market.[35]

Other resources that your family background provides you can be segmented in threefold:

- **Economic:** economic capital is characterised by the financial support parents offer their children with respect to educational (e.g., tuition) or unemployment costs (e.g., financial support in times of unemployment, and the search for a new occupational position).

- **Culture** can take form in credentials, such as advanced educational degrees, but it also shows in status markers unrelated to formal education, such as cultural participation, verbal skills, and extracurricular activities.

- **Social networks**: a broad social network may be advantageous when applying for a position on the labour market.

Signalling effect on your career progression

Your family and social background assists employers with their decision making at the early stages of your career. Once individuals enter the labour market, employers will increasingly select based on actual performance, not on signals related to this background.

As a result, parental resources will lose importance when employers gain access to other performance signals.[36] Whereas **resource theories** insist that there are increasing family effects across the life-course of your career, **signalling theories** propose decreasing effects.

In fact, signalling theories propose that, when screening potential employees, employers have little information on the productivity of the individuals they hire. To solve this information problem, employers screen applicants on signals assumed to predict unobserved skills. When a potential employee has recently entered the labour market, employers' hiring decisions are based on a limited set of signals often highly associated with the employee's family background (e.g., educational level, informal references).

However, as individuals advance in their careers, employers gain access to a broader range of productivity indicators, such as job performance or employment records.[37] Signalling theories predict that, once we have entered the labour market, employers will increasingly select on actual performance, not on family or social background. Therefore, the effect of your family background on your career diminishes as you progress on your career journey.

In Candice's and Ronald's example, this means in the early career stages when they enter the world of work, Candice might have some advantage as employers will rely on her family background of well-known parents to predict employability whereas Ronald might struggle because employers could judge him, using his disadvantaged background.

Other potential background influences

There is also a belief that the occupational status of those from the same family who grew up in the same neighbourhood is influenced by **neighbourhood effects**. This influence is likely to change over the life-course, as people tend to live in their parental neighbourhood until young adulthood, but often move away and form their own families as they grow older.[38]

Sibling similarity due to neighbourhood effects will thus decrease at later life stages because siblings are likely to move to different regions and become exposed to different environments and labour market characteristics. The neighbourhood effect thus becomes less important over the life-course of a career but does not disappear (as research has shown that later neighbourhoods of siblings are more similar than those of unrelated individuals).

Sibling peer effects also have an impact on your career. As siblings generally spend a lot of time together, they influence each other in their aspirations, values, and academic behaviours.[39] This means you are more likely to be impacted or influenced by your siblings in your career choice or the opportunities available are more likely to be influenced by them.

Social origin might affect career success beyond labour market entry and potentially increases inequalities across individual lives.[40] In South Africa, there was a period where children who had attended what was known as Model C schools (well-funded schools, with parents who could afford higher fees) were preferred in the job market as compared to those who came from rural or "township schools".

Whether you choose to believe the signalling theory or the resources theory, what these two theories affirm is that when prospective employers do not have any tangible data with which to make their hiring decisions, they tend to revert to your background to predict future performance. It can be your social background, your family background, your neighbourhood, or your sibling. They will use whatever background they have access to.

Managing Your Background Effects Stage is therefore all about an awareness of the fact that your entire background can affect your career journey. At times, there is little we can do to change our backgrounds, as we are born into our respective families. However, we can be deliberate in limiting the effect by providing prospective employers with data sources they can rely on in their decision making.

Effectively communicating your career capital in a way that highlights what makes you stand out to employers or educational institutions should be your focus. The key is to shift the focus from your background to the strengths and value you bring to the table.

For example, instead of Ronald being seen just as someone who came from a poor neighbourhood and underperforming school, the focus is on the attributes and track record he's built. In doing this, you limit the impact of your past circumstances, which you largely have no control over, and you bring the focus to what you have control over: your track record, your talents, and your attributes.

An effective strategy for achieving this is by expanding your educational and qualification portfolio. By acquiring various qualifications, you provide valuable signals to employers, offering them essential data for decision making. These qualifications serve as indicators of your dedication, perseverance, and intellectual prowess, showcasing characteristics that position you as a valuable and promising candidate in the job market.

Obtaining a certificate in common systems and platforms that are often used such as Microsoft, Salesforce, Google Analytics shifts the focus of the interview with a prospective employer to "what made you decide to do this certificate".

Simultaneously, you cultivate a strong appetite for personal growth and exploration. Anything that can enhance your profile beyond the impact of family or social resources is a worthwhile asset. Acquiring relevant work experience plays a crucial role in setting you apart for the positions you aspire to. This practical exposure offers prospective employers valuable insights into your capabilities, aiding them in making informed decisions about your suitability for the role in question.

As you build your personal brand, you slowly detach yourself from some of your background effects, thus taking a step towards achieving autonomy. This involves shaping your career ideas and perspectives, seeking inspiration from diverse sources while purposefully disentangling yourself from the inherent impacts of your background.

Potential Derailers of Managing Your Background Effects Stage

If Stage Three is not managed deliberately, there is an inherent risk of placing excessive emphasis and reliance on the advantages that come with your personal background, such as your family networks and family's social standing, etc. They may offer initial advantages but could diminish in value as your career progresses.

It's important to keep in mind that positive background effects are beneficial in the early stages of our careers; however, their impact tends to wane in the later career phases. This is the time when you need to have developed your own career capital to rely on. It becomes crucial to shift the focus towards building a robust career capital rather than perpetually relying on the family's career capital.

Another potential pitfall in the stage of background effects is succumbing to self-pity regarding your background and its effects on your career. Thinking, "I won't get that job because of my family background," can impact a person's self-esteem and outlook on life, leading them to feel trapped and less capable than others with more advantages. Albert Bandura, an influential social cognitive psychologist best known for his social learning theory, suggests that individuals internalise the expectations and attitudes prevalent in their environment.[41] For someone from a disadvantaged background, this might mean absorbing the belief that they are less likely to succeed, which can lead to feelings of self-pity and helplessness when they compare themselves to those from more privileged backgrounds.

To pull yourself out of self-pity and imposter syndrome, you can adopt the practice of cognitive reframing. This involves consciously changing the way you think about your background and experiences. Instead of viewing your background as a limiting factor, you can reframe it as a source of unique strengths and resilience. For instance, recognising that overcoming challenges has made you more adaptable and resourceful can help shift your mindset from self-pity to self-empowerment.

A significant pitfall during the stage of managing background effects is over-reliance on a single source of career capital, which can hinder long-term career development. An over emphasis on one type of capital, such as networking (social capital)—while neglecting others like education (cultural capital) or relevant work experience (economic capital)—can create an imbalance that may limit career opportunities.

For example, a professional who invests heavily in networking might secure introductions and interviews but may lack the skills or qualifications to convert those opportunities into career advancement.

Research shows that a diversified approach to career capital is more sustainable. For instance, studies in career development emphasise the importance of "human capital"—skills, knowledge, and experience—in combination with social capital to enhance employability. Relying solely on one type of capital can lead to stagnation or missed opportunities.

To address this pitfall, individuals should adopt a balanced approach to career development, akin to the principles of "portfolio management" in finance, where diversification reduces risk and enhances returns. Practically, this involves setting clear career goals and regularly assessing the balance of your capital investments, ensuring you are developing not just your network but also your skills, qualifications, and practical experience.

In the next section, we will explore the specific challenges tied to these risks and discuss practical practices you can adopt to successfully mitigate them, ensuring that you continue moving forward in your career.

Key Challenges of the Managing Your Background Effects Stage

Navigating Stage Three presents its own set of tests and challenges, with the first one being "Failure to Launch." This challenge tests your ability to detach from the influences of all your background affects— social, family, or neighbourhood. It revolves around your capacity to autonomously craft your unique career identity, cultivate your personal career capital, and construct a career narrative that propels you forward on your career journey. Essentially, it's a test of your independence and the extent to which you can break free from the confines of familial or societal expectations, forging your own path.

Overemphasis on family expectations is one of the pitfalls to navigate during this stage. A person from a family that places high value on a particular profession, such as medicine or law, may feel pressured to pursue that particular career path, even if it does not align with their passions or strengths.

This can lead to career dissatisfaction and burnout. Hornstra and Maas's research highlights the enduring impact of family background on occupational status, where family expectations can shape career choices across different life stages. This influence can be particularly strong when families have a history or tradition in specific professions, leading individuals to internalise these expectations and pursue careers that may not align with their true interests. To navigate this challenge, individuals should engage in self-reflection and career counselling to identify their own passions and strengths.

Setting personal goals that align with one's values, rather than solely following family expectations, is crucial. Open communication with family members about personal career aspirations will help manage expectations and reduce pressure, allowing individuals to pursue more personally fulfilling careers.

Another potential challenge is *limited access to social capital*; if you come from a disadvantaged socioeconomic background, you may lack the network or connections that could provide career opportunities, mentorship, or guidance, making it difficult to access good jobs.

A study by Hornstra and Maas indicates that siblings from lower socioeconomic backgrounds often experience similar limitations in their career trajectories due to a lack of social capital. This reinforces the idea that social networks play a crucial role in career advancement, and those without access to such networks may struggle to achieve upward mobility.

Building social capital outside of your immediate family and community is essential. This can be achieved by seeking out mentors, joining professional organisations, and participating in networking events. Engaging in internships, volunteer work, or online communities related to your field of interest can also expand your professional network, providing the necessary support and opportunities for career advancement.

Another challenge could be internalisation of low expectations. If you grow up in an environment where low expectations are set due to socioeconomic status, you might internalise these expectations, leading to self-limiting beliefs and a lack of ambition or confidence in pursuing higher goals.

Hornstra and Maas's research suggests that the impact of family background, including socioeconomic status, can lead to internalised low expectations. This internalisation can manifest in self-limiting beliefs, where individuals from disadvantaged backgrounds may doubt their abilities to achieve higher-status occupations, perpetuating a cycle of limited career mobility.

Overcoming self-limiting beliefs requires developing a growth mindset, which involves recognising that abilities and intelligence can be developed through dedication and hard work. Techniques such as positive affirmations, setting incremental goals, and celebrating small achievements help build confidence. Surrounding yourself with positive role models and supportive peers who encourage ambition can foster a more aspirational mindset, helping you to break free from the constraints of your background.

However, by adopting specific practices, you can proactively manage these impacts and steer your career in the desired direction. The following paragraphs will delve into some of these practices, offering you tools to effectively navigate the background effects stage and ensure your career stays on track.

Success Strategies to Navigate the Managing Your Background Effects Stage

Being aware of background effects: being aware of and managing background effects is an essential aspect of navigating your career journey effectively. It is crucial to identify and understand the potential influences that your family, community, and society may have on your career path.

This involves recognising the resources, both tangible and intangible, that your family may provide, such as financial support, education, or professional connections. Evaluate whether these provide an advantage you can use in building and progressing your career. Can you use these advantages in progressing your career? Additionally, consider the cultural influences that may impact your choices and preferences in your career.

Deliberately managing the impact of background effects: this is about doing something to either make use of your positive background effects or to limit the negative impact of your background effects. Positive effects don't need managing because they often are visible on their own. It is the negative effects that you want to focus on managing; this involves building career capital to dilute the negative effects.

For example, acquiring relevant work experience to allow employers to hire you based on your track record instead of background signals.

It's a good idea to create a clear plan that outlines how you will leverage your background's advantages and mitigate any potential challenges. For instance, if you come from a family with extensive professional networks, explore ways to independently build your own connections and broaden your network. Actively seek out opportunities to gain experience, skills, and knowledge that are relevant to your chosen field, ensuring that you have concrete and objective data to showcase your capabilities to prospective employers.

This approach helps level the playing field and allows you to be evaluated based on your merit and qualifications, rather than solely on your background. This approach will also work if you come from a family with no networks; the idea is to build your own career capital that you can be evaluated on instead of relying on background signals.

Building your autonomous career: this involves taking the time to define and set short-term to immediate career goals that are aligned with your personal aspirations and ambitions. By doing so, you establish a clear direction for your professional journey that is independent of any external influences, such as family expectations or societal norms. This approach empowers you to pursue a path that resonates with your own values, interests, and long-term objectives.

To summarise, the stage of managing background effects is preoccupied with the effects of your background—be it family, community, or neighbourhood—that can either impact your career journey positively or negatively. Research shows that background effects tend to play a prominent role in the early parts of our careers but the impact might dwindles in the later stages. Mastering this stage requires you to be aware of these effects and be deliberate in managing their impact on your journey.

Stage Three requires you to be intentional in managing the influence of background effects on your career. As the story of Candice and Ronald shows, factors like parental resources, signalling effects, neighbourhood, and sibling dynamics shape the opportunities you encounter or the barriers you face. These influences often operate subtly, yet they can have long-lasting consequences on how employers perceive you.

Parental resources, such as education or financial stability, might signal to employers that you come from a privileged background, while those from under-resourced backgrounds may be perceived as lacking support or skills. Similarly, the reputation of your neighbourhood and the achievements of your siblings can influence employers' assumptions about your capabilities or work ethic, often without any direct knowledge of your professional qualifications.

The key message here is that when employers don't have tangible data about your skills and experience, they may rely on your background for employment decisions. This is why it's essential to focus on building valuable career capital, such as your work experience and track record, to provide employers with concrete evidence of your abilities.

Navigating this stage successfully requires you to be aware and understand the background affects you bring and be deliberate in using them to your advantage. Where they may pose challenges, it's about limiting their negative impact. You must be intentional in controlling the narrative around your background, ensuring it does not become a limiting factor but instead highlights your strengths.

Stage Three Coaching Questions

What past influences are still shaping your career choices today? How can you actively minimise any negative effects while amplifying the positive ones to drive your career forward with purpose and clarity?

Stage Four – Your Career Anchors

Ever experience the urge to quit your job every day, questioning how you have landed in this dissatisfying role? That nagging feeling of discontent leaves you wondering about the source of your daily work agony: the frustration you feel but can't pinpoint the cause. All you know that is each day you go to work, and it kills you inside. Have you thought about what could cause that feeling?

In Stage Four: Anchoring your Career Home, we tackle that feeling of dissatisfaction head-on, unpacking the source of your discontent and understanding why each day at work feels like a struggle. This stage is your guide to dissecting some fundamental factors that could be contributing to the emotional toll of your professional life, offering clarity and a path to a more fulfilling career.

Stage Four is sometimes known as the home and roots stage. It is like the strong foundation of a building that holds everything together. It's situated at the bottom of the wheel, and it's all about things related to home, safety, family, and how we feel. These things greatly affect whether we feel settled, comfortable, and secure in our careers. Think of it as your "career home". This is where you can retreat to your own private space whenever you need to reflect before you make big career decisions.

Overview of the Career Anchors Stage

A career anchor is an overriding concern or need that operates and constrains career decisions. It's something you will not give up if you have a choice. It's part of your self-concept, which you will not give up when it comes to career decision making. It reflects a set of needs that are at the top of your hierarchy within your self-image. These can be thought of as the values and motives that you will not give up if forced to make a choice.[42]

Your anchors become part of your career identity discussed in Stage One. Your career anchors are the evolving self-concept of what you are good at, your needs and motives, and the values that govern your work-related choices. You do not have a career anchor until you have worked for a number of years and have had relevant feedback from those experiences. But once your career anchor develops, roughly five to ten years after you start working, it becomes a stabilising force that guides and constrains your future career choices.

They provide a mechanism for understanding our perceived talents, values and motives. When developing the career anchors model, Schein chose the term "career anchors" because he believed the combination of talents, values and motives would pull us back to a specific career path, like an anchor. In his view, the primary career anchor, the one that is most important, is the one thing that you would not give up if forced to make a choice between two career moves.[43]

Most of us are not aware of our career anchors until we are forced to make choices pertaining to self-development, family, or career.

This would explain the unexplained feeling of dissatisfaction that we sometimes have with our jobs. Understanding your career anchors is one way of taking ownership of your career.

Common types of career anchors

Edgar Schein developed various categories of career anchors as part of his research to gain a deeper insight to what values and motives drive our careers. First he interviewed forty-four alumni from the MIT Sloan Schools of Master's degree program in management over a thirteen-year period. Through these interviews, he noticed common traits among the individuals he studied and sought to categorise these commonalities.

He further conducted interviews with hundreds of professionals in different fields during their early and middle stages of their careers over a thirteen-year period to assess if these categories were applicable to a broader spectrum of occupations and professions. This resulted in following eight career anchor categories:

1. Security/stability: If your career anchor is security and stability, your primary focus is on finding jobs that provide economic security and long-term stability. You're less concerned with the nature of the work itself and more with how well your employer can offer job permanence, solid benefits, and a reliable retirement plan.

The concept of "golden handcuffs"—incentives that make staying in a job more appealing—perfectly aligns with your priorities. While you may have various skills and values, nothing is more crucial than achieving a sense of security and stability in your career.

Examples include civil servants, who enjoy stable employment in government positions; educators, who often benefit from tenure and consistent contracts; and healthcare professionals, such as nurses and doctors, who typically have strong job security in a high-demand field.

Other roles in large corporations, like financial analysts or administrative managers, often offer stability through established career paths and benefits packages, appealing to those who seek long-term security in their careers.

Individuals anchored in security/stability are those who experience the most severe problems because of the shift in organisational policies from guaranteeing "employment security" to touting "employability security." This shift implies that the only thing you can really expect from your employer is the opportunity to learn and gain experience, which presumably makes you more employable in other organisations.

However, what this means internally to those that value security and stability is that the base of security and stability must shift from dependence on an organisation to dependence on yourself, which can take a while to get used to.

2. Autonomy/independence: If autonomy and independence are your career anchor, your top priority is having control over your work life. You prefer to avoid organisational routines, rules, dress codes, fixed work hours, and any other forms of regimentation. You are likely drawn to roles where you can work independently, such as a teacher, consultant, or entrepreneur.

Some organisational roles might still appeal to you, like field sales or positions in research and development, where you can maintain a level of autonomy. However, you'd likely feel dissatisfied if promoted to a higher-paying job at headquarters, where your independence is restricted. Examples include freelance writers, who choose their projects and schedules; independent consultants, who provide expertise on a contractual basis without direct supervision; and entrepreneurs, who start their own businesses and make key decisions independently. These roles often work autonomously to explore their ideas and express their creativity without constraints.

A significant challenge for those with this career anchor is deciding whether to focus on honing their unique skills—the specialised expertise that first made them valuable—or to broaden their skillset and eventually move into a management or administrative role. Balancing the desire for autonomy with the potential need to diversify your abilities can be a key consideration in your career path.

Individuals anchored in autonomy find the occupational world an easier place to navigate. The autonomy anchor is aligned, with most organisational policies promising only employability. The self-reliance that is increasingly required in managing your career is already part of the psychological makeup of this group.

In his research, Schein found that, as we age, our need for autonomy increases, leading to fantasies of opening up our own businesses, becoming consultants, working part-time, and finding other ways to reduce our dependence on any particular organisation or job.

3. Technical-functional competence: If your career anchor is technical or functional competence, your sense of identity is strongly tied to your specific talents or skills, and you're driven to apply and develop those skills at increasingly advanced levels. You're motivated to seek challenges that allow you to further your expertise within your area of specialisation.

While you might consider moving into management or administrative roles within your technical field, you would likely resist moving into general management; it would mean stepping away from using your core skills.

Examples include software developers, who specialise in programming and software engineering; data analysts, who utilise statistical tools to interpret data; and engineers, such as civil or mechanical engineers, who apply technical knowledge to design and construct systems and structures. Other roles like medical specialists, IT consultants, and research scientists also exemplify this anchor, as they rely on deep technical skills and knowledge to excel in their fields.

You seek validation primarily from others who recognise and value your expertise. If a job doesn't challenge you, you might consider leaving unless financial necessity forces you to stay. In such cases, you would likely find ways to continue practising your skills outside of work, either through side jobs or hobbies. A key risk in many organisations is that your technical skill could lead to promotions into general management roles, which you may find unfulfilling and might not excel in.

Some people discover as their careers unfold that they have a strong talent and high motivation for a particular kind of work. For example, someone who takes on an engineering job discovers that they like engineering and are very good at it; others have similar feelings about financial analysis—they discover that they have the talent for and like managing money.

Still others like data processing because they have a talent for analysing certain kinds of problems while some discover that they are good at sales or marketing. As these people move along in their careers, they further discover that if they are moved into other areas of work, they are less happy and less skilled; they begin to feel "pulled back" to the area they are competent in and like.

They build their sense of identity around the content of their work, the technical or functional area in which they are succeeding, and develop increasing skill in that area, becoming the modern version of the craftsman whose ambition is to become better and better in the craft.

4. General managerial competence: If this is your career anchor, your ultimate goal is to reach a high-level position where success is measured by the overall performance of the organisation you lead. While you recognise the importance of technical or functional skills for advancing in your career, you won't feel truly accomplished until you're in a general management role, overseeing and integrating multiple functions.

Examples include corporate executives, such as CEOs and COOs, who set strategic direction and ensure operational efficiency; operations managers, who coordinate daily activities across departments; and project managers, who lead cross-functional teams to deliver complex initiatives. These roles require strong leadership skills, a broad understanding of business functions, and the ability to integrate various aspects of an organisation to drive success.

To excel as a general manager, you come to understand that you need a mix of strong motivation, the ability to analyse and synthesise information, interpersonal skills, and emotional resilience—especially in making difficult decisions regularly without being overwhelmed by them. Your core identity and sense of achievement are closely tied to the success and growth of the organisation you manage.

Most people look up to and might want to believe that this is their anchor, because of the perceived great rewards that are presumed to go with high-level general management jobs; but increasingly, the technical/functionally anchored person recognises that the skill set and emotional makeup that is needed for such jobs is fundamentally different.

You must be highly motivated to exist in the increasingly political environment, you must have analytical and financial skills, high levels of interpersonal competence to function in teams and in negotiations, and, most important of all, you must have the emotional makeup to make highly consequential decisions with only partial information.

5. Entrepreneurial creativity: If this is your career anchor, you have always had a strong desire to create something of your own—a business, product, or service—where your success is a direct result of your creativity and effort. You likely began starting ventures even in school, and the idea of launching new enterprises is always on your mind, even if you currently hold a more traditional job.

Examples include start-up founders, who develop and launch new businesses; venture capitalists, who invest in promising startups; and product managers, who drive the development of innovative products. Consultants who help companies innovate and improve their processes also embody this anchor, as they leverage their expertise to create value and foster entrepreneurial growth within organisations.

While making a lot of money is part of your vision, it's not the primary goal; rather, it serves as a measure of how successful you are in bringing something new into the world. Your ventures are often personal extensions of yourself, which is why you might name them after yourself. You'd consider working for a company only if it allowed you to develop your own projects with full control or to retain ownership of your innovations. However, you're not inclined to be a minority shareholder or to share credit for your creations with others.

More and more people are attracted to the idea of starting their own businesses, and as the world becomes more dynamic and complex, opportunities for those with an entrepreneurial mindset will grow significantly. The demand for new products and services, especially in areas like information technology, biotechnology, and emerging technologies, will continue to rise. With the increased global mobility available today, entrepreneurs can easily move to those regions most receptive to their ideas. The ever-changing complexity of industries will place a high value on creativity, which is the core of this career anchor.

6. Service or dedication to a cause: If this is your career anchor, your career is driven by core values that you aim to fulfil through your work. These values might include:

- "making the world a better place"
- "creating a more humane work environment"
- "developing products that save lives or combat hunger," and similar ideals.

You will only stay in a job or organisation if it enables you to pursue and realise these values. Careers that fall under the "service or dedication to a cause" anchor include roles such as social workers, who advocate for vulnerable populations; non-profit managers, who lead organisations focused on social change; and educators, who strive to impact students' lives positively.

Additionally, healthcare professionals like nurses and doctors dedicate themselves to patient care, while environmental activists work to promote sustainability and protect natural resources. All these careers reflect a commitment to making a meaningful difference in society and prioritising the well-being of others.

More and more young people as well as mid-life career occupants report that they are feeling the need not only to maintain an adequate income but also to do something meaningful in a larger context. As the world becomes more conscious of large scale problems such as the environment, the growing gap between the developed and the underdeveloped world, the problems of race and religion, product safety, privacy, overpopulation, social responsibility issues around health and welfare, and new kinds of organisations and careers are being created to address these issues.

The information technology explosion has made all of the world's problems highly visible and thus drawn the attention of the more service-oriented. Research conducted by Wrzesniewski and his colleagues highlights how individuals with a strong service orientation derive a sense of meaning and purpose from their work.[44] Their study categorises work into three types: job, career, and calling.

Those with a calling, akin to Schein's dedication to a cause anchor, view their work as a fundamental aspect of their identity and often pursue careers in non-profit sectors, healthcare, education, or social work. This perspective underscores that individuals are motivated not just by financial rewards but by the impact they can make in the lives of others.

The service anchor combined with the entrepreneurial anchor is already creating new organisations devoted to recycling, privatising health care and welfare, and managing environmental problems through products that use less energy to waste management, and so on. In turn, such organisations will absorb a lot of the technologically unemployed as well as attracting some of the best and brightest of the new generations.

7. Pure challenge: If this is your anchor, you require the kind of work that will always permit you to feel that you are overcoming "impossible" barriers, meeting very difficult challenges, or winning over tough competitors. The kind of work you do is less important than the fact that it allows you to win out over opponents or problems. You tend to define situations in terms of winning and losing, and you get true satisfaction from it.

Examples of careers that typically align with this anchor include roles such as management consultants, who analyse and resolve intricate business problems; research scientists, who explore unknown territories in their fields; and software engineers, who develop innovative solutions to technical challenges.

It's more about defining your career in terms of overcoming impossible odds, solving unsolved problems, and winning out over your competitors. According to Edgar Schein, this group is growing in number, but it is not clear whether more people are entering the labour force with this predisposition or it is an adaptation to the growing challenges that the world is presenting to us.[45]

In any case, there will not be a shortage of challenges to be met, so long as this group is willing to become active learners as well since the nature of these challenges will itself evolve rapidly with technological change.

8. Lifestyle: if this is your anchor you feel that your work life and career must be integrated with other aspects of your total life: your family situation and your personal growth needs. You will therefore seek situations that allow you to make that integration even if it means some sacrifices in relation to the career. This situation comes up most clearly if you have a career involving a spouse, and the two of you need to make joint lifestyle decisions.

You will decide how each of you will balance personal and professional needs, where you will live in terms of joint job opportunities, whether and when to have children, and how to handle situations, where your organisational careers might require one or the other of you to make a career compromise. You tend to seek integrative solutions rather than letting career concerns dominate the decision .

Examples of careers aligned to this anchor include freelance writers and artists, who often choose flexible schedules to pursue their passions; wellness coaches, who emphasise healthy living; and remote tech professionals, who enjoy the freedom to work from anywhere.

Additionally, roles in hospitality, like travel consultants or yoga instructors, allow individuals to integrate their personal interests into their professional lives, fostering a harmonious blend of work and lifestyle.

How can you identify your career anchor?

Now that you are aware of the different career anchors, how can you identify yours? As you navigate your career journey, you will discover that one of these eight categories is your anchor, the thing you will not give up, but most careers also permit the fulfilling of several of the needs that underlie different anchors.

You will discover your career anchors as you are faced with key career decisions. For example, as a coach, I can fulfil my need for autonomy, security, technical/functional competence, and to be of service to others. I only discovered that my anchor was autonomy when I left corporate employment and thought I was looking for another job. I attended multiple interviews and received multiple job offers, but I could not get myself to accept not even one of those offers.

Eventually, I realised that the problem was not the job offers and the companies making the offers. The problem was me and what was important to me. I learned that we become aware of our anchors when faced with a situation that threatens what is important to our career. It can either be a job shift, a promotion, losing your job, a geographical or functional move. You don't have to wait for dilemma to discover your anchors; these are some of the ways you can narrow them down:

- Identify all the major choices you have made in your career from school life onwards, relating to jobs and career.

- Figure out what the reasons were for making those choices. Once the reasons have been identified, look for patterns in those reasons. If several patterns are revealed, suggesting that you have been able to meet multiple needs in your career thus far, it is important to project future choices and invent hypothetical situations which would force a resolution between different categories. Ask yourself: if I were to make a career decision in future, which anchor will be the most important.

- You can also use the career anchor questionnaire I have provided on the *Master Your Career* website. Use this questionnaire with a coach, mentor, or accountability partner (www.thetalentintel.com/master-your-career-tools).

In this stage, we find ourselves metaphorically in *the dressing room* of our careers, similar to returning home before embarking on a new endeavour. This sacred space serves as the platform where we retreat, pause, reflect on our anchors, and rejuvenate before stepping out into the world once more. It forms the foundation, the very essence, and the soul of our career journeys.

Just as actors retreat to their dressing rooms to prepare for the stage, we too retreat to our career homes and our roots to ensure that we are adequately equipped and mentally prepared before venturing out into the world. In this space, we metaphorically stand before mirrors adorned with lights, representing the illumination and clarity we seek as we ready ourselves for the next act along our professional journey.

This stage invites us to honour the sanctity of our inner centre, recognising it as the cornerstone in our career's narrative. It allows us to take time to reflect, recharge, and realign with our authentic purposes. In doing so, we strengthen ourselves with the necessary confidence, clarity, and conviction to face the challenges and triumphs that await us beyond the threshold of our career homes. It's crucial because it's where we tap into our inner selves to create a career that's not only successful but deeply fulfilling and aligned with our true values.

Next, we will explore the positive characteristics that make the "Anchoring Your Career" stage so effective.

Positives of the Career Anchors Stage

When everything is going well in your professional journey, this stage becomes a beacon of stability, self-awareness, and meaningful connections. At the Career Anchors Stage, you develop a strong sense of self that feels both genuine and deeply rooted in every aspect of your work.

One of the remarkable characteristics of the fourth stage is that it serves as a *foundation and a private world within you*. It becomes your inner centre of gravity, providing a sense of safety and sanctuary. In this space, you find relief from the external demands and pressures of your career. It's the place where you can be yourself, free from the need to perform or conform to societal expectations. This authenticity allows you to connect with your true self, enabling you to make decisions and choices in alignment with your values and aspirations.

Stage Four represents a home. It is a *place where you retreat to find safety, security,* and *sanctity* in the midst of life's challenges and uncertainties. Here, you feel a profound sense of belonging, not only to your career but to the world at large. It is the stage where you establish a firm foundation for your professional journey, allowing you to thrive and contribute meaningfully to your field and community. When you master these characteristics, you can experience a deep sense of fulfilment and purpose in your professional life.

Potential Derailers of the Career Anchors Stage

While this stage holds the potential for great strength and stability in your career, it is imperative to be mindful of the negative characteristics that may emerge if left unattended. A *hyper-focus on external achievements at the expense of your career anchors* can lead to a disconnect from your authentic self and, ultimately, the derailment of your career journey.

It is not uncommon for people preoccupied with careers and outer achievements in the world to be caught up with activity and external happenings that we might neglect and lose touch with the "I" that is underneath it all".

What this means is that we are overly occupied with what we are doing, seeing, a feeling that we forget about the "I" that is doing all the work. In the process, we ignore or compromise our career anchors because we are driven by external circumstances.

In some cases, this preoccupation with external achievements can result in *a loss of balance and perspective.* The relentless pursuit of success and recognition may overshadow the need for a holistic approach to your career, which encompasses professional accomplishments as well as personal fulfilment and well-being. Neglecting this balance can lead to a sense of discontentment or even a crisis of identity, as you grapple with the realisation that your career no longer aligns with your deeper sense of self.

Key Challenges of the Career Anchors Stage

During the Career Anchors Stage, the primary task is to assemble the various fragments of our career that we've gathered over time and *build them into a cohesive foundation, akin to building a career home.* This serves as a fallback—a steadfast base to return to—should our career face challenges. It's your base as you engage in the evolving nature of work, where you increasingly engage in multiple roles, with multiple employers, and sometimes even pursue multiple careers simultaneously.

Challenges experienced during this stage extend to *having lingering career regrets emanating from career decisions not aligned to your career anchors that you might have made earlier in life.*

An example is a client who came to me for coaching in a state of deep frustration. On paper, he had what many would consider a successful career, but something was gnawing at him. He felt trapped, stifled, and perpetually at odds with his job; yet he couldn't quite put his finger on why.

As we delved deeper into our sessions, it became clear that his discomfort stemmed from ignoring a fundamental part of his professional identity: his career anchor. You see, he thrived on entrepreneurial creativity and autonomy. He was the type of person who loved to innovate, make decisions, and see his ideas come to life without excessive interference.

However, in his current role, he felt like his wings were being clipped. Every time he and his team came up with a new solution, they had to submit their proposals to the innovation team for approval. This process not only slowed down the implementation of ideas but also made him feel as though the decisions that should have been his to make were being handed over to others in higher positions. The control and independence he craved were completely absent.

He was frustrated and disillusioned feeling that his potential was being smothered by layers of bureaucracy. They were wearing him down, and he felt increasingly disconnected from his work. Yet in all this frustration, he couldn't see the root of his problem. He only knew that he was unhappy, so he began to look for an escape.

When he first approached me for coaching, he was in the final stages of transitioning to a new job. He believed that a change of scenery would be the solution to his woes. But as we peeled back the layers during our coaching sessions, a startling realisation hit him— in a true "aha" moment.

The job he was preparing to move to was nearly identical to the one he was trying to escape: the same structures, the same restrictions, and the same lack of autonomy. It was a role that once again ignored his need for entrepreneurial creativity and independence, the very things that defined him and brought him joy.

He realised that he had been on the verge of making a lateral move—one that would have landed him in the same cycle of frustration, simply because he hadn't recognised his career anchors. He is not the only one, most of us navigate our careers unaware of our career anchors. We attribute our dissatisfaction to external factors or blame others for our career dissatisfaction.

Edgar Schein's work on career anchors pointed out the congruence between your career anchor and work environment that would lead to greater job satisfaction and increased organisational commitment. He also suggested that individuals in incongruent environments either leave their organisation or need to find a way to fulfil their career anchors outside of work through hobbies and other interests.[46]

Another potential stumbling block involves *resisting change and failing to adapt* to evolving professional landscapes. Clinging to your anchors and resisting to adapt in a way that impedes personal and career growth and hinders progress is common at this stage. For example, individuals anchored in general management enjoy responsibility and achievement and measure their success in terms of status, number of promotions and income.

They will be affected by the growing trend of removal of management layers in organisations leading to what is described as delayered organisations. In the last twenty years many organisations have implemented flatter organisational structures, limiting opportunity for the hierarchical progression that was provided for by traditional approach to careers. One of the impacts of removing the opportunity for this type of progression is the feeling of dissatisfaction among those employees who are holding onto their general management career anchors.[47]

Similarly, people who hold tightly to security and stability as their career anchors and resist adapting to change in the workplace will find it increasingly difficult to cope with growing job insecurity. In the past, jobs were more secure and often lasted a lifetime within a single organisation.

However, the idea of "a job for life" is now rare, meaning that most of us will need to change jobs multiple times. This reality poses challenges for those whose careers are deeply anchored in security and stability.

Understanding your career anchor is crucial for aligning your career choices with your intrinsic values, leading to greater job satisfaction and success. I examine various anchors, such as security/stability, autonomy/independence, technical-functional competence, general managerial competence, entrepreneurial creativity, and service or dedication to a cause, each reflecting different priorities and motivations that influence career decisions.

I have highlighted the importance of intentionally aligning your career with your career anchor to achieve fulfilment. I have also addressed the challenges that may arise when there is a misalignment between your career anchor and your job or organisation, such as dissatisfaction with job security or unfulfilled aspirations. The next section will focus on practices you can adopt to address these challenges and help you maintain alignment between your career and your anchors .

Success Strategies for the Career Anchors Stage

Identifying your career anchors

The first crucial practice for managing career anchoring challenges is identifying your career anchors. This process is akin to establishing a career foundation: a personal space where you can retreat and reflect before undertaking significant career changes.

This "space" isn't necessarily physical but represents a mental and emotional refuge where you can evaluate your career decisions. By identifying and reviewing your career anchors, you align your choices with what matters most to you at that moment. To assist with this, a questionnaire is provided on our web page to help you identify or reassess your career anchors effectively.

Identifying and reviewing your anchors helps you align with what is important to you at that particular moment. It is an opportunity to express your fears and seek advice and support, where you are having to make decisions that deviate from your anchors.

Having an accountability partner outside of work partner who reminds you when deviating from your career anchors, such as a mentor or career coach, can also be helpful.

Another important practice is ensuring congruence between your job, your employer organisation, and your anchors. Congruence in the context of career anchoring refers to the alignment between your career anchor, the job you hold, and the organisation you work for. Ensuring this alignment is crucial because it directly impacts various aspects of your professional life.

When there is a good fit between your personal values and motivations (your career anchor) and the characteristics of your job and employer, it leads to greater work effectiveness, job stability, and overall well-being.

This is supported by research conducted by Feldman and Bolino which found that a strong match between your career anchors and your work environment is associated with increased job effectiveness, improved psychological well-being, better work role adjustment, and reduced role conflict.[48]

Similarly, a study by Igbaria, Greenhaus, and Parasuraman that focused on General Managerial and Technical-Functional and anchors revealed that employees who experienced alignment between their job and career anchors reported higher job and career satisfaction, greater organisational commitment, and a lower intention to leave their positions. These findings support the idea that congruence between your career anchors, your job, and your employer are vital to succeed with your career.

One of the ways of ensuring congruence is testing each job and organisation you choose against your career anchors. This involves using your career anchors as a key criterion when making career decisions. For example, during job interviews, ask questions to determine if the role and organisation align with your core values and motivations.

If, like my client, you have a strong career anchor in autonomy and independence, you should inquire about the level of decision-making authority you and your team will have, especially regarding innovation and new ideas. In this case, it will be important to understand the company culture on decision making and how much freedom employees enjoy to make choices about their projects. By asking these questions, you assess whether the job and organisation will meet your needs and avoid incongruence frustrations.

To summarise, *managing your career anchors* stage is all about understanding the core values and motivations that shape your professional life. Think of your career anchor as a guiding star, helping you make choices that resonate with what truly matters to you. We explore different career anchors like security/stability, autonomy/independence, technical-functional competence, general managerial competence, entrepreneurial creativity, and service or dedication to a cause. Each of these anchors represents different priorities and drives, influencing how you choose your roles and organisations.

To ensure your career aligns with your anchor, it's essential to check that your job and employer match your core values. This means using your career anchors as a key factor when considering new opportunities. For example, if autonomy is important to you, make sure the role offers the freedom to make decisions and innovate.

When there's a strong match between your career anchor and your job, you'll experience greater job satisfaction and better performance. So, as you navigate your career, ask the right questions and evaluate job opportunities against that which matters the most to you—Your career anchors.

Stage Four Coaching Questions

What are your core career anchors, and how closely is your current career path aligned with these fundamental values? What bold actions are you willing to take to bridge the gap between where you are now and truly want to be?

Stage Five – Leveraging Your Strengths and Talents

Tom had always been the kind of person who felt deeply, who saw the world in vibrant colours and had a wellspring of creativity bubbling just beneath the surface. But somewhere along the way, he lost touch with that part of himself.

Each day, he put on a suit that felt more like armour and walked into an office that seemed to drain the life out of him. It wasn't just the monotony of the job—it was the feeling that he was living someone else's life, following a path that was never really his.

As the years went by, Tom started to feel like a stranger in his own skin. He'd look at his reflection and see a man who had traded his dreams for a steady pay check and societal approval. The talents and passions that once defined him were now locked away, gathering dust in the corners of his mind.

It was as if he were carrying a bag full of untold stories and unexpressed ideas, but every time he tried to open it, something held him back. The spark that once lit up his eyes was fading, replaced by a growing sense of frustration and emptiness.

Stage Five marks a crucial point where the focus shifts from dissatisfaction to self-discovery and professional contentment. It focuses on expressing one's talents and strengths, breaking free from the frustration of conformity. This stage isn't just about surviving in a career; it's about thriving by tapping into your unique abilities and unleashing your creativity. Throughout this chapter, I provide practical guidance and insights to help you connect with your authentic selves, transforming your career from mere survival to a fulfilling journey of self-realisation and purpose.

The fifth stage of your career is a vibrant phase characterised by self-expression, creativity, and celebration. It's a time of fertile growth, where the seeds of creation are sown. This stage governs not only artistic and dramatic expression but also the literal act of bringing new things into existence.

This marks the inception of a deep yearning to communicate and express oneself through various forms of creation, whether it be through art, innovation, or even in the literal sense of bringing new projects and ideas to life.

During this stage, there's an innate desire to test our capabilities through close encounters and experiences. We seek to gather our own unique set of experiences and truly live, experiment, and take calculated risks to witness the outcomes. Within these experiences, the true realisation of our career aspirations takes shape. The activities in this stage not only yield professional growth and accomplishment but also bring immense joy and satisfaction, reinforcing our sense of individuality and uniqueness.

This observation is confirmed by Robert Greene who emphasises that ea*ch of us is born with a profound uniqueness, encoded in our very DNA.*[49] Each one of us is a singular phenomenon in the universe, with a genetic makeup that has never before existed and will never be replicated. This exceptional individuality first manifests itself in childhood through innate inclinations.

Take Leonardo Da Vinci as an example; for him, it was his insatiable curiosity about the natural world around him, expressed through a distinctive artistry. Similarly, others may be drawn to visual patterns, foreshadowing an affinity for mathematics, or they might find themselves captivated by specific movements or spatial arrangements.

At the moment of our birth, a seed of uniqueness is sown within us, yearning to grow, transform, and ultimately blossom to its fullest potential. Our life's mission is to nurture this seed and articulate our individuality through our endeavours. Maintaining a strong connection to this vital life force increases the likelihood of fulfilling what Robert Green refers to as our **Life Task** and attaining mastery.

However, this force can be weakened by the influence of a powerful factor in our lives: the *societal pressure to conform*. This pressure may emanate from well-meaning parents steering us towards a career path deemed secure and lucrative. If these counterforces become formidable, they can destroy our connection to our true selves, causing our inclinations and desires to mirror those of others.[50]

This can lead us down a perilous path, resulting in a career choice that is fundamentally mismatched to our authentic selves. In this case, our passion and enthusiasm will gradually wane, resulting in a decline in the quality of our work. We begin to seek fulfilment and pleasure outside of our professional endeavours. As our engagement with our career diminishes, we fail to stay attuned to industry shifts, inevitably falling behind the curve and paying the price for our complacency.

When faced with decisions, we flounder, relying on the choices of others, as we search for an internal compass to guide us. In doing so, we destroy our connection to the destiny imprinted upon us at birth. If you have been ignoring your calling towards your life task, fear not. The journey towards mastering our **Life's Task** can begin at any point in life, for the dormant force within us remains ever-present and ready to be reawakened.

Overview of the Stage of Leveraging Your Strengths and Talents

Stage Five is characterised by the urge to expand and radiate outwards, much like the sun.[51] It deals with our *innate longing to be acknowledged for our individual uniqueness and special qualities.* This desire to charm and impress others with our distinct worth and value is deeply rooted in our early experiences.

During this stage, two dominant principles come to the forefront. Firstly, *there's a strong desire to be liked and appreciated for our specialness and uniqueness.* This desire is a fundamental aspect of our human nature, reflecting a need for recognition and acceptance that motivates us in our pursuit of personal and professional fulfilment. This is where our need to be acknowledged for ideas we contribute at work comes from. Think about how angry we get when someone takes credit for our work.

Secondly, *there's a profound drive to create from within ourselves.* This creative impulse emerges as a natural expression of our inner selves, reflecting our unique perspectives, talents, and passions.[52] Think of how dissatisfied we get if we work in an environment where our creativity is stifled. Where you are not allowed to bring your ideas. This often becomes a big source of dissatisfaction with your job.

However, our innate drive for recognition is often countered by the pressures to conform to societal norms and incentives for meeting expectations. This can lead to a *suppression of our authentic selves as we strive to fit into prescribed moulds.* You become an "adapted child" as your individuality is stifled. Recognising and reclaiming our uniqueness becomes a crucial aspect of navigating the fifth stage, allowing you to authentically express yourself.

Stage Five also provides a powerful *platform for creative expression and self-empowerment.* It's a period where we unleash our *unique identity,* tapping into our inner talents. Through this *creative outpouring,* we generate stunning works of art, whether in our professional pursuits or personal endeavours. This is primarily driven by an inherent sense of joy and pride in creation, aligning with the very nature of our authentic selves.

This stage revolves around our innate *desire to express oneself creatively.* The yearning to generate something novel and unique that can be attributed to our career. Whether it's a ground-breaking idea, an innovative solution, or a work of art, this creative impulse fuels our drive to contribute something distinctive to our field.

Additionally, Stage Five invites us to embrace recreation and *rediscover our inner child.* Acts of pleasure, leisure, and activities that reinforce our lively spirit find a home here. It's a phase where we learn to strike a balance between the demands of work and the importance of play in our career. Recognising the significance of both work and leisure enables us to maintain a harmonious and fulfilling professional life.

Stage Five encourages us *to take calculated risks and step out of our comfort zone to try out our unique talents.* This is a pivotal phase where we use our talents, strengths, and passions to distinguish ourselves from others and cultivate a sense of uniqueness or specialness. It requires courage, self-belief, and the willingness to see projects through to fruition. The act of taking risks becomes a means of gathering experiences, fully living, testing our capabilities, and embracing the unpredictability that comes with pursuing our passions and aspirations. It's a transformative process that leads to personal and professional growth, allowing us to step into our full potential.

Identifying your talents

This is the stage where we first identify our innate talents. According to Markus Buckingham your talent is your naturally recurring patterns of thought, feeling, or behaviours that can be productively applied.[53] Our talents feel so natural that they seem to be common sense. We tend to downplay them thinking: Doesn't everyone see the world as I do? Doesn't everyone feel a sense of impatience to get this project started? Doesn't everyone want to avoid conflict and find common ground? Can't everyone see the obstacles lying in wait if we proceed down this path?

François Gagné, a Canadian psychologist and researcher renowned for his work in the field of gifted education and talent development, confirms that when you are talented in something, you have the ability to perform an activity to a degree that places your achievement within at least the upper ten percent of peers who are active in that field.[54] Talent implies the presence of well above average natural abilities. You cannot be talented without first being gifted.

However, it is possible for well-above-average natural abilities to remain simply as gifts and not become translated into talents; think of the well-known phenomenon of academic underachievement among intellectually-gifted children.

If you are talented in a particular field, you will have an ability above others, and you don't need to try hard to use it. You will excel with ease and grace. You have a certain aura in your ability that others wish to emulate and from which others draw inspiration."[55]

Buckingham introduced a tool to help you identify your dominant talents; it involves a process of self-observation: engaging in various activities, noticing how quickly you grasp them, how you effortlessly skip steps in the learning process and even add your own unique twists. Pay attention to whether you become so absorbed in the activity that you lose track of time. Through this self-exploration, your dominant talents will gradually reveal themselves, providing the foundation for you to refine them into potent strengths.

This always has a way of showing up at work; for example, you become the go-to person for a particular activity. It might even be something that has nothing to do with your job. An example is you become the Master of Ceremonies each time there are important work functions. You become the go-to person for people experiencing system or technical issues.

In this stage of showcasing your talent, the focus is on turning your innate talents into strengths. Developing a strength in any activity hinges on possessing specific natural talents. A strength refers to "consistent near perfect performance in an activity."[56]

Turning your innate talents into strengths involves acquiring *factual knowledge* and *experiential knowledge*. It involves acquiring *skills* that brings structure to your experiential knowledge. In acquiring a skill, you learn to formalise your accumulated knowledge to a sequence of steps that if followed will lead to acceptable performance. A skill enables you to avoid trial and error when performing an activity. By learning a skill, you get better at doing something. However, having a skill in something does not cover your lack of talent in that specific area.

While it's possible to *build a strength with knowledge and skill in any area*, it's impossible to do so without the innate talent for it. Therefore, the key to building your strengths lies in identifying your dominant talents and then honing your talents with the right knowledge and skills.

Unfortunately, some of us underestimate the true essence of our talents and may not even be aware of our unique talents. There's a common misconception that with enough practice, almost anything can be learned. This leads some to accumulate a vast array of knowledge and skills in hopes of bettering themselves in a general sense. However, this approach often falls short of leveraging their true talents.

To fully capitalise on your strengths, it's essential to ask yourself what your specific strengths are, and how you can use them effectively. Identify the powerful combinations that set you apart from others. Look inward and pinpoint your strongest traits and then reinforce them through dedicated practice and continuous learning. Seek out or create a role that allows you to apply these strengths on a daily basis. By aligning your professional life with your unique strengths, you'll find yourself becoming more productive, fulfilled, and ultimately, more successful.

When you study the careers of successful individuals, a common thread emerges—the ability to recognise and harness their strengths, structuring their lives in a way that allows these strengths to flourish. This process involves identifying recurring patterns of behaviour and then cultivating these patterns into genuine and productive strengths, ultimately propelling your career to new heights.

The truth is that we each have specific areas where we consistently stand out, can do things, understand things, and learn things better and faster than other; this is our strength zone. When we find ourselves in this zone, we are magnificent, self-assured, and flushed with success.[57]

How you use or misuse your talent at work

Each employer has their own definition of what they regard as talent. The definition tends to be subjective and often tailored to fit their unique organisational context. For instance, at Gordon Ramsay Holdings, talent is synonymous with the creative flair exhibited by chefs. At Google, talented individuals are referred to as "Googlers", are characterised by qualities such as confidence, innovative thinking, and are known for challenging norms. PricewaterhouseCoopers, on the other hand, identifies talent as individuals possessing attributes like drive, applied intelligence, and a willingness to take on challenges, regardless of their role or function within the organisation.

Recognising that each company will have unique talents that they value more than others is imperative for your career journey because if you possess talents that are not a priority to a specific organisation you will not be regarded as talent. It does not mean you don't have any talents. Depending on how an organisation defines talent, you may find yourself in a pool of recognised "top talents" or, conversely, in a group that may not be perceived as highly talented.

This distinction is inherently tied to the nature of the industry and specific work conducted by the organisation. As such, understanding your talents and strengths and aligning with prospective employer's definition of talent is crucial for your success and career advancement. You want to align yourself with organisations that value your strengths and talents .

Positive of the Stage of Leveraging Your Strengths and Talents

This area of Stage Five is characterised by a deep-seated desire to be *recognised and appreciated for our individual uniqueness and special qualities*. It's a fundamental aspect of human nature that remains deeply embedded, driving us to seek acknowledgement for our distinctiveness.

Identifying your unique talents, strengths, and passions is one of the great characteristics of this stage. Connecting with who you are and the unique characteristics that you bring is a good focus areas of this stage.

Generativity is a key characteristic of Stage Five. This term encapsulates our capacity to produce and create, which becomes a vital expression of our inner selves. The ability to bring forth something unique and meaningful is a powerful force that propels us forward in our career journey. It signifies a deeper level of contribution and impact, as we actively engage in the act of creation—be it in our professional endeavours or in other aspects of our lives.[58]

Experimentation, taking risks, being open to try out new things so as to change your career trajectory. Openness to try out new things allows you to experiment with different areas and discover your talents and strengths. It would be difficult to know what your innate talents are without any experimentation and having to try different things.

Potential Derailers of the Stage of Leveraging Your Strengths and Talents

Despite this inherent drive to be celebrated for our distinctive qualities, our work environments and culture often encourage and incentivize conformity and meeting work expectations. This can lead to a *suppression of our authentic selves, as we strive to fit into prescribed moulds.*

On the other hand, the *overuse of creativity* leads to the tendency to be forever creating new things without seeing them to fruition or completion. Think of someone who always comes up with brilliant ideas and gets started with the creation process, and no one ever knows how it opens out because in the middle of the projects, they grow excited by something new.

Taking risks is also another great characteristic of this stage; however, an overuse of risk taking might lead to negative consequences and negative impact on your career.

An over emphasis on having fun and leisure and the overuse of the child archetype might create a personal brand of someone who is playful, cannot be relied upon and taken seriously. Such perceptions will impact what career opportunities are available to you. If you are perceived as childish, playful, and never serious about anything, it is unlikely that you will be trusted with more responsible jobs and projects. This in turn, can be limiting to your career.

Key Challenges of the Stage of Leveraging Your Strengths and Talents

Are you suppressing your unique characteristics that make you unique? One of the challenges that individuals may encounter during this stage is the temptation to suppress the unique characteristics that set you apart. In an effort to conform to societal or organisational norms, there can be a tendency to downplay or even hide the very traits that make them special. This could stem from a fear of standing out too much or concerns about being misunderstood or undervalued.

However, succumbing to pressure can stifle creativity, limit innovation, and ultimately hinder personal and professional growth. It is crucial to recognise the value of your uniqueness and find ways to integrate it into your career journey, rather than suppressing it. Embracing and celebrating what makes you distinct can lead to greater fulfilment and success in the long run.

Are you allowing external forces to dictate what your talents and strengths are? Another challenge that may arise in this stage is the inclination to follow popular opinion or conform to widely accepted notions of talents and strengths. Allowing external forces, whether societal norms or industry trends, to dictate what is deemed valuable in terms of skills and abilities can lead individuals to neglect their true, unique talents.

For example, there is a growing trend of young people who see themselves as social media influencers. While most young people might try this out, some will soon realise that they do not have innate talents or strengths in this area.

Going with such trends can result in a disconnect between your authentic strengths and the perceived expectations of others. It's essential to resist this inclination and instead, delve deep into introspection to discern what truly sets you apart. In doing so, you can ensure that you are tapping into your genuine talents, rather than adhering to externally imposed definitions of what constitutes strengths in your respective field. This self-awareness and conviction in your abilities is key to achieving genuine mastery and success in your career.

Are you trying to build strengths that have nothing to do with your talents and focusing on addressing weakness instead of developing your strengths? A prevalent challenge encountered during this stage is the tendency to divert energy towards building strengths that are unrelated to your innate talents. Individuals may become fixated on trying to excel in areas that do not align with their natural inclinations. This can lead to investing lots of effort and diluting your potential impact.

Additionally, there may be a tendency to overly focus on addressing weaknesses rather than leveraging and refining your existing strengths. While it is important to address our areas of improvement, the primary emphasis should be on cultivating and harnessing your talents that are already present.

By channelling efforts towards areas of genuine talents, you can maximise their impact, achieving a level of mastery that is rooted in authenticity and genuine passion. This practice not only leads to greater career satisfaction but also fosters a more meaningful and impactful professional journey.

Success Strategies for the Stage of Leveraging Your Strengths and Talents

During the stage of expressing your talents, certain practices will help you connect with your true talents, strengths, and passions; maximising them are crucial.

Are you identifying your innate talents and turning them to strength? A pivotal practice is the identification and clarification of your innate talents, followed by the deliberate process of transforming them into strengths through knowledge and skill-building. This practice is fundamental for achieving true mastery and fulfilment in your chosen field.

This starts with thorough examination of your natural inclinations, recurring patterns of thoughts, feelings, and behaviours. These are the tell-tale signs of your inherent talents. By recognising and acknowledging these unique attributes, you lay the groundwork for harnessing them to their fullest potential.

Once you have identified your innate talents, the next step is to embark on a journey of continuous learning and skill development. This involves seeking out relevant knowledge and honing the skills that complement your natural strengths. This process not only enhances your existing talents but also equips you with the tools necessary to amplify them further.

Do you embrace your journey towards mastery? To master a field, you must love the subject and feel a profound connection to it. The key to mastery is choosing places of work and jobs that offer the greatest possibilities for learning and practising, avoiding choosing learning paths that are easy and comfortable. This process never ends; you must adopt a mindset that is open to continuously discovering and learning new ways of practising your talents.

Are you taking responsibility to nurture your unique strengths and talents? It is your responsibility to nurture and develop your unique strengths and talents. It's not the responsibility of your employer to develop your strengths; yet we leave this important task to them. Our employers will only invest in developing talents and strengths they need.

It only makes business sense to build talents that will add value to the business. Development opportunities provided by most employers are geared to building and growing talents, strengths and skills that they need to meet "the job requirements," or the business requirements." This means if your talents do not match what they are looking for, you will focus on developing strengths and skills that are not connected to your innate talents.

Organisations will identify, nurture, and develop the talents they need; everything else is irrelevant. This is the nature of business focused career frameworks.

Do you try to match your talents to the right organisations? Matching your talents and strengths to the right organisations can significantly impact our career journeys. It's imperative to seek out employers who not only recognise but also appreciate the unique skills and abilities you bring to the table. When your talents are valued, they are more likely to be nurtured and cultivated, leading to professional growth and fulfilment.

Tomas suggests looking at talent as "personality in the right place"– meaning when your attributes are matched to the right task, context or environment, they will represent important weapons for you, as well as crucial performance drivers for the organisation.[59]

Conversely, if there is a poor match, you will be at best, irrelevant and at worst counterproductive. Your natural strengths and talents may be an asset to certain jobs and companies but not others. Make it your mission to know which employers are suited for your strengths and talents.

In summary, Stage Five of your career journey focuses on connecting with your talents, strengths, and passions. This stage is critical because it is where you allow your natural inclinations to shine and invest time and energy into nurturing them. Much like an artist honing their craft, this stage is about honing your innate abilities, developing them further, and applying them meaningfully in your career.

The positives of this stage are that it encourages you to work from your strengths, which can lead to greater fulfilment, creativity, and success. When you align your career with your talents, you feel more engaged and motivated, and you are also more likely to excel and stand out.

However, there are potential derailers to be mindful of. One of the key risks is falling into environments or roles where your talents are stifled or you feel compelled to conform to norms that don't allow you to express your natural abilities. When this happens, you may find yourself disengaged, frustrated, or underperforming because your true strengths are not being utilised.

Another challenge is being unaware of your own talents or allowing external pressures to drive you into roles that don't align with your passion or natural abilities. If you aren't mindful, you can end up in a role that requires skills you may have competence in but don't find joy or fulfilment in.

To navigate this stage effectively, it's important to make time for self-reflection and identify your natural talents and strengths. Seek feedback from those around you to gain insight into what you do well and what energises you. Another useful practice is deliberately placing yourself in environments and roles that value and leverage your unique strengths. Avoid spaces or organisations that encourage conformity over creativity, as these may suppress your talents.

Lastly, continually invest in nurturing and developing your strengths towards mastery—whether through additional learning, mentorship, or experiences—so that you are constantly growing in the direction of your natural abilities.

By being intentional about your career choices and ensuring alignment between your talents and your work, you can build a fulfilling career that plays to your strengths while allowing you to make a meaningful impact in your field.

Stage Five Coaching Questions

What unique talents and strengths are you currently showcasing in your role, and which ones are waiting to be unleashed? How might embracing those hidden strengths transform your career?

Stage Six – Bringing Your Whole Self to Work

I knew something had to change the moment I realised I'd lost my laugh. That simple, joyful part of me was gone, and with it, my smile. Everyone around me thought I had the perfect job, a role most people would dream of; but deep down, I knew something wasn't right. Without my laughter, I wasn't fully myself, and I had to figure out why.

From the outside, it was a dream position, but internally, I felt like something essential had slipped away. My smile, the one that always came so easily, was fading. Worse, I had lost my trademark laugh, the one that used to fill rooms with joy and ease.

At first, I couldn't quite articulate what was wrong. There was nothing wrong with the job itself or the company; it was a fantastic environment with great people. But something in the culture, something intangible, made it difficult to bring my whole self to work. Slowly, I began to feel like I was leaving important parts of myself at the door each day. I knew I had to make a change.

I made the difficult decision to take a sabbatical and return to studying. It wasn't easy. I couldn't even explain to my closest family and friends why I was leaving such a great role. But deep down, I understood. I needed to reconnect with myself, to rediscover the joy and authenticity I had lost. This sabbatical wasn't just about finding a new career direction; it was about reclaiming the parts of me that had been pushed aside. It was a decision I had made for my soul, knowing that if I didn't act, I would continue to drift further from who I truly was.

This is one of many stories from many of the clients I coach, they share a sense of frustration and disconnection from their work environments, feeling like they can't bring their true selves to the office. One client expressed it perfectly: "It's honestly frustrating. I keep feeling like showing up as my true self at work is just a fantasy. It's like I constantly have to pretend to be someone I'm not just to be accepted and respected."

Another voiced exhaustion, saying, "I'm so tired of being overlooked for growth opportunities just because I don't have that dominant, hard-driving personality my bosses seem to favour." These concerns are not unique. Time and time again, I hear from clients who feel drained by the need to fit into work cultures that seem to stifle their individuality and authenticity. They often grapple with the pressure to wear a mask just to get through the day, only to return home feeling depleted.

By the time they seek help, it often feels like they're at a breaking point: a "fix me or I'll have to leave" situation. The conversation usually centres around how they can change themselves to fit into the expectations of their boss, their work environment, or others.

There's this urgent need to "dress self" because the real self seems to be the problem: it's not fitting in, not staying hidden at home.

Of course, our true selves do come with us to work. This tension between who we are and who we feel we need to be is a common issue in many workplaces, and it's exactly what we'll explore in the Bringing Your Whole Self to Work Stage.

This chapter delves into these challenges and explores how to reclaim your full self in a work environment that may not always seem to welcome it. At its core, the Bringing Your Whole Self to Work Stage involves the integration of everything you bring—your personal values and identity into the work environment. It's about aligning the essence of who you are with the dynamics of the workplace, encompassing interactions with the organisation, colleagues, and superiors.

These interactions serve as a mirror, reflecting back to the earlier stages of your career, prompting a re-examination of selfhood:

- Stage One: Creating your career identity
- Stage Two: Developing your career capital
- Stage Three: Anchoring your career
- Stage Four: Managing background effects
- Stage Five: The utilisation of your innate talents

All the stages so far have provide a platform to explore and deal with your personal choices and motivations according your personal characteristics. The sixth stage moves the focus from self to how the self engages with the external world of work. As you engage and navigate the complexities at work, you receive feedback that leads to further self-discovery.

During this stage, your personal traits meet up with the characteristics of your work environment and interpersonal relationships at work. This is a pivotal stage where our internal and external worlds converge, prompting a continuous process of self-adjustment to align with the demands and realities encountered in the professional arena.

Overview of the Bringing Your Whole Self to Work Stage

Stage Six intricately *explores the dynamic relationship between our inner selves and the external world of work.* It delves into the connection between our inner purpose, wishes, and aspirations, and the practicalities of day-to-day work life. This stage requires us to engage with the realities of our working lives, assessing whether our working life aligns with our inner purpose, and making adjustments to resolve any conflict.

We learn to bring together our thoughts, emotions, and physical self as we balance our inner world with the outer work environment. We blend the different parts of who we are—mind, body, spirit, and feelings—into a way that works smoothly. This is when we really explore how our inner thoughts and emotions connect with the world of work.

As we navigate this stage, we undergo adjustments or refinements to our identity in response to the realities encountered in our professional world. This encounter manifests in various aspects:

- Our approach and execution of work
- Interactions with colleagues, defining the nature of co-worker relationships
- Coping with authority and managing subservient positions
- Establishing connections with those providing support

- Tailoring our time management and preferred work environment
- Infusing the tasks in our daily work with the appropriate energy
- Balancing the relationship between work and personal health
- Navigating the impact of work overload or unemployment

Consequently, *our attitude towards work and our preferences undergo development during this stage.* Some of us find solace in structured and stable work environments, appreciating clearly defined requirements that allow for a methodical and unhurried approach.

By contrast, others hate such structures, preferring a work setting free from the constraints of complying with a boss's demands. The sixth stage becomes a defining period where our personal inclinations and work-related preferences formulate the unique approach we each take towards our professional journeys.

This is where you explore if your career anchors discovered in Stage Four aligns to your job, to your employer's or bosses expectations. Misalignment often causes dissatisfaction and the need to either fix yourself by ignoring your career anchors to fit the job and your employers' expectations.

The dynamics of *establishing and maintaining relationships with co-workers plays out.* It serves as the area in which your work character takes shape, defining how you respond to authority, behave as a subordinate, and interact with those in subordinate roles. The dynamics of collaboration and hierarchy play out in this stage, shaping the interpersonal aspects of your professional identity.

How you treat and are treated by your peers and superiors plays a crucial role in determining your approach to teamwork, leadership, and the overall work environment during this stage. This is where your career identity defined in Stage One meets up and gets tested by others. Who you believe you are, how you perceive yourself against how others perceive you.

How you are perceived by others is shaped by your characteristics as a person of service, This is defined by your approach to helping and contributing to others. Simultaneously, the way you engage others and receive help is also moulded, influencing how you engage with and appreciate the assistance you receive. This platform becomes a transformative period where your disposition towards service, whether providing or receiving, evolves and develops, contributing to your overall professional and personal development.

The Bringing Your Whole Self to Work Stage serves as a platform where you witness the results of the experiments you conducted in Stage Five. It *reveals how your career decisions and experiments from the previous stage influence your career journey.* The outcome determines the success or challenges you face in your journey. For example, trying out a new skill in order to expand your talents to meet the challenges and demands of your work environment.

The stage lands itself as the *battleground for career success* and a testing ground for mental health, physical well-being, and the emergence of any psychological or physical issues resulting from work-related experiences. It is where we experience the reactions of others, the repercussions of our experimenting, the rejection of an unwelcoming culture, and the demands to change to meet the expectations.

For example, the focus of coaching with Tom after he presented the problem articulated at the beginning of this chapter was on him learning to manage the draining characteristics of his working environment reducing the negative impact on his well-being.

In response to all these expectations and demands, *you embark on a journey of self-discovery, learning to distinguish between your authentic self and external influences.* This involves a process of understanding "what is me" and "what is not me." You are forced to go back to the earlier stages and refine your sense of identity and career identity in Stage One, clarifying personal values in Stage Two, principles, and authentic aspirations.

Self-awareness is crucial for maintaining your individuality amidst multiple influences you encounter at work. In the end, you are constantly faced with the challenge of deciding what part of you changes and what in your authentic self you do not want to temper with.

These challenges significantly influence your physical, mental, and spiritual well-being. For example, Maggie, one of my coaching clients, found herself struggling with a manager who demanded that she present herself in ways that conflicted with her authentic self. She felt that she was constantly expected to be more aggressive in dealing with her team. With her manager constantly saying, "You have to speak the language that they will understand" and labelling her as a "softie", over time, this dissonance between who she was and who she was required to be took a heavy toll on her mental and emotional health. The pressure to conform led her to experience emotional exhaustion, ultimately resulting in a mild mental breakdown.

Given the extensive portion of our life we spend at work and the role workplaces play in shaping our social identity, the impact of professional experiences filters in our overall health and well-being.[60] This main task during this stage focuses on building a balanced relationship between your inner self and the work environment, helping you grow both personally and professionally, while supporting your overall well-being and spiritual needs.

This is what is commonly known workplace spirituality (or spirit friendly workplace) when a work environment recognises that employees have an inner life that nourishes and is nourished by meaningful work taking place in the context of community.[61]

Positives of the Bringing Your Whole Self to Work Stage

When you are being intentional in navigating the "bringing self" to work stage, you can observe certain characteristics that indicate that everything is going well. If you want to check your alignment, here are some good signs:

Bringing inner self to work involves embracing a sense of self-awareness and understanding about who you are, the meaning of your actions, and the contributions you make within your professional environment.[62] The focus is now on aligning your personal values and beliefs with your work, fostering a deeper connection between your inner identity and the tasks you engage in during your daily professional life. Such connection promotes authenticity, fulfilment, and a meaningful integration of self into the workplace. It results in what others have called workplace spirituality.

When there is congruence between your inner self-concept and your work, you experience a heightened motivation. In other words, when the nature of your work aligns with your inner self and core identity, you are more likely to experience increased motivation and fulfilment.[63]

Conversely, when there is misalignment or *incongruence between your inner self-concept and your work, it can lead to demotivation and potentially adverse work situations*. When the tasks, values, or overall nature of the job diverge significantly from your inner identity, it can create a sense of discord, potentially impacting motivation levels and overall job satisfaction.

Another element that impacts our sense of being able to bring our true self at work is meaningful work. Meaningful work transcends the mere completion of cognitively meaningful tasks; it encompasses a deeper dimension that links with personal joy and a connection to a greater purpose. It is not only about the nature of the tasks but also involves a profound sense of fulfilment and joy derived from one's professional endeavours.[64]

Meaningful work connects what you do at work to the bigger picture of what's important in life. It's more than just completing tasks; it's about feeling mentally involved, emotionally fulfilled, and having a sense of purpose that matches your personal values and how you contribute to society.

According to Michael Lerner, a well-known American Social Scientist, *we all desire a meaningful connection between our day-to-day job responsibilities and a larger purpose in life*.[65] Beyond seeking competence and mastery, we aspire to engage in work that holds social meaning or value.[66] It is critical to have a sense of calling through meaningful experiences, especially within the context of work.[67]

These findings highlight a fundamental human need for work that goes beyond mere tasks, resonating with a deeper purpose and societal significance while providing a sense of fulfilment and connection to something greater than the individual job itself.

To confirm the importance of spiritual alignment to your work, Asmos and Duchon conducted a study involving 696 individuals in four Midwestern hospitals. Their finding was: having *work that is meaningful and purposeful is one of the most crucial elements of a successful and fulfilling career.*

The indicators of meaning at work were statements such as "I see a connection between my work and the larger social good of my community" and "The work I do is connected to what I think is important in life".[68] This shows that we feel a deep sense of satisfaction and connection to something bigger when our work is not only personally meaningful but also helps the community and matches our overall life values.

To achieve this, requires *aligning ourselves with suitable jobs that enable the authentic expression and thriving of your inner self, rather than opting for work environments that compel suppression and concealment of your true identity.* This underscores the idea that a well-suited job facilitates the alignment of personal values, strengths, and characteristics with the demands and culture of the workplace, fostering an environment where you can be yourself and contribute meaningfully.

Other factors that influence our feeling of whether we are able to bring our whole self to work is the existence or lack thereof a sense of community. As spiritual beings, *we live in connection with other human beings.* This means activities like sharing, mutual obligation, and commitment that foster connections among people are important to us. Jane Dutton refers to this as "high-quality connections,".[69] Belonging to a community plays an important role in nurturing the spirit at work, contributing to the overall sense of connection and well-being.

Similarly, with the decline in traditional sources of community such as neighbourhoods and memberships in churches, we bring our need for community to work. There is a collective hunger for community in the workplace, and productivity is greatly enhanced when such a community is found.[70]

An analysis of management practices that either support or harm workplace morale, highlights that one of the key things people value at work is the sense of belonging to a larger community or feeling interconnected with others.[71]

Our colleagues play a crucial role in determining job satisfaction. This becomes even more pronounced as individuals spend an increasing amount of time at work, and work takes on a more prominent role in shaping our social identity. The nature of social relations within the workplace and the quality of interactions with colleagues becomes increasingly influential in overall job satisfaction.

When your job and the work environment provide meaning, self-determination, self-expression, and the pursuit of goals and activities that aligns with your values, you achieve a state of what is called eudaimonic well-being. Eudaemonic well-being is about experiencing a deep sense of fulfilment and purpose in what you do. It goes beyond simply feeling happy or satisfied in the workplace; it's about finding meaning and personal growth through your job.[72]

When we experience eudaemonic well-being, we are aligned with our values, passions, and strengths, helping us feel that we are making a positive impact and achieving our potential. This type of well-being is often fostered in environments that encourage continuous learning, purpose-driven work, and opportunities for self-development.

When we experience happiness, pleasure and satisfaction in our work, we achieve hedonic well-being. When we achieve hedonic well-being we experience job satisfaction, positive relationships with colleagues, and a sense of enjoyment in our daily tasks. While it enhances short-term happiness, hedonic well-being doesn't necessarily lead to long-term fulfilment or purpose.

Another great outcome when this stage is managed well is physical well-being. *Given the significant impact of these factors on our personal lives, health and well-being* become a focal point during this stage, as it encompasses the various health issues arising from our daily duties and routines.

During the Bringing Your Whole Self to Work Stage, the goal is to fully align your personal values and beliefs with your professional life. When everything is going well, you'll notice that you feel more connected to your work because it reflects who you are on a deeper level. This stage is all about authenticity—being true to yourself at work. When your job aligns with your inner self, it brings a sense of fulfilment and motivation, making your work more meaningful and satisfying.

However, when there's a mismatch between your true self and your work, it can lead to feelings of stress and demotivation. Companies that ask employees to leave their personal selves at the door can unintentionally create a work environment that stifles authenticity.

This separation between personal identity and professional roles can make it difficult to bring your whole self to work, leading to dissatisfaction and a lack of true engagement. Being able to connect your work to a greater purpose and feeling part of a community at work are also key factors in thriving during this stage.

Potential Derailers of Bringing the Whole Self to Work Stage

When not in control of this stage and things don't go well certain characteristics take centre stage. *Health issues stemming from your job and related challenges become prevalent.* As we navigate this stage, issues arise from a lack of boundaries, overworking, and difficulty balancing work and home activities. Such challenges may lead to burnout, frustrations, and, in many instances, physical and mental illnesses.

The toll of these difficulties can significantly impact your well-being and professional performance. The American Psychology Association conducts an annual stress in America survey and each year it has found that work is cited as a significant source of stress by a majority of Americans.[73]

This is supported by a 2022 survey by the American Institute of Stress, which found that 5 percent of Americans report having low stress levels, and 76 percent report that stress harms their productivity.[74]

In the majority of the corporate coaching work I do, managing stress is often cited as one of the key results that the coachee must focus on. The type of stress reported by my coaches emanates from feeling less than adequate when comparing themselves to workplace demands.

Experiencing *job loss, especially through redundancy,* can exacerbate the negative characteristics of Stage Six. The aftermath of unemployment may trigger self-worth issues, prompting you to question your life's purpose. This crisis of identity can result in diminished confidence, making it challenging to recover and secure gainful employment. For those of us who have long defined our self-worth by our job, this stage poses the additional challenge of understanding and redefining ourselves outside the context of previous employment.

Key Challenges of the Bringing Your Whole Self to Work Stage

At Stage Six, you will encounter several tests and challenges that ultimately impact your career and may impact your well-being, these include: certain job stressors affect your well-being at work. These include the challenge stressors: those that have to do with workload, and time pressure. Hindrance stressors, on the other hand, relate to role confusion or strain in work relationships at work. Failure to manage any form of job stressors will negatively impact our well-being .[75]

- *Work-life balance*: maintaining a healthy work-life balance becomes a central challenge during this stage; if not effectively managed, it can lead to various health issues. The paradox lies in successfully adhering to daily work routines while simultaneously prioritising your personal health and a wholesome lifestyle. Striking a balance becomes crucial to prevent burnout, stress-related illnesses, and ensure sustained well-being.

- *Balancing short-term and future-focused work*: another challenge arises when navigating the delicate equilibrium between short-term routine work and activities with a long-term future-focused perspective. Revisiting previous stages like your career capital is helpful in navigating this stage.

The risk lies in becoming overly engrossed in day-to-day tasks, potentially neglecting strategic, future-oriented activities that are crucial for achieving your career goals. Effective management involves balancing both aspects to ensure sustained professional growth and development.

- *Balancing service to self and service to others*: Stage Six presents the challenge of maintaining a balance between serving others and practising self-care. A risk emerges when we prioritise service to others or prioritising work at the expense of our well-being. Striking a harmonious balance between being a great employee and attending to personal needs is vital for sustained personal effectiveness and fulfilment during this stage.

Successfully navigating these challenges requires developing self-awareness, which will help you focus not only on the work aspect of your life but also your holistic well-being and recognising the interconnectedness of your professional and personal life.

Success Strategies for the Bringing Your Whole Self to Work Stage

There are practices you can adopt to effectively navigate the challenges of Stage Six. In this section, we discuss some of the practices and tools you can use to deal with challenges of *this* stage and stay on track on your career journey.

The first important practice is *being proactive* in influencing your own work environment and getting involved in crafting your job, making sure that you derive meaning from it. You can proactively influence your job to add components that are meaningful to you. You can also avoid elements that can be stressors.

Practices

Creating personal meaning and purpose: to address the challenge of balancing short-term and future-focused work, you can adopt the practice of deriving personal meaning and purpose from your career. This involves aligning daily tasks with broader career goals and personal aspirations. By finding intrinsic value and fulfilment in your work, you can make even boring mundane work activities exciting by creating meaning and aligning them to your personal purpose.

Bringing inner self to work: deliberately bringing your full self to work is a practice that involves authenticity and emotional intelligence. It goes beyond leaving emotions at the door and encourages you to integrate your personal values, beliefs, and emotions into your professional identity. By embracing vulnerability and authenticity, you can foster genuine connections with colleagues, contributing to a positive work environment.

Adopt prosocial behaviour that builds connections at work: deliberately building healthy connections at work is another crucial practice during this stage. This involves adopting a mindset that intends to actively build positive relationships with colleagues, superiors, and subordinates.

Yes, there will always be situations that make it difficult to attain this. For example, as part of Maggie's coaching plan, she focused on building connections at work to help her learn from colleagues who demonstrated the tough behaviours expected by her boss, but in a way that aligned with her own values.

She identified a colleague who consistently commanded respect without being aggressive and asked him to be her accountability buddy. In forming this connection, Maggie was able to observe his approach, learn from his experience, and receive valuable feedback on how she was progressing in practising this behaviour. This relationship not only provided her with practical insights but also helped her stay aligned with her values while developing the leadership qualities her boss required.

However, if your approach and intention is about fostering supportive networks, you can navigate the challenges of the work environment more effectively. Creating a sense of community and interconnectedness contributes to a positive work atmosphere and enhances your overall well-being.

Establishing work-life boundaries: one crucial practice involves setting clear boundaries between work and personal life. This might be difficult in the age where our physical work environment and work environment is the same.

However, you can create structured routines that designate specific times for work-related activities and personal endeavours. This separation helps in preventing burnout and maintaining overall well-being.

By consciously dedicating focused time to work and personal life, you can cultivate a healthier work-life balance. Reducing job-related technology that forces you to ignore the boundaries

Developing self-care recovery routines: this practice will help bring awareness whenever you are encountering situations at work that are misaligned to who you are, what you value and have a negative impact on your overall well-being. *Beyond awareness of these situations is having a recovery routine that assists in dealing with situations.* In particular, this will focus on personal reflection on the interaction between yourself and your workplace:

- What am I happy about in my work?
- Why is my work important to me?
- How does it align with my personal purpose?
- What do I need to let go of in my work?

The Bringing Your Whole Self to Work Stage is a crucial point in your career journey that emphasises the integration of who you are, your personal values and identity within the workplace. At its core, this stage helps you to align who you are with the dynamics of your work environment.

This alignment includes navigating interactions with your organisation culture, colleagues, and superiors. Navigating this stage depends on work done in earlier stages of your career, such as creating your career identity, developing career capital, anchoring your career, and managing background effects.

During this stage, your personal and career identity faces real-world challenges, resulting in feelings of either being accepted or rejected by your work environment. The valuable skills amassed as career capital must be tested in the workplace; you will start to see how your background influences your daily work life. This stage is characterised by active feedback, acceptance, and rejection of personal characteristics.

Positives of this stage include having alignment between your inner self and your work, which results in experiences of heightened motivation and fulfilment. Establishing and nurturing connections at work fosters an environment, where you can thrive as your true self while being productive.

Potential derailers may arise if this stage is poorly managed. One major challenge is achieving work-life balance, which is essential for preventing health issues. Your task is to navigate the balance between short-term tasks and long-term goals, as well as between serving others and practising self-care. If not managed intentionally, this stage can impact your well-being, affecting your spirituality, confidence, and self-esteem.

To successfully navigate this stage, strategies such as creating personal meaning and purpose in your work, bringing your inner self to the workplace, adopting prosocial behaviours to strengthen connections, and establishing clear work-life boundaries are recommended.

In conclusion, Stage Six offers a powerful opportunity to align your personal values with your work environment. By embracing both your unique qualities and the demands of your role, this stage allows you to discover more about yourself, unlocking personal and professional growth. When you navigate it with intention, it can bring increased job satisfaction and a deeper sense of purpose in your career. All of this enables us to be our true self while also being productive members of society and impacting our world.

Stage Six Coaching Questions

What traits do you hold back at work, and what's driving your discomfort in fully expressing your true self in that environment?

Stage Seven – Navigating Career Shocks

David's career seemed to be going well. A bright, highly-educated man, he had been with one company for ten years, having joined straight from university. Over that time, he grew as a professional, developing his skills and building his reputation as a high performer. But after a while, David became restless. He was eager to explore new opportunities and see if his success could translate to other industries. So, when he received an offer from a fast-paced tech firm, he jumped at the chance to leave his comfort zone and try something new.

When he started his new job all was going well, but after two months David started feeling like things weren't going as smoothly as he had first thought. He struggled with the new environment and constantly felt unsure of his role. Used to having a close relationship with his manager, he now found himself needing someone to interpret what was expected of him. Before he could find his footing, David was informed his job was being made redundant.

Was it really about the job, or was it he who hadn't adapted? The shock shook David's confidence. When he came to me for coaching, he was eager to get back on track, find a new role, and prove his worth. In no time, David landed another great job at a blue-chip company. But just six months in, history repeated itself—his job was once again made redundant, and David was left wondering where things had gone wrong.

When we restarted the coaching sessions, David still only wanted to focus on job searching and preparing himself for interviews. He believed that his biggest challenge was finding another job. However, as the coaching progressed, David discovered that his challenge wasn't only about finding a new job. In fact, he concluded that if he continued to look for a new job without addressing the real issue, chances were that he would face the same challenge.

The missing piece was his ability to build and nurture professional networks. He had relied too heavily on his boss and hadn't invested in informal networks that could have helped him integrate and adjust to company culture and avoid career shocks. David learned that success wasn't just about qualifications; it was about relationships, both inside and outside of work, that support career growth and resilience. By intentionally focusing on building these networks, David's integration into his next role was smoother.

David's story introduces us to Stage Seven of the career journey—one focused on navigating career shocks that are brought about by the changing world of work. It's a stage where the relationships and networks you nurture become the sources of resilience and pillars that support your career, especially when you are faced with unexpected changes.

In Stage Seven, the focus shifts from just understanding yourself and your career as an individual to seeing how you fit into the larger world. It's all about the people you meet, the relationships you build, and how you work with others—whether in business partnerships, on teams, or in personal relationships. This stage is about balance, mutual exchanges, and learning to understand yourself better through your interactions with others.

Up to this point, the earlier stages have been about discovering your career identity and preferences. Now, in Stage Seven, you start to adjust those ideas based on external realities, like the opportunities and challenges you encounter and how the relationships and networks you build can sustain your career journey. during this stage, you discover that your career isn't something that happens in isolation but is shaped by your environment and the people around you.

You begin to understand the vital role that others play in dealing with career challenges that you encounter in your career. It prompts a shift from a self-centred approach to a collaborative mindset, recognising that working in partnerships is what will make your career a success.

The acknowledgement of interdependence becomes a driving force, leading us to subordinate ourselves to the collective goals and objectives shared with others. This transition brings forth conflicts and challenges, which, rather than being obstacles, serve as opportunities for personal and professional growth.

The conflicts inherent in Stage Seven manifest into career shocks and become instrumental in driving adjustments both within ourselves and the dynamics of our professional relationships. We learn to navigate and resolve conflicts and shocks, honing our interpersonal skills and adaptability. This stage pre-empts a transformative period where the focus expands beyond self-mastery to the mastery of collaborative efforts.

Overview of the Managing Career Shocks Stage

A career shock is a distinct and impactful event that triggers deliberation about potential career transitions such as acquiring new skills, searching for a new job, changing occupations, or retiring.[76] These events can throw us in unexpected directions. Some events may be completely unanticipated, such as an injury, illness, or job loss. Others, such as a relocation, marriage, or pregnancy, may be planned, though the impact and consequences of the event can be more disruptive than expected.

Whether planned or not, such events may cause us to pause and re-think our careers and even life directions. David's career shock initially presented itself as a technology upgrade that led to his job being redundant; however, the pattern of being the only one being declared redundant just after starting a new role became evident. David was forced to explore whether there could be more than what meets the eye.

Navigating and managing career shocks brings a realisation that our individual prowess alone is insufficient for mastering your career. In this stage, the importance of networking and working with others becomes clear. You realise that your success is linked to the relationships you build.

This stage is about discovering how to work well with others and how different personalities can affect your career growth. As David discovered he needed to learn to build both formal and informal networks when he joined a new employer to facilitate his integration.

As we navigate this stage, we start to understand the kinds of personalities and work environments that suit us best. We identify the colleagues and leaders whose working styles complement our own. Such an awareness helps us adapt to the realities of the workplace, accepting that some things are beyond our control.

We come to see that the world of work is a larger system that requires collaboration. Building strong relationships and networks becomes essential for career growth. We realise the importance of cooperation and learn to distinguish between situations we can control and those influenced by others.

As a result, relationships take centre stage, and the significance of social capital becomes important. We recognise that connections with others provide access to a wealth of knowledge and privileged social networks. It encompasses the advantages gained through social relationships, offering valuable insights and connections that can facilitate effective negotiation and advancement within society.[77]

Studies on social capital, such as those by Ronald Burt, a prominent sociologist, renowned for his theory of "structural holes, emphasise the importance of networks and relationships in career advancement, noting that individuals with strong relational networks tend to have access to more opportunities and support within their career when navigating career shock.

In this stage, we are challenged to be adaptable, resilient, and be deliberate in our professional interactions. We learn to move away from a self-centric approach in life towards a more holistic and objective approach.

Positives of the Managing Career Shocks Stage

When all is going well during this stage we focus on mastering our networking; we try to develop and maintain relationships with others who have the potential to assist us in our work or career.

This involves understanding who to collaborate with and who might pose challenges.

It is made up of a series of goal-directed interpersonal interactions with network contacts that build and maintain professional relationships and that comprise the mutually- beneficial exchange of resources that are instrumental for our work and career success.[78]

A number of studies have demonstrated that networking has positive outcomes on our careers, such as salary growth over time. In simple terms, putting effort into networking is an investment in future success, and those who do it tend to be happier with their careers.[79]

This is supported by researchers, Michael and Yukl, who studied networking behaviour with a sample of 247 managers from a diverse group of companies. The focus was on internal networking (interactions with others in the organisation) and external networking (defined as interactions with outsiders such as clients and suppliers). The researchers found that having a strong network provides a cushion when experiencing career shocks.[80]

Employees who have a network of contacts both inside and outside organisations are able to increase their individual social capital, especially the part related to work. Networking becomes indispensable for work execution, achieving professional satisfaction and managing the future of the job.[81]

Adaptability and resilience are important characteristics of this stage. From a career perspective, resilience refers to the capacity to continue making progress toward current career goals with the resources and strategies already developed. While adaptability involves reformulating your goals and/or strategies to adapt to new work and career realities, resilience and adaptability are important when experiencing *career shocks*.[82]

Holistic career perspective: the Stage of Managing Career Shocks marks a departure from a self-centric career approach to a more holistic perspective. We learn to view our careers as part of a broader system shaped by external forces. This broader outlook helps us in making career choices with open eyes, considering both personal needs and external requirements.

When everything is going well during Stage Seven, we cultivate our networks, honing the art of building connections and discerning collaborative partners. We develop adaptability and resilience, embracing change and bouncing back from career shocks, recognising the limited control we have over external factors.

This stage fosters a holistic career perspective, shifting from a self-centric approach to understanding careers within the broader context of external forces, influencing thoughtful and objective career choices. However, at times, this stage can take a negative turn with bad characteristics if not managed intentionally.

Potential Derailers of the Managing Career Shocks Stage

When career shocks arise, they demand that you learn and adapt. Failing to adjust can trap you in a cycle of repeated challenges, often stemming from the same source. Without an awareness or the willingness to address the situation, these shocks keep recurring. In David's case, he overlooked a pattern: each time he joined a company, his role became redundant within a few months.

Another negative trait of this stage is succumbing to career shocks. This often happens when individuals fail to address or cope with challenges effectively. For some, this leads to wellness issues, low self-esteem, and eventually abandoning their jobs or careers altogether. They may start to believe they're not good enough or undeserving of a fulfilling career. This pattern typically occurs when people face repeated career shocks without finding a way to confront or resolve them, leading to deeper emotional and professional setbacks.

On the flip side, there is also the risk of becoming too self-centred, neglecting the needs of others in pursuit of personal goals. The real challenge lies in striking a balance between personal interests and those of the people around you.

Another bad trait of this stage is the difficulty in handling uncertainty that comes with career shocks. These shocks often push you into unfamiliar territory, bringing vulnerability and discomfort. This is where you learn to engage with the aspects of the workplace that are beyond your control. The real challenge is managing the resulting uncertainty, insecurities, and self-doubt, while staying confident and adaptable.

Key Challenges of the Managing Career Shocks Stage

Mastering Stage Seven requires us to grasp several key challenges and lessons that revolve around adapting to external forces, fostering meaningful relationships, and maintaining a balanced perspective. The challenges encountered during this stage are intricately tied to relationships and the quality of the ones established in the workplace.

First, individuals need to understand the dynamic nature of the external world and acknowledge that our careers are intertwined with broader societal forces. This lesson emphasises the importance of adaptability and resilience in the face of constant changes in the professional landscape. By recognising that external factors are beyond personal control, individuals can navigate uncertainties more effectively. This requires a realisation that your career depends on others and that you might not have total control over their influence in your career.

Second, the lesson of cultivating meaningful relationships becomes crucial at this stage. Building networks, cooperating with colleagues, and engaging with diverse personalities are integral components. This highlights the value of camaraderie, teamwork, and open communication in navigating the complexities of the external social environment. We must learn to build relationships with an objective and essential quality perspective, recognising that it is one way of influencing how others impact your career.

Additionally, we must learn to manage uncertainty and insecurity. As they step into the world with limited control, feelings of vulnerability and insecurity may arise. The message here is to develop coping mechanisms, resilience, and a confident approach to dealing with the uncertainties.

In this stage, it's important to accept that change is a constant. With change often come career shocks, and the decisions we make during this period are frequently reactions to these unexpected events. Success depends on embracing change and adapting to new situations, such as a shift in leadership, a department restructure, or even a complete career change. The groundwork laid in earlier stages—from defining your career identity (Stage One), building career capital (Stage Two), addressing background effects (Stage Three), strengthening career anchors (Stage Four), connecting with your strengths (Stage Five), to bringing your whole self to work (Stage Six)—determines how prepared you are for these shocks.

Dealing with these shocks may require revisiting earlier stages to strengthen key foundations. Doing so can propel your career forward by solidifying aspects that might have been overlooked, ultimately accelerating your growth. Embracing this process is vital for navigating career shocks and making thoughtful adjustments.

The main lesson to learn at this stage is that your career does not exist in isolation. For example, imagine someone in a senior marketing role, who has always thrived on individual performance and overlooked the influence of others in her career. She might have an outstanding record of delivering projects, but her relationships with key stakeholders, like senior executives or cross-functional teams, might be weak. When a significant promotion opportunity arises, she is overlooked in favour of a colleague who has built stronger relationships with decision-makers.

This is a career shock—a moment where failing to recognise and "manage" those who impact your career causes an unexpected negative outcome. To avoid this, it is essential to be aware of the role others play in shaping your career and to actively foster connections, mentorships, and alliances to support your growth.

Success Strategies for the Managing Career Shocks State

Mastering Stage Seven requires adopting a *mindset that acknowledges the interconnectedness of your career with external forces and the role others play in developing your career. Embracing a cooperative mindset that values collaboration and mutual support means recognising* that career success is not achieved in isolation; instead, it involves building meaningful relationships, navigating change, and understanding the dynamic interplay between individual goals and collective success.

To effectively master Stage Seven, consider adopting cooperative practices. Actively engage in networking activities, both in-person and online, to *build a robust professional network*. Prioritise relationship-building by offering support and contributing value to your network, knowing that these investments will strengthen your connections and enhance your professional influence. Emphasise collaboration over competition and be intentional about building a reputation as a supportive and valuable member of your professional community.

Adopt resilient and adaptable practices when dealing with career shocks: when managing career shocks, it's important to first deal with the psychological and emotional impact that arises and then nurture a growth mindset. It starts with acknowledging and processing emotions triggered by these events. However, do not get stuck in a loop of overthinking, which can lead to rumination.

Rumination happens when we obsessively replay negative thoughts, often making situations seem worse than they are. For instance, David's challenge was dwelling on not understanding why he was losing his jobs when he was so good at his job and so skilled.

Effectively navigating career shocks involves not only acknowledging emotions but also actively engaging in constructive ways to process and navigate them. Instead of succumbing to destructive emotions, such as anger, anxiety, resentment, self-doubt, sadness, or frustration, individuals can adopt proactive strategies.[83]

One effective approach is *connecting to our emotions*, which involves embracing and fully experiencing negative emotions without resistance, judgement, or attempts to banish them. By allowing yourself to sit with these emotions without struggling against them, we gain a deeper understanding of our feelings and the triggers behind them.

Another beneficial practice is *"going through emotions,"* where you take intentional actions aligned with your plans and priorities, regardless of your current emotional state. For example, you might feel depressed and angered by the proposed restructuring at work. The strong urge to stay in bed and not go in might be tempting, but adhering to your plan for early morning exercise and choosing to move forward despite the prevailing depressing motions will serve you well.

This proactive approach helps you navigate challenges by focusing on your goals and commitments, contributing to increased resilience and adaptability. For David, his action plan focused on applying for a new job, being ready to present himself for interviews and building networks and integrating successfully after being offered a job.

Adopting a growth mindset: encountering career shocks can create doubts about whether you have the required ability to achieve your career goals. In such instances, the fundamental assumptions or mindset people hold about the plasticity of the capabilities in question can significantly influence what they do next.

When you hold a fixed mindset about particular abilities, whether in the technical, operational, marketing, administrative, leadership, or some other domain, you perceive them as largely immutable and thus presume that the scope to develop them substantially is innately limited.

Statements to yourself or others such as "I'm too old for this" or "This is just not one of my strengths and that's never going to change," are hallmarks of a fixed mindset about the ability in question. After you have encountered setbacks, research has shown that what flows from a fixed mindset includes reluctance to seek feedback about how you could get better, systematically experiment with new strategies, or generally engage proactively in the kinds of development initiatives that enable ability improvement. Fixed mindsets are often validated by acting as a self-fulfilling prophecy.[84]

When we hold a growth mindset, on the other hand, we tend to assume that if an ability is presently inadequate, it means it has not yet been sufficiently developed. A growth mindset assumes that abilities can be cultivated; this cues us to respond to setbacks by engaging in a search for strategies to acquire and build certain abilities so that the person can move forward.

Adopt strategic networking practices: establishing meaningful connections with others not only fosters professional relationships but also contributes to building resilience. Research conducted by Silbert (2016) and colleagues highlights the psychological resilience that a robust professional network can provide in the face of various shocks.[85]

Their study found that possessing a large professional network acts as a buffer against adverse effects resulting from unexpected career events, such as a poor performance evaluation, negative political incidents, or even job loss. The professionals studied in this research demonstrated a remarkable ability to bounce back from these unforeseen challenges.

Moreover, those with expansive professional networks often maintained, and in some cases, strengthened their sense of professional identity. There are five types of networking behaviour that are fundamental strategies to enhance and grow your professional connections, drawing insights from research by Forret and Dougherty, who developed the concept of networking behaviours:

1. **Maintaining contacts:** this refers to the regular effort to stay in touch with people who could be of assistance to you in your career. It is crucial for keeping relationships active and is often about reciprocity—helping others as much as they help you. Strong, ongoing relationships serve as a bridge to new opportunities.

2. **Socialising:** engaging in casual, informal interactions within your professional circle. This could be in-person or virtual and is often more about bonding over shared interests or personal experiences than strictly work. Socialising helps to build rapport and trust with peers, colleagues, and mentors, which can facilitate stronger professional connections.

3. **Engaging in professional activities**: participation in activities directly related to your profession, such as attending conferences, joining professional organisations, or participating in industry-specific events. These engagements allow you to meet new people in your field and stay updated on current trends, which may increase your perceived value within your professional network.

4. **Participating in the community:** networking can extend beyond the workplace or industry. Participation in community activities, charity events, or social organisations can widen your network and help you connect with individuals outside your usual professional circles. These networks can provide fresh perspectives and additional opportunities for collaboration or mentorship.

5. **Increasing internal visibility:** this involves making yourself more noticeable within your organisation. It includes actively

participating in meetings, taking on leadership roles, or volunteering for visible projects. Being recognised internally helps to build influence, establish credibility, and attract opportunities for career growth within your company.

In Stage Seven, your resilience and resourcefulness are tested as you face career shocks. This stage emphasises the importance of building strong networks and being adaptable. Your ability to navigate these shocks effectively relies on nurturing relationships and maintaining a resilient mindset, which will help you make decisions that can propel your career forward.

Managing Career Shocks, is about effectively dealing with unexpected disruptions in your professional journey. Career shocks can be anything from sudden job loss, restructuring, market changes, or personal challenges like illness or family needs that impact your work. These shocks are inevitable in most careers, but the way you manage them significantly influences your long-term success. How you respond determines your ability to harness the positives that come from such disruptions.

This stage presents an opportunity for personal growth, reinvention, and adaptability. When faced with a career shock, you are forced to reassess your goals, values, and the direction of your professional path. Successfully in navigating this stage can lead to greater resilience, renewed purpose, and sometimes even a more fulfilling career trajectory.

One of the major derailers at the Managing Career Shocks Stage is succumbing to fear or anxiety, which may cause you to make rushed or reactive decisions rather than thoughtfully assessing the situation. Another potential derailer is dwelling too much on the negative aspects of the shock, which can lead to a victim mentality and ultimately stagnation.

Over time, this paralysis may prevent you from moving forward, keeping you stuck in uncertainty and unable to seek out new opportunities. These derailers are compounded by the key challenge of staying adaptable in the face of change.

The disruption of routine and security can cause emotional stress and may lead to self-doubt or confusion about your career path. Another challenge is ensuring you have the necessary resources, such as a strong professional network, financial security, or personal support, to weather the shock. To counter these challenges, certain practices should be adopted to ease the navigation through this stage.

To manage career shock successfully, adopting a growth mindset is important, viewing the challenges brought about by career shocks as opportunities. The following practices can be helpful: first, take time to assess and reflect on the situation.

Rather than reacting immediately, reflect on what caused the shock and use this moment to realign with your long-term goals. Doing so will enable you to leverage support networks effectively. Adopting strategic networking behaviours is one of the effective ways of navigating career shocks.

Stage Seven Coaching Questions

What strengths, skills, and inner resources can you draw upon to navigate career shocks and how will you harness them to emerge stronger and more resilient on the other side?

Stage Eight – Navigating Career Transitions

I often think of myself as the Queen of Transitions. In my career, there's hardly a type of transition I haven't navigated. Reflecting on some of the major changes I've gone through, one of the most profound was leaving a full-time job to return to studying.

The shock of not having a steady income hit me hard, and although no one had forced me to make that decision, I had been fortunate to receive a scholarship to study abroad. It was an exciting opportunity, but the uncertainty that came with it was undeniable.

When my studies were over, I remember the deep worry about whether I'd be able to land a job at the same level I had left. The scholarship came with a condition: I had to return to Johannesburg, my home, and work there for three years.

This meant another transition, both personally and professionally. Fortunately, I found a position as an HR Director, covering Sub-Saharan Africa, which was an incredible opportunity but came with its own set of challenges.

After three years in Johannesburg, yet another shift came: this time to London, where my role expanded to include Europe, the Middle East, and Africa. Just when I thought I had settled, my role was made redundant. Once again, I faced a major decision: should I stay in corporate and search for another job or transition out and start my own business? I chose the latter, stepping into the unknown but with the confidence that each transition before had prepared me for this one.

Career transitions are broadly defined as "any process of change or movement in one's work or professional role".[86] The transition could be a shift within the same organisation or a complete change in career direction, and it often involves a period of adjustment.

Over the course of our professional life, we will navigate a range of career transitions. There are transitions that are triggered by your life phase such as transition from school to work, from work to retirement. There are other transitions triggered by personal choices such as work-to-work or unemployment-to-work transitions.

Successfully managing career transitions is crucial for long-term career success, work adjustment, and overall well-being. Research shows that individuals who navigate these transitions effectively tend to experience better career satisfaction, adaptability, and work-life balance. These transitions often demand the development of new skills, building relationships in new settings, and dealing with the stress of uncertainty, which, if managed well, can significantly enhance a person's career trajectory and future opportunities.

Overview of the Managing Career Transitions Stage

Career transitions often go beyond minor changes, such as job rotation or enrichment, and instead involve major shifts in work content and context. Whether the transition is voluntary or involuntary, it often requires a period of adjustment, learning, and realignment of career goals to ensure successful integration into the new role or environment.

There are different types of transitions that your career will go through over the course of your career:

Vertical transitions (promotions or demotions)

Vertical transitions involve moving up or down within a hierarchy, typically signifying promotions to higher responsibility roles or demotions to less challenging ones.[87] These transitions often bring changes in status, income, and professional identity, requiring new skill sets and adjustments to power dynamics. My transition from a Sub-Saharan Africa role to a Europe Middle East and Africa role was a vertical transition because it entailed a bigger scope of work.

Horizontal transitions (lateral moves)

Horizontal transitions refer to lateral movements within an organisation or across industries, where the role level remains constant but the job function or environment changes. These transitions are a means of acquiring new experiences and skills without upward movement, often fostering versatility and broader professional exposure.[88] Your move may be from your current role to a new role at the same level, be it within the same employer or to yet another employer in a horizontal transition.

Voluntary vs. involuntary transitions

Voluntary transitions are initiated by the individual, such as career changes for personal growth or lifestyle reasons. Involuntary transitions, such as layoffs or forced career shifts, are externally driven and often involve navigating emotional and financial challenges. Voluntary transitions are often planned while involuntary transitions often come as an unexpected career shock. When my role was made redundant, that was an involuntary transition.

Organisational vs. occupational transitions

Organisational transitions occur within the same occupation but across different companies, often driven by the search for better opportunities.[89] Occupational transitions involve a complete change in profession, requiring the individual to acquire new skills and potentially retrain, as seen in mid-career shifts or second careers. When I transitioned from being a Human Resources professional to a full-time career coach, that was an occupational transition.

Regardless of the type of transition, experiencing a career transition often brings instability, change, and uncertainty, which can be stressful. Career transitions share common characteristics that define the nature and complexity of the change. These characteristics influence how individuals experience the transition and how they navigate it. Key among these are the degree of controllability, the magnitude of change, and the level of ambiguity involved.[90]

One important characteristic is the degree of controllability, which refers to how much the transition is initiated by one's own choice. For instance, if you lose your job due to your company relocating to another province, this transition is considered low in controllability because it was imposed by external factors. On the other hand, if you have been planning for years to start your own business by the age of forty, this would be a high-controllability transition, as it aligns with your long-term personal goals.

Another characteristic of career transitions is magnitude, which refers to the extent of change involved. A transition with a high magnitude, such as switching both your career field and job level, may present more challenges than simply moving to a new employer within the same field. For example, a software developer becoming an executive in a new company faces a greater magnitude of change compared to a developer moving to a different firm but staying in the same role.

Ambiguity is another defining factor in transitions, relating to how clear or uncertain the next steps are. Some transitions are filled with uncertainty, while others are straightforward. Consider someone who has always known they wanted to be an actor. The path is clear, and the steps are well-defined.

By contrast, an individual who has never given much thought to their career path may struggle with deciding what to do next, especially in the case of job loss. The level of ambiguity they face depends on how many options are available and how equipped they are to make informed choices about their next move.

Another characteristic of the Managing Career Transitions Stage is duration, which refers to the time it takes you to fully navigate the transition. Transitions typically unfold over a period of days, months, or even years, requiring thoughtful reflection and adjustment. Throughout this process, you often need to reevaluate your goals, update them as you gather new information, and make decisions about when to stay the course or adapt your plans.

This extended period allows for continuous learning and adjustment, making career transitions a gradual, evolving experience rather than a single event.

Another important characteristic of career transitions is personal circumstances, which can deeply impact how someone experiences and manages change. These circumstances include everything from financial stability and family responsibilities to social support and where you live.

For example, if you have some savings tucked away, the pressure of a career change might feel less daunting compared to someone who's living pay check to pay check. Your family situation matters too, such as having young children or caring for an elderly parent can add layers of complexity to any transition. And let's not forget the role of friends and community. If you've got a strong support system or know people who have been through similar transitions, it can make the journey a lot smoother.

On the other hand, factors like a tough job market or the work situation of a partner can make the process more stressful. These personal circumstances shape how each person approaches their transition.

Positives of the Managing Career Transitions Stage

Career transitions and transformation can be tough; however, navigating this stage of your life can bring about the change your career requires. When all is going well in this stage, your career becomes more and more adaptable.

Career adaptability requires you to ask yourself, am I *ready* to deal with whatever changes that get thrown at me by the changing world of work? Do I have the right *resources* to be able to manage these changes? Do I know how to *respond* to the changes and career shocks brought about by these unexpected changes? What *outcomes and results* am I driving for as I navigate and adapt to these changes?

Readiness

Adaptive readiness is the personality trait of flexibility, of willingness to change. It involves strengthening certain personality traits that helps you adapt to workplace changes.

The principal characteristics are:

Tenacious goal pursuit: cultivating tenacious goal pursuit brings a number of advantages when navigating the dynamic world of work. If you possess this trait, you will demonstrate relentless determination and resilience in pursuing your objectives, allowing you to weather the storms of career shocks. The unwavering commitment to your goals enables you to withstand setbacks fostering adaptability in the face of changes in the work environment. This trait empowers you to bounce back from career challenges, as it instals a mindset geared towards overcoming obstacles and persistently working towards desired outcomes.

Flexible goal adjustment: in conjunction with tenacious goal pursuit, flexible goal adjustment is important in the dynamic landscape of the world of work. While tenacity provides the drive to relentlessly pursue your career objectives, flexibility allows you to recalibrate your goals in response to evolving circumstances. This characteristic allows for alignment with emerging opportunities and challenges.

Imagine relentlessly pursuing a goal, when career prospects in that area are known to be dwindling because that particular field is changing due to new technology. You could end up building skills that will be obsolete by the time you finish your studies. Flexibility in goal pursuit enables you to take advantage of unforeseen prospects that come up as you pursue your goals and navigate career shocks more effectively. It fosters a resilient and agile approach to goals, while recognising that circumstances may change. Ultimately, a combination of tenacious goal pursuit with flexible goal adjustment equips you to navigate the complexities of the modern workplace with dexterity and strategic insight.

Learning goal orientation: in addition to tenacious goal pursuit and flexible goal adjustment, fostering a learning goal-oriented mindset is paramount in navigating the ever-changing world of work and managing career transitions triggered by the shifts in this dynamic landscape. A learning goal orientation involves a focus on acquiring new skills, knowledge, and experiences, emphasising personal development and adaptability.

In the face of career shocks or changes in the workplace, individuals with a learning goal orientation approach challenges as opportunities for growth. This mindset encourages continuous learning, enabling you to stay relevant and resilient in the face of evolving job demands.

A commitment to learning also facilitates the acquisition of transferable skills, making you more versatile and better equipped to transition smoothly in response to changes in the world of work. Embracing a learning goal orientation not only enhances adaptability but also positions you to thrive in the face of career transformations and uncertainties.

Proactive personality: if you are proactive you take initiative, anticipate potential challenges, and actively seek opportunities for growth and advancement. This is beneficial when facing career shocks or unexpected shifts in the professional landscape. If you are proactive, you are more likely to engage in strategic career planning, skill development, and networking, enabling you to stay ahead of industry changes and position yourself favourably in the job market.

Embracing a proactive mindset empowers you to be an architect of your career, proactively steering your professional journey, and effectively managing the uncertainties associated with the changing world of work.

Readiness helps you adapt to workplace changes through tenacious goal pursuit, flexible goal adjustment, a learning goal orientation, and a proactive mindset. By cultivating these traits, you become more resilient in the face of career shocks and better equipped to navigate evolving job demands. However, to truly thrive in a changing work environment, another essential practice is resourcefulness.

Resourcefulness

Career adaptability resources are like strengths or abilities within ourselves. We can use these strengths to solve problems that come with new, complex, and unclear challenges in our career, like adopting new tasks, switching jobs, or facing difficulties at work.[91] These resources shape the strategies we use to adjust and handle changes.

Career transition resourcefulness framework is made up of four career "adapt-abilities": concern, control, curiosity, and confidence.[92]

Concern involves your awareness of and preparation for your career future. If you have a high level of concern, you strategically plan for your career future. Concern indicates the extent to which you are aware of and prepare for your own career future.

Control centres on the beliefs you hold about your personal responsibility for career preparation and your perceptions around the level of control you have over your career situation and future, while those with a strong sense of control often take proactive measures and exhibit personal responsibility.

Control reflects beliefs about personal responsibility for preparing your career and the perceived personal control of your career situation and future. If you believe your career aspirations are achievable, you are more likely to persistently work towards these goals, even in the face of difficult career shocks.

Curiosity, on the other hand, signifies your inclination and ability to explore professional environments, including learning about various types of work and job opportunities. It triggers you to explore and learn about diverse career paths, contributing to adaptability in the face of change. Curiosity reflects the personal tendency and the ability to explore professional environments, for example by exploring and learning about types of work and occupational opportunities available for someone with skills and experience similar to yours.

Lastly, *confidence* plays a key role in your perceived self-efficacy in resolving the stumbling blocks you may encounter while navigating this stage. Confidence empowers you to navigate challenges and take advantage of opportunities during career transitions. Confidence is demonstrated by your perceived self-efficacy to resolve problems encountered during transitions and your ability to successfully do what is necessary to overcome obstacles.

These career "adapt-abilities" are the resources that each one of us can develop so that we are able to manage career transitions and adapt to career changes. In essence, resourcefulness equips individuals to effectively manage career changes, demonstrating flexibility, resilience, and a proactive approach to their professional journey.

Potential Derailers of the Managing Career Transitions Stage

The Managing Career Transitions Stage is one of the most volatile and unstable stages as it is all about change, transitions and transformation. In such situations, you are already responding to something that has gone wrong and a lot more can be challenging during this stage.

For example, my coaching client, Sarah, was a mid-level manager in a manufacturing facility that suddenly underwent restructuring, leading to the elimination of her department. Faced with the unexpected loss of her role, Sarah had to quickly transition into job searching, upskilling, and adapting to new industry demands. During this volatile stage, she experienced uncertainty, financial strain, and emotional stress, all while trying to navigate her career transition.

One of the potential challenges during this stage is having a strong *desire to conform to social norms and seek high levels of acceptance.* These traits may hinder career adaptability resources, making it difficult to navigate career transitions effectively.[93] This often plays out in situations, where you know you should transition out of particular job or company; however, due to the yearning to be perceived in a particular way by family, colleagues or society as a whole, you may choose to remain in a job that no longer serves you and that doesn't align to your career goals.

Challenges encountered in the early stages of your career journey often resurface in Stage Eight, influencing your work relationships with colleagues and bosses. The archetypes associated with our earlier experiences, especially those resembling child archetypes, tend to manifest in this stage. Challenges may include unresolved issues related to authority, collaboration, and interpersonal dynamics.

For instance, if early career stages involve struggles with authority figures (such as continuous conflict with your team leader), similar challenges may arise in interactions with bosses during Stage Eight. Recognising and addressing these recurring patterns becomes crucial for personal and professional growth, as it allows you to navigate workplace relationships more effectively and break free from persistent challenges rooted in their early career experiences.

Another significant challenge encountered in Stage Eight is *the fear of change,* which is deeply connected to the potential losses experienced during this transformative phase. The darkness associated with such losses can challenge your sense of personal control, particularly when facing the uncertainties that come with job loss, changes in employment benefits, and a shift in position power.

Events such as redundancies, organisational restructuring, or even transitions to new employers or professions may trigger these fears. Navigating these changes requires resilience and adaptability as you grapple with the emotional and psychological impact of letting go of familiar roles, statuses, and workplace structures. It requires embracing the unknown and building the capacity to thrive amidst change.

Another challenge in Stage Eight is the *potential failure to take responsibility* for the transformation and regeneration that is forced upon you. The inherent pain of this process can give rise to feelings of resentment, blame, and even deep-seated hatred towards those perceived to have initiated or instigated the change. Resistance to accepting personal responsibility may block your ability to fully engage with the required adaptations and may prolong the healing process.

This challenge highlights the importance of embracing a mindset that encourages self-reflection and accountability, ultimately fostering a more constructive approach to navigating the complex dynamics of career transformation during Stage Eight.

Key Challenges of the Managing Career Transitions Stage

Career transitions are complex processes requiring a solid foundation, often established in the initial stages of one's career journey. These transitions can be difficult to manage if fundamental elements from earlier stages are not clearly defined and addressed.

For example:

Career identity in Stage One: the challenge of navigating transitions can often be linked to the lack of a well-defined career identity. Research has shown that identity plays a pivotal role during transitions, as individuals who have a clear understanding of their career goals and aspirations are better equipped to manage change.[94] When career identity is ambiguous, people may struggle to determine their next steps, leading to confusion and indecision.

The process of **developing your identity** is important during significant life transitions, such as entering a new career or educational phase, highlighting that a well-formed identity facilitates smoother transitions by offering a clear sense of direction. If your career story—your long-term vision and purpose—remains undefined, transitions may feel overwhelming and lack clarity.[95]

Building career capital in Stage Two: a major difficulty in career transitions is identifying and leveraging one's career capital—skills, networks, and experiences that have been built over time. Studies on career transitions highlight that individuals who successfully transition to new roles tend to have a well-developed portfolio of skills and contacts.[96]

If you haven't invested in growing your career capital, it becomes challenging to market yourself in new environments or industries. Career capital isn't just about possessing skills but understanding where and how these skills can be applied in different contexts, something that requires strategic foresight developed earlier in one's career journey.

Managing the background effects in Stage Three: the role of personal background—such as family, socioeconomic status, or early career experiences—can be another critical factor in career transitions. Research suggests that background effects, including confidence and self-efficacy issues, may become especially pronounced during times of transition.[97]

If left unresolved, these background influences can diminish self-belief at critical points when career decisions need to be made. Confidence, built through both personal growth and external validation, is essential during career transitions as it shapes one's ability to adapt and make informed decisions in a rapidly changing career landscape.

Career anchors in Stage Four: anchors, as identified by Schein, are internalised guides that help individuals make choices about their professional lives. When these anchors are not well-defined, transitions become far more challenging. Understanding your intrinsic motivators—whether autonomy, security, or creativity—helps to filter career opportunities and choose roles that align with your long-term aspirations.

Lacking clarity on career anchors might lead you to pursue roles that don't align with your true values, causing repeated career dissatisfaction and prolonging the transition process.

Talents, strengths, and passions from Stage Five: lastly, if you lack clarity on your innate talents, strengths, and passions, transitions can become disorienting. Career researchers agree that aligning one's next career move with their core strengths leads to better long-term job satisfaction and performance.[98]

Without a clear sense of what you are good at and what you enjoy doing, the transition to a new role might feel like grasping at straws, as you may not be able to confidently assert what type of role or industry would suit your unique capabilities.

Contextualising experienced changes and navigating complexities of unexpected transformations can be a challenge if perceived negatively. The ability to embrace change positively, even in the face of crises is helpful in such situations

In the case of expected or self-induced change, the challenge can be on the *miscalculated impact of the transition*. The impact of changing jobs, the impact of starting your business, or the impact of changing industries can be miscalculated, leading to inadequate preparation. When John, a previous coaching client, decided to leave his executive job at a utility company and ventured into starting his own business, he never anticipated that his new company would require him to play multiple roles at once. He found himself being an IT manager, HR Manager, Sales and Marketing etc. He struggled with the concept of being an entrepreneur. Nothing could have ever prepared him for this.

The big challenge in this stage is *resisting change*. Have you seen people who remain in jobs holding to the idea of what the job was when they were first hired? When change comes, they try to push it under the mat and try to act as if nothing is changing hoping that the change will go away. Some people hold on to the job, allowing the most atrocious things to be done to end. Think of situations where you ask yourself, "Why hasn't this individual left already?"

In conclusion, the challenges encountered during career transitions are often rooted in the foundational work that was (or was not) addressed in the earlier stages of your career journey. Without a well-defined career identity, strong career capital, or a deep understanding of your background effects, career anchors, and personal strengths, transitions can become overwhelming and disorienting. These foundational elements serve as a roadmap to help you navigate the inevitable uncertainties and opportunities of career transitions.

It's crucial to recognise that transitions are an inherent part of any career, making it all the more important to have those career fundamentals in place. By ensuring that these essential building blocks are solid, you equip yourself with the tools needed to effectively manage shifts in your professional journey.

Preparing for these transitions requires intentional reflection on the lessons from earlier stages and continuous growth. This reflection enables you to enter the next phase of your career with confidence, clarity, and resilience. The next section focuses on practices that can help minimise the impact of these challenges.

Success Strategies for the Managing Career Transitions Stage

Navigating the career transitions stage requires more than just reacting to changes; it calls for a proactive mindset and strategic practices that can help you manage uncertainty and transform challenges into opportunities.

In the next paragraphs, we will explore the mindset and key career practices that will empower you to navigate career transitions with confidence and purpose.

Adopting a boundaryless career mindset: the boundaryless career mindset represents a significant shift in how we perceive and navigate our career journeys. Unlike the traditional notion of a career tied to a single organisation, this mindset acknowledges the dynamic nature of today's work landscape, fostering the realisation that organisational changes are constant challenges as is the idea of lifelong employment with a single employer. Adopting a boundaryless career mindset brings a proactive approach to career management.[99]

Embracing a boundaryless career mindset means recognising that skills and knowledge are portable assets. It requires a continuous commitment to staying alert and vigilant, fostering adaptability, and openness to moving where your expertise are most valued. Instead of fixating on job security within a single organisation, individuals with this mindset prioritise employability. This shift involves actively seeking diverse experiences, honing leadership skills, and building a versatile skill set that transcends organisational boundaries.

Adopting a protean career mindset attitude: the term "protean" derives from the Greek god, Proteus, known for his ability to change forms, symbolising adaptability and self-direction. Hall used the concept to describe a career mindset that is flexible, self-directed, and driven by personal values rather than external factors such as organisational loyalty or traditional career paths.

This mindset emphasises the importance of individuals taking control of their own career development, adapting to changes in the environment, and aligning their work with their personal values and life goals.

The Protean Career model reflects the changing nature of careers in the modern world, where individuals are less likely to follow a linear path and more likely to experience multiple career changes throughout their working lives. The protean career attitude goes beyond traditional notions, framing a career as a calling and a means of self-fulfilment.[100]

At its core, this mindset recognises your strengths and talents as tools for a unique mission. It acknowledges the workplace as a stage, where personal abilities can be harnessed to fulfil your unique purpose.

A key tenet of the protean career mindset is realising that you own and self-direct your career. This approach empowers you to shape your career journey according to your values and beliefs, distinct from organisational expectations. In contrast to conforming to external standards, if you adopt a protean career attitude, you will navigate your journey based on personally-defined goals. Embracing this mindset signifies a departure from conventional career paradigms, encouraging a more self-aware, values-centric, and self-directed approach to professional development.

Placing a high value on a protean career attitude might result in higher *goal-setting* and a greater investment of effort because you feel responsible for your career and want to act according to your own values and aspirations.

Having a learning goal-oriented mindset: the learning goal-oriented mindset underscores the intentional pursuit of knowledge, skill acquisition, and valuable experiences within any given professional environment. This mindset instills a *sense of purposeful learning*, emphasising the importance of continuously expanding your capabilities regardless of the job or setting. It fosters a proactive attitude that rejects the tendency to underestimate or downplay the significance of any role.

Within this mindset, you can recognise that *every job or environment provides a unique opportunity for growth and development*. Instead of viewing certain positions as mere stepping stones, the learning goal-oriented mindset encourages you to actively seek out opportunities to enhance your skills and gather diverse experiences. It involves a strategic approach, thinking beyond the immediate tasks at hand and thinking how each role contributes to your personal and professional growth.

Furthermore, this mindset prompts you to *consider how you can effectively communicate and leverage the skills and experiences you have acquired*. By being mindful of the value derived from your learning journey, you can articulate your contributions and capabilities in a way that aligns with your career goals.

Adopting a proactive mindset: a proactive mindset is crucial during times of career transition or transformation, *embodying a sense of ownership and self-direction in one's career journey*. This mindset transcends short-term thinking, emphasising the importance of taking decisive actions in the present to lay the groundwork for future career goals. Proactivity involves a forward-looking approach, where you actively plan and prepare for your career journey, recognising that the choices made today shape the possibilities of tomorrow.

In the context of career transition, a *proactive mindset means steering your own course and not waiting for external cues or directives*. It also means taking initiative to set long-term career objectives and actively pursuing them. This extends to interactions with superiors and colleagues, where you assertively communicate your career aspirations, intentions, and plans.

For instance, proactively engaging in discussions with a current boss about future career moves or approaching leaders in a desired department well in advance, even before positions become available, exemplifies the proactive mindset.

By embodying a proactive mindset, you not only take charge of your career journey but also *cultivate a sense of empowerment and agency*. Rather than being passive recipients of career changes, those with a proactive mindset actively shape their professional destinies, influencing the direction of their careers with purpose and foresight.

Career planning: career planning plays a pivotal role in mastering the career transition stage, particularly when experiencing career shocks. Having a well-thought-out career plan provides you with a strategic roadmap that aligns with your long-term goals and aspirations. In the face of unexpected transitions or challenges, a career plan serves as a valuable reference point, offering predefined options and directions.

While unplanned transitions may demand quick decision making, a pre-established career plan empowers you to respond in ways that align with your intended career journey. This proactive approach not only helps maintain focus amid uncertainties but also ensures that decisions made during critical moments are in harmony with one's overarching career objectives.

Career exploration: is all about behaviours aimed at gaining access to information about occupations, jobs, and organisations not previously within your immediate field. It involves the deliberate gathering of relevant information to inform the progress of your career.

In the context of career transitions, career exploration serves multifaceted purposes. It *facilitates the establishment of coherent career plans*, enabling you to pursue a work life that is personally meaningful. Moreover, it equips you with the tools to navigate rapid changes and effectively manage diverse transitions.

While its significance is particularly pronounced in Stage Eight, career exploration is recognised as a lifelong and adaptive function, integral to the broader concept of career adaptability. As you navigate this transformative stage, the practice of career exploration empowers you to make informed decisions, fostering adaptability and coherence in your evolving career journey.

In summary, career transitions are a pivotal stage in any professional journey, marked by shifts that may be significant or subtle, vertical or horizontal, voluntary or involuntary. The positives of this stage include the opportunity for personal and professional growth, as transitions can open doors to new skills, roles, and industries.

They provide a chance for individuals to realign their careers with their evolving values, strengths, and passions. Transitions can also enhance your career flexibility, making you more resilient to future changes and better able to adapt to dynamic work environments.

However, career transitions also come with potential derailers. Emotional reactions to change, such as fear, uncertainty, or insecurity, can lead to poor decision making or even career paralysis. Without adequate preparation, transitions may result in a loss of career momentum or even a sense of professional identity.

The challenge of financial instability during a transition period can become a major concern, especially if the shift involves a period of unemployment or retraining. Family responsibilities and the lack of social support can further complicate the experience, making transitions harder to manage.

Key challenges during career transitions often revolve around managing uncertainty, maintaining a clear sense of career direction, and ensuring financial and emotional stability. Professionals need to develop the emotional resilience to face the stresses associated with change, while also being mindful of their long-term career goals. Additionally, understanding and adapting to new workplace dynamics or industry expectations can be particularly daunting when the transition involves moving into unfamiliar territory.

To navigate this stage effectively, it is crucial to adopt a proactive and adaptive mindset. Embracing a boundaryless mindset allows you to view opportunities beyond the confines of a single organisation or industry, while a protean mindset helps you remain flexible, prioritising personal values and continuous growth.

Engaging in career planning practices, such as setting clear career goals and maintaining a network of professional connections, will ensure you are prepared for transitions before they occur. Continuous learning and skills development are essential practices to stay relevant in a constantly evolving job market.

Furthermore, being mindful of personal circumstances—such as family, financial stability, and social support—will help you better manage the emotional and logistical challenges of transitions.

Ultimately, career transitions are an opportunity to reinvent and realign your career. By preparing early, cultivating a mindset that embraces change, and staying adaptable, you can confidently navigate transitions and create a career path that aligns with your long-term purpose and values.

Stage Eight Coaching Questions

What transformative change have you been hesitating to embrace? What steps or mindset shifts can empower you to feel fully prepared for this exciting new chapter?

Stage Nine – Finding Purpose and Meaning in Your Career

Pearl sat at the edge of her desk in the small, dimly lit apartment she had grown accustomed to in Poland. The hum of machines from the manufacturing facility next door had become a familiar backdrop to her daily routine, but today, it felt more like a distant echo than a source of pride. Her gaze drifted to the framed photograph on her desk: a snapshot of her former team in Kenya, full of bright faces and hopeful smiles.

A year and a half ago, Pearl had been in a different world. Her company's manufacturing operations, which once thrived in Kenya, had been shut down and relocated to Poland. The move had been a blow not just to the local economy but to Pearl's sense of purpose. Her role had transformed from a leader fostering growth and development in a developing world to a specialist overseeing a new facility in Europe.

The company had offered her a significant retention bonus and a crucial role: managing the start-up of the machinery in Poland. It was an opportunity that couldn't be ignored, given her unique skill set and experience. She had accepted the challenge, driven by a sense of duty and the excitement of new professional growth. Yet as the facility settled into its operations and Pearl's role shifted from start-up manager to ongoing overseer, she found herself grappling with an unsettling sense of disconnection.

In Kenya, her job had been more than a career; it was a calling. She had thrived on mentoring young talent, creating jobs, and contributing to the development of a community she cared deeply about. Her work aligned seamlessly with her personal purpose of uplifting developing regions. It wasn't just about the tasks she performed; it was about the impact she made every day.

Now, in Poland, Pearl's job felt less meaningful. The sense of purpose she once derived from her work seemed to have dissipated. She had become a cog in a well-oiled machine, her contributions less visible, and her impact less immediate. The daily grind of the new facility, while professionally fulfilling, left her questioning whether she was still living her purpose or merely going through the motions of her role.

As Pearl reflected on her journey, she couldn't ignore the growing realisation that her career transition had altered her sense of meaning. The experiences and challenges she faced while relocating and settling into a new environment shifted her perspective. The alignment she once felt between her job and her personal purpose now seemed elusive.

Sitting in her apartment, Pearl felt a deep need to reassess her career journey. She wondered if there was a way to reconnect with her sense of purpose or if she needed to redefine it entirely. The questions were daunting, but they were also a call to action: how could she align her current role with the passion that once drove her? How could she find new meaning in her career that resonated with her personal values?

As Stage Nine unfolds, we learn about creating purpose and personal meaning from our job and our career. This chapter is a reminder that achieving this alignment is an ongoing process that requires proactive and intentional actions.

In Stage Nine, after overcoming the career shock and transitions of the previous stages, we emerge feeling renewed and wiser. As we begin to settle into our new circumstances, we often confront the challenging question, "What does it all mean?" We start to reflect on how our experiences align with our deeper sense of purpose and reason for being, seeking clarity on the meaning and direction of our career journey.

Aligning your career with your personal purpose means ensuring that your professional life reflects and supports your core values, beliefs, and long-term aspirations. According to Mark Savickas in Career Construction Theory, this alignment involves crafting a career that integrates personal narratives with work experiences, thus creating a cohesive story of one's professional life.[101] Savickas emphasises that when we align our career paths with our personal purpose, we experience greater satisfaction and fulfilment.

For instance, in Pearl's story, her alignment with her personal purpose was evident when she worked in Kenya. Her role in working with those not so fortunate matched her passion for creating opportunities and mentoring young talent.

However, after relocating to Poland, Pearl began to question whether her new role still resonated with her core values and long-term goals: the search for meaning and purpose and looking for something greater out there that explains our career choices and career experiences. We yearn to create significance and meaning from our career experiences.

Searching for meaning in your job involves understanding how your work connects to your sense of identity and purpose. In his research on meaningful work, Michael Steger defines it as the extent to which individuals see their work as purposeful, significant, and contributing to the greater good.[102] For work to be meaningful, an individual must identify a personally significant contribution they make through their efforts. Meaningful work reflects the subjective experience that one's job or career aligns harmoniously with the broader meaning and purpose of their life. It also empowers individuals to feel that their work positively impacts others or society.

In Pearl's case, her work in Kenya felt meaningful because it allowed her to contribute to local development and mentor young talent, directly aligning with her personal mission. This sense of significance and contribution gave her work a sense of purpose that went beyond daily tasks.

However, after relocating to Poland, Pearl struggled to find the same personal and social impact in her new role, causing her to question whether her work still held the same meaning for her.

Aligning your purpose with your work leads to the experience of meaningful work. The two are closely interconnected: meaningful work cannot truly be achieved without aligning your job or career with your personal purpose. When your work reflects your core values, beliefs, and sense of purpose, it creates a deeper sense of significance and fulfilment. Without this alignment, work can feel disconnected, lacking the personal impact that gives it meaning.

Overview of the Stage of Searching for Purpose and Meaning

The primary characteristic of Stage Nine revolves around the *quest for meaning, guidelines, goals, and a sense of purpose*. As humans, we inherently seek meaning, desiring absolutes and steadfast ideals to aspire to, along with principles that can guide our lives. The absence of meaning can evoke a sense of emptiness, leaving us feeling as though there is nothing to live for, no hope, no reason to strive, and a lack of direction in life.

Psychologists often link psychological issues, such as neurosis, to the absence of meaning and purpose. In this stage, the exploration of profound existential questions becomes a central theme, as we grapple with the need to establish a meaningful framework that provides direction, purpose, and a sense of fulfilment in our career journey.[103]

Another distinctive characteristic of the stage of searching for meaning involves deeper exploration of intellectual and spiritual realms, reflecting journeys of the mind. During this stage, *we strive to attribute philosophical, meaningful, or spiritual perspectives to the unfolding narrative of our career journey*. When significant events occur in our career, we try to identify philosophical or spiritual significance in relation to these experiences.

The ninth stage is marked by a deep introspection into the broader implications and interconnectedness of our professional path, prompting us to seek profound meaning and purpose beyond the surface-level events. The lens through which we view our career broadens, encompassing not only practical aspects but also the philosophical and spiritual dimensions, contributing to a richer and more holistic understanding of the unfolding journey.

An example is when someone faces a job loss; instead of seeing it solely as a setback, they begin to reflect on what this change means for their life's purpose. They might consider how this event can redirect them towards a career that aligns more closely with their passions or values, prompting them to explore new fields that resonate with their personal purpose. This shift in perspective allows them to view the situation not just as a challenge but as an opportunity for growth and rediscovery. It leads to a career path that feels more meaningful.

Stage Nine is marked by the endeavour to comprehend the essence of our relationships within a collective context. During this stage, *we develop career foresight, showcasing the ability to envision our career journey beyond its current state.* This forward-looking perspective emphasises a focus on the future and an anticipation of what is yet to unfold in our professional journey. It is characterised by a deliberate attempt to create a comprehensive understanding of everything transpiring in our career, going beyond immediate circumstances to gain insight into the broader context.

For example, the practice of aligning significant career events to the vision you have for your career. Typically, the career shocks and the career transitions that you experience in the last two stages are aligned to the broader contexts of your career

Positives of the Stage of Finding Purpose and Meaning

When your work aligns with your personal purpose and becomes meaningful, you begin to experience certain characteristics that define a deeply fulfilling career which are demonstrated by:

1. Self-transcendent: a key characteristic of meaningful work is its self-transcendent nature, you feel that your work contributes to something greater than yourself. This sense of transcendence allows you to connect your personal efforts to a broader societal impact, creating purpose and meaning beyond the individual level. Abraham Maslow, known for his Hierarchy of Needs, placed self-transcendence at the top of his pyramid, emphasising that the highest form of human motivation is the desire to contribute to others.

For example, a garbage collector may find meaning in his work when he sees how his daily efforts contribute to creating a cleaner environment for future generations. Similarly, a professor might find her work meaningful when she sees her students graduate, understanding that her teaching has contributed to their personal success and the community.

2. Poignant / sentimental: meaningful work is often poignant, encompassing not only positive experiences but also challenging, emotionally charged moments. Research shows that the most meaningful moments often arise during difficult times. Nurses, for example, may find profound meaning in easing a patient's final moments, even though the experience is painful.[104]

Similarly, a lawyer who dedicates years to securing a life-changing verdict for a client may find the work deeply meaningful, even though the journey was difficult. These experiences are richer and more memorable because they involve overcoming challenges and having a lasting impact.

3. Episodic: meaningful work tends to be episodic, arising in specific moments of significance rather than consistently throughout your career. No one experiences meaningfulness in their work continuously, but rather during peak moments that are highly emotional and impactful. Research by social scientists highlights these moments as highly memorable, often becoming part of your life narrative.

For example, one actor who was interviewed in a study of meaningful work summed this feeling up well: "My God, I'm actually doing what I dreamt I could do; that's kind of amazing." These peak moments are rare but create lasting significance for the individual.

4. Reflective awareness is another characteristic of meaningful work. Often, meaningfulness is not realised in the moment but in retrospect, after you have had time to reflect on your work's broader significance. Research shows that people frequently become aware of their work's meaningfulness when they step back and connect it to their broader life purpose.

For example, an academic might reflect on decades of research and realise its significance only when it leads to technological advancements. Similarly, a street sweeper may look back at a clean street and realise how their work contributes to a healthier environment for the community. Meaningfulness emerges from thoughtful reflection, rather than immediate emotional responses, as you connect your work to broader life goals.

5. Personal: meaningful work is also personal, deeply connected to your life experiences and values. It goes beyond workplace engagement and extends into how work relates to one's personal identity and relationships. Researchers have found that meaningful work often carries personal significance, such as fulfilling family expectations or aligning with one's life goals.

For instance, a musician may find a performance especially meaningful when a family member attends and expresses pride. Similarly, an entrepreneur may be motivated to succeed not only for personal achievement but also to honour a family legacy. This intertwining of work and personal life elevates the sense of meaning in your career.

Authors Catherine Bailey and Adrienne Madden conducted a study in 2016; they interviewed 135 people working in ten very different occupations and asked them to tell stories about incidents or times when they found their work to be meaningful and, conversely, times when they asked themselves, "What's the point of doing this job?"[105]

The study found that meaningfulness tended to be intensely personal and individual; it was often revealed to employees as they reflected on their work and its wider contribution to society in ways that mattered to them as individuals. People tended to speak of their work as meaningful in relation to thoughts or memories of significant family members such as parents or children, bridging the gap between work and the personal realm. Interviewees talked of unplanned or unexpected moments during which they found their work deeply meaningful.

The study also found that meaningfulness appeared to be driven up and decreased by different factors. Interviewees tended to find meaningfulness for themselves rather than it being mandated by their managers. If employers want to destroy that sense of meaningfulness, that was far more easily achieved. The feeling of "Why am I bothering to do this?" strikes people the instant a meaningless moment arises, and it strikes people hard.

If meaningfulness is a delicate flower that requires careful nurturing, think of someone trampling over that flower in a pair of steel-toed boots. Avoiding the destruction of meaning while nurturing an ecosystem generative of feelings of meaningfulness emerged as the key leadership challenge.[106]

What we can learn from this study is that you are the only one who can create meaning from your work because it is personal. Your employer can only create conditions that enable you to do the work at your best possible self and reflect on the impact you are making and the meaningfulness of that impact.

Finding meaning and purpose in your work can sometimes seem abstract, theoretical, or even impractical. However, these characteristics offer practical indicators that help us understand how meaning and purpose manifest in our work lives. If you're uncertain whether your work truly aligns with your purpose, reflecting on whether you've experienced any of these traits can provide clarity. The next section explores the challenges and downsides that may arise during this stage.

Potential Derailers of the Stage of Finding Purpose and Meaning

The downside of Stage Nine is the *tendency to seek meaning for every event that happens in your career*. While the quest for meaning is a positive aspect, over analysing every occurrence can lead to an *excessive search for significance, potentially causing stress and anxiety.* This inclination to interpret every detail may result in an overwhelming desire to find profound meaning in even mundane or random events. It's important to strike a balance, acknowledging that not every event may carry deep symbolic meaning.

This aspect highlights the need for discernment, encouraging us to distinguish between meaningful patterns and the ordinary fluctuations of a dynamic career journey. An awareness of this helps in maintaining a healthy perspective and prevents the undue burden of attributing excessive significance to every twist and turn in your professional life.

Alexis is a great example of how this can unfold; she is a dedicated professional in the advertising industry who sought profound meaning in every twist of her career journey. She often found herself caught in a web of overthinking and stress, ascribing excessive importance to even the most routine aspects of her job.

This constant quest for profound meaning started to hinder her ability to navigate the dynamic and often unpredictable nature of the advertising world. As time went on, colleagues noticed that Alex's over-analysis resulted in indecisiveness and a lack of adaptability.

Unfortunately, this eventually took a toll on Alex's professional relationships and overall well-being. The need to find meaning in every moment, although well-intentioned, became a stumbling block in Alex's career progression.

Lack of long-term career perspective: similarly, navigating your career without a long-term perspective, assuming that it will naturally unfold without deliberate planning, can be a potential drawback during Stage Nine. This lack of foresight may lead to a reactive rather than a proactive approach to career development. Individuals who take each day as it comes without a long-term plan may miss valuable opportunities for growth and find themselves unprepared when faced with career shocks.

A strategic, long-term career perspective involves setting goals, envisioning the desired trajectory, and planning steps to achieve those objectives. Without this perspective, we risk becoming complacent, relying on the belief that our career will unfold without active engagement. This mindset may hinder the pursuit of meaningful opportunities and the ability to navigate transitions effectively.

Lack of a practical action plan for your career: relying solely on meaning and beliefs without practical plans for one's career can have potential negative impacts on our professional development. While faith and belief can provide a source of inspiration and guidance, the lack of concrete, actionable plans may result in a lack of tangible outcomes. Believing in a higher power is meaningful, but it needs to be complemented by proactive steps and strategic actions to navigate the complexities of the career journey effectively.

The danger lies in passivity, when you may adopt a mindset of leaving everything to fate without taking charge of creating actionable plans that deliver your career aspirations. Without practical plans and actions, opportunities for growth and development may be overlooked or missed entirely.

It's essential to strike a balance between faith and proactive engagement, leveraging one's religious beliefs as a source of strength and guidance while actively participating in career planning and decision making

Discarding employment opportunities: exclusively seeking jobs that align with what you deem to be your personal purpose and values can have potential negative impacts on your career. One notable consequence is the limitation of employment opportunities. When you narrow your job search solely to roles that perfectly resonate with your ideals, you may inadvertently restrict your options, especially in dynamic job markets offering diverse opportunities.

Narrowing your focus on jobs that perfectly align to your personal purpose can lead to extended periods of unemployment or underemployment, overlooking that discovering meaning and purpose in your career is an evolving journey.

While the pursuit of meaning in your career is important, overanalysing every detail and lacking a long-term perspective can lead to stress, indecisiveness, and missed opportunities. Balancing your sense of purpose with practical career planning is essential to avoid passivity or limiting your job prospects. Let's explore the common tests and challenges you may face in the quest for meaning and purpose, and how to navigate them effectively.

Key Challenges of the Stage of Finding Your Purpose and Meaning

Quest for meaning: the quest for meaning in every career event poses a challenge during Stage Nine. You may find yourself *overanalysing and overinterpreting situations, attempting to extract profound significance from every aspect of their professional lives.* This relentless search for meaning can lead to unnecessary stress and hinder the ability to navigate career events with clarity.

The challenge is to balance the need to derive meaning and ability to move on and take each experience as it comes. I can think of a number of situations when I was coaching clients going through career transitions as a result of career shocks; moving to action follows the time spent seeking meaning from unfavourable career events.

To overcome this challenge, it is beneficial to develop a discerning mindset. Recognising that not every occurrence requires a profound meaning allows you to focus on the inherent purpose and impact of specific experiences. By adopting a balanced and realistic interpretation of career events, you can derive meaningful insights without overwhelming yourself in the quest for constant meaning.

Long-term career perspective: maintaining a long-term career perspective becomes a challenge in Stage Nine, where you may assume that your career future will unfold organically without the need for deliberate planning. Overlooking the importance of a well-defined long-term plan can leave you unprepared for future opportunities and challenges.

To overcome this challenge, a proactive approach to career planning is essential. You need to set clear goals, envision their desired journey, and formulate actionable steps for long-term success. Embracing strategic career planning ensures that you are equipped to navigate your professional journey with purpose and direction, contributing to a more fulfilling and sustainable career.

Lack of career vision: a significant challenge in Stage Nine revolves around the lack of a clear vision for your career. When individuals fail to cultivate a long-term perspective and instead navigate their professional lives day by day, it often results in last-minute actions that lack strategic impact. Oftentimes, this might lead to dissatisfaction, demotivation and lack of engagement. "I don't know what comes next in my career after this" is the statement I often hear as a reason for needing coaching.

Successful career transitions and advancements demand careful planning, extensive networking, and the continuous acquisition of knowledge and skills. Waiting until an ideal job opportunity is advertised is a reactive approach that always proves to be too late.

Visionary career planning involves anticipating future moves, proactively building networks, and acquiring the necessary expertise well in advance. *Overcoming the challenge of lacking a career vision requires a shift toward strategic thinking and proactive career management.* By setting long-term goals, you can align your actions to your envisioned career journey, ensuring that each step contributes to the larger narrative of your professional journey.

Overcoming this challenge empowers you to make intentional decisions, fostering a sense of control and purpose in your career. It highlights the importance of foresight and preparation in navigating the complexities of the evolving professional landscape.

Success Strategies for the Stage of Finding Your Purpose and Meaning

Adopting a holistic career code / principles: you can enhance your career mastery by developing a comprehensive career code. This involves defining a set of moral principles, ideals, beliefs, and ethical standards that guide your professional choices. For instance, believing in the value of hard work for salary advancement or recognising the importance of building a robust track record for career excellence.

By consciously shaping a career code, you create a framework for interpreting and deriving meaning from your career experiences. This practice promotes a sense of purpose and coherence, aligning actions with deeply held values and principles, which contributes to a fulfilling and meaningful professional journey.

Cultivating a long-term career vision: a crucial best practice in Stage Nine is cultivating a long-term vision for your career. This involves proactively planning and strategizing for future moves, well before ideal opportunities arise. Instead of reacting to immediate job openings, you should focus on building networks, acquiring relevant skills, and staying informed about industry trends.

A clear career vision enables individuals to make intentional and impactful decisions, ensuring that each step contributes to their overarching career trajectory. This practice empowers you to navigate the dynamic and uncertain nature of the professional landscape with purpose and foresight.

Embracing continuous learning and adaptability: in the rapidly-evolving world of work, adopting a mindset of continuous learning and adaptability is an important best practice for career mastery. Stage Nine calls for an active commitment to acquiring new skills, staying updated on industry trends, and embracing change. Those who prioritise learning remain agile and resilient in the face of evolving challenges.

This fosters a proactive approach to career development, ensuring that you are well-prepared for the ever-changing demands of your profession. Embracing continuous learning becomes a key driver for success in Stage Nine, promoting adaptability and sustained career growth.

In summary, the stage of finding meaning and purpose in your career is a deeply introspective and transformative phase. It is marked by expansive thinking, where individuals strive to understand the greater purpose behind their professional lives. This stage presents a platform to align one's career with their personal values, beliefs, and long-term vision, offering a sense of fulfilment and clarity about their path.

A positive aspect of this stage is the development of career foresight—the ability to see beyond immediate roles and tasks to understand how your work contributes to a larger narrative, both for yourself and for the world around you.

However, Stage Nine also comes with potential derailers. One of the primary challenges is the tendency to overanalyse or seek profound meaning in every career event. This can lead to frustration, especially in roles or tasks that may not seem immediately aligned with personal purpose.

Another potential risk is becoming overly fixated on finding jobs that are perfectly aligned with your personal values, which can limit opportunities and reduce career flexibility. It's important to strike a balance between seeking meaningful work and maintaining a practical perspective.

Key challenges in this stage include avoiding the trap of constantly questioning the purpose of every career decision or experience. This constant reflection can lead to indecision and stagnation if not balanced with action and practical considerations. Additionally, one might face the difficulty of reconciling personal values with the demands of the current job market or organisational culture, leading to internal conflict or dissatisfaction.

To navigate this stage effectively, adopting a balanced mindset is crucial. Cultivating a comprehensive career code—grounded in your personal values but adaptable to different career situations—can help you stay focused. Embracing a long-term vision, rather than seeking immediate fulfilment in every task, enables you to stay patient and resilient.

Continuous learning and growth are also vital, as they allow you to explore new perspectives and remain adaptable in an ever-changing career landscape.

By mastering this stage, you not only create a purposeful career path but also lay the foundation for your legacy—how your career contributions will be remembered and appreciated in the long term. Balancing meaning with practicality ensures that you remain grounded, adaptable, and fulfilled as you continue your professional journey.

Stage Nine Coaching Questions

What deeper sense of meaning and purpose do you gain from your current work, and how does it align with your personal values and long-term aspirations?

Stage Ten – Your Ambition and Career Legacy

Title: The Producers

Scene: Max Bialystock's office

(The stage is set in a small, run-down office filled with faded posters of Max's past Broadway flops. A cluttered desk with piles of paperwork dominates the space. MAX BIALYSTOCK, a flamboyant and ambitious producer, paces energetically, while LEO BLOOM, his anxious accountant, stands nervously by the desk, clutching a stack of financial records.)

Max Bialystock: *(With dramatic flair, his eyes gleam with excitement)*
Don't you see, Leo? This is it! This is our moment! Our time to create a legacy like no one's ever seen! We'll produce the biggest flop in Broadway history—and that's how we'll win. We'll be legendary!

Leo Bloom: *(nervously, glancing at the records)*
But Max...that's crazy. What if it works? What if it's a hit? We'll be ruined.

Max Bialystock: *(laughing heartily, dismissing Leo's concerns)*

A hit? Leo, no one wants a hit! They want a sensation! They want scandal, controversy, something so bad it's brilliant. And we're going to give it to them. This...is how you build a brand, my boy. Think about it. Max Bialystock, the man who defied the rules and turned failure into fame. That's my legacy. That's what they'll remember.

Leo Bloom: *(hesitant, fidgeting with the papers)*

But Max...what if...what if people don't see it that way? What if they think we're just failures?

Max Bialystock: *(leaning in closer, his voice filled with conviction)*

Leo, listen to me. Success isn't about being good. It's about being remembered. You see, in this world, you don't get to decide your legacy by playing it safe. You have to take risks, make bold moves, and make sure everyone knows your name. Even if we fail, they'll be talking about us for years. That is the power of branding, Leo! It's not just about what you do, it's about how you're remembered.

Leo Bloom: *(gaining confidence, a spark igniting in his eyes)*

So... even if we lose, we win?

Max Bialystock: *(grinning widely, brimming with enthusiasm)*

Exactly! We're not just producing a play, Leo. We're producing our legacy. The spotlight is waiting for us. And when the curtain falls, we'll get our standing ovation, whether it's for genius or insanity. Either way, we win.

(Max slaps Leo on the back with a flourish, both men's faces lighting up with wild ambition as they turn to face the door, symbolising the entrance to their audacious future.)

(The lights dim slightly, highlighting their hopeful expressions as the stage fades to black.)

End scene[107]

The tenth stage is like stepping onto the grand stage in a theatre, where all eyes are on you under the main spotlight. This is the moment when the rules and expectations of the world come into play, and your role is defined by how you are seen: your achievements, reputation, and the respect you've earned. It's your time to stand in the spotlight, showing the world who you are and what you've accomplished, while being recognised and rewarded for your performance.

Stage Ten is like the grand finale of a performance, where we step forward to make a lasting impression. It's the moment in our career when we strive to stand out and be remembered. Here, we take centre stage, presenting our achievements and earning recognition. Just as an actor shines in the final act, this stage is about leaving a legacy and making a meaningful contribution. It's our time to showcase our brilliance and let the world see the impact we've made.

If your career journey were a grand performance unfolding across the twelve stages, the tenth stage would be that moment when you step into the spotlight and receive a standing ovation. It's the culmination of your efforts, where your achievements and contributions take centre stage. In this stage, you bask in the applause, showcasing the best of what you've offered throughout your career.

This is your time to shine, leaving a lasting impression on the audience. Stage Ten is the encore, the applause, and the acknowledgement of a career well-played.

Overview of the Stage of Ambition and Career Legacy

Stage Ten represents the culmination of your personality's fulfilment, achieved through the personal satisfaction derived from using your abilities and talents to serve and influence society. It is the arena in which your *career achievements are crafted,* and the *recognition and awards you receive* are a reflection of the impactful work you do.

This stage is the manifestation of your *professional legacy,* reflecting the imprint you've left on the world through your career journey. It often takes the form of your CV, your LinkedIn profile, portfolios as well as recognition certificates you have received in your career over the years.

We *engage in a reflective process* where we take stock of our entire career journey. This involves a comprehensive assessment of our achievements, as well as an acknowledgement of any missed opportunities or setbacks. It's a moment of introspection when we may evaluate the overall career journey and reflect on the significance of our professional endeavours. For some, this stage prompts contemplation about the fulfilment of their career goals and aspirations.

There may be a poignant realisation of whether the career journey aligns with their deepest aspirations or if there's a sense of unfulfilled potential. It's the point where we revisit the question of whether our careers have been a meaningful and purposeful endeavour or if there's a need for recalibration and redirection.

This reflective process is crucial for shaping the narrative of one's professional legacy and determining the ultimate impact of our career journey.

Positives of the Stage of Ambition and Career Legacy

Because this stage unfolds on the world stage it revolves around issues of *personal branding,* concerns about how we wish to be perceived by others and how we portray ourselves to them. It captures the qualities for which we seek admiration, praise, respect, and regard. Through these qualities, we aspire to attain *honour, achievement,* and *recognition.*

This stage represents the attributes we want to be remembered for and the contributions we desire to leave as our *legacy* in the world. The compelling desire for esteem and acknowledgement stems from the tenth stage, shaping our public identity and the impact we aim to make in society.

The Stage of Ambition and Career Legacy is defined by a strong focus on career ambition and status, where your contributions to society and personal reputation become key priorities. As you concentrate on these aspects, it's normal for career-related worries to arise. Success in this stage is driven by your personal goals and ambitions.

From a career perspective, your ambition is demonstrated by persistent and broad aspirations for success and achievement. It often translates into a desire for advancement within your current organisation or profession, such as seeking promotions or leadership positions within your career.

There is an assumption that those that have high career ambition will achieve career success which has been proven by various studies, including studies by Hirschi and Spurk, who consistently affirmed the positive correlation between ambition and career success.[108]

This belief was supported by a study done by Barrick and colleagues, which found that ambition is strongly linked to higher achievement in both education and career. The study highlights that ambitious individuals tend to take deliberate actions toward their goals, leading to greater career success. Additionally, the research showed that this success often results in increased life satisfaction and longevity.[109]

This driving force compels us to set ambitious goals, strive for excellence, and actively pursue avenues for career advancement. As a result, ambition becomes a powerful catalyst for personal and professional growth, propelling us toward higher levels of achievement and success in our chosen fields. [110]

With ambition comes a desire to be known and perceived in a way that will facilitate career success. This is why Stage Ten also focuses on our public image, personal brand, and career brand. This focus brings a strategic approach to creating, positioning, and maintaining a positive impression of ourselves as professionals, commonly known as *personal branding*.

Personal branding has become important in the contemporary employment landscape, which is marked by increased flexibility in work arrangements. This necessitates us to adopt a more market-oriented mindset. Personal branding brings this mindset by emphasising the deliberate process of establishing a unique and positive personal identity, conveying a distinct promise to our target audience through a differentiated narrative we tell about ourselves.

As we navigate Stage Ten, crafting and managing our public image, our personal brand becomes an integral aspect of positioning ourselves for success and recognition in the professional sphere.

The core focus of personal branding is deliberately coordinating certain activities to align with a defined direction, targeting a specific audience. To be more effective in our personal branding, we differentiate how we market ourselves, by emphasising our unique and valued characteristics in comparison to others.

This *communicates benefits and promises to deliver outcomes* that are highly valued by others. It is not only about projecting our distinctive traits but also about fitting seamlessly into the expectations of a particular field or context.

Personal branding relies significantly on *technology as the primary conduit* for conveying imagery, such as logos, photos, and work samples, alongside the associated storytelling to the target audience. The digital era has ushered in a paradigm shift in how we shape and present our professional identities. Social media platforms, personal websites, and online portfolios serve as virtual spaces where personal branding strategies unfold. The use of technology amplifies the reach of our personal branding efforts and allows for dynamic and interactive storytelling.

Whether through curated online profiles, multimedia presentations, or engaging content dissemination, technology provides the tools to craft a compelling narrative that resonates with your intended audience. Leveraging technology has become a pivotal aspect of personal branding where the visibility and impact of our professional image are intricately linked to digital mediums and online platforms.

A number of studies suggest that personal branding plays a pivotal role in achieving positive career outcomes. These outcomes encompass the accrual of social capital, financial rewards, and expanded career opportunities. This was confirmed by a Taiwan study by Cheng and his colleagues, which studied 195 employee-supervisors from various industries in Taiwan. The study found that individuals who employed deliberate self-promotion behaviours showed greater career satisfaction compared to those who did not employ such behaviours.[111]

In 2019, Gorbatov and colleagues embarked on a study to explore the ins and outs of personal branding. Their research sought to test the characteristics and outcomes of personal branding. Their findings shed light on the crucial role personal branding plays in our individual career success. Amongst the key findings, it emerged that our attitudinal predisposition, specifically the aspiration for career achievement, is the principal characteristic that drives successful personal branding.

This implies that those of us with a deep-seated desire for career advancement and accomplishment are more inclined to actively partake in personal branding endeavours. It serves as the driving force behind the strategic (deliberate) cultivation of their professional identity.

It explains what drives some people to invest time, effort, and creativity into crafting and promoting their personal brand. In the end, the research confirmed the interconnected dynamics between career ambition and the intentional practice of personal branding.[112]

Personal branding goes beyond simply standing out—it also enhances career success by building social capital. Those who actively promote their value and share their achievements often develop stronger social networks and resources. This increased social capital provides access to valuable information, resources, and influential sponsors, which significantly boosts career satisfaction. Overall, personal branding plays a crucial role in both self-promotion and developing a supportive network that helps advance career goals aligned to our career ambition.

Our ambition also links to the legacy we want to be known for. *We are concerned about leaving a lasting legacy that recognises our efforts and contributions throughout our careers. This is like passing oneself through the corridors of time and generations. It involves creating continuity from the past, weaving a narrative that connects our historical roots with the present and extends a guiding thread into the future.*[113]

Just as we find meaning in our lives by constructing narratives Stage Ten extends the narrative-building process from the preceding stage into the future, the legacy we are shaping and leaving to the world of work for the generations that follow.

In the context of our careers, a legacy is forged from the lessons of the past, the core values we hold in the present, and the beliefs we have about the future. This unique blend of identity, values, and history creates what is passed along as a legacy.

The underlying driver of creating a career legacy is our desire, to assist future generations by imparting hard-earned knowledge, values, and beliefs, thereby contributing to the wisdom that guides the ongoing journey of individuals in the professional landscape.

Mastering Stage Ten is about addressing personal preferences relating to your career ambition, building your personal brand, and defining the impact and legacy you want to leave for the future generations. However, such success can be impeded by multiple factors discussed in the next section.

Potential Derailers of the Stage of Ambition and Career Legacy

One of the characteristics that can be a derailer during this stage is *being overly ambitious*, without investing in the necessary work that will help you achieve your career ambitions. Think of someone who always complains and laments about how they have been in a particular job for a long time and have not moved up the ladder, but they show no evidence of having invested in growing themselves to prepare for career growth.

Interestingly, they will be clear on what their ambition is: articulating where they are meant to be at what stage of their life. However, that normally shows up as *having empty ambitions without doing the necessary work, which often is a major source of dissatisfaction.*

Because this is the stage when your career becomes public, *negative personal brand* or negative publicity resulting from the mistakes you have made in your career might be a derailer. A number of us have made mistakes in our past careers that we have not dealt with or moved past. For example, losing a job due to a particular mistake which becomes what we are known for.

Imagine being known as a bad leader or being known as someone who is not trustworthy or someone who cannot deliver on commitment. All that can negatively affect your future career prospects. During Stage Ten, it becomes important to address any negative career perceptions about you by investing in deliberate efforts to boost your personal brand.

Unrealistic personal brand: becoming *overly concerned about your public image, creating and sharing particular achievements and legacy that do not reflect reality.* Have you heard of someone who will go all out to create a social media persona and lifestyle that is not a true reflection of their actual life? This results in overly attractive CV, and social media profiles such as LinkedIn. Obviously, this will attract employers, however employers come with an expectation that you will leave up to the attractive brand that you have created.

Failure to deliver or live up to expectations results in misalignment. You end up with a person with an attractive CV or LinkedIn profile with a list of high profile employers but short employment stints and lack of depth in all the high profile projects that they may have been involved in. They try to leave just before their employer discovers that they oversold their experience.

Key Challenges of the Stage of Ambition and Career Legacy

One of the significant challenges that comes with this stage is grappling with a sense of inadequacy and questioning the tangible outcomes of your professional endeavours. Despite navigating various challenges, overcoming obstacles, and accumulating a wealth of experience, you may find yourself contending with feelings of emptiness and a perceived lack of concrete achievements. This can lead to self-doubt and a profound questioning of the overall worthiness and impact of your career.

Some questions that might come out during coaching related to this stage are:

- I have been through so much in my career, but what do I have to show for all that?
- Others ask themselves: was it all worth it?
- Was my career worth all the sacrifice and pain I have been through?
- Is this it?

Navigating this challenge requires a deep dive into self-reflection, acknowledging and reminding yourself and appreciating the value you have created throughout the journey, while recognising that personal growth, resilience, and wisdom gained are substantial accomplishments in themselves.

It requires reframing the narrative from a focus solely on tangible achievements to a more holistic understanding of the richness and depth that your entire career journey brings.

Recovering from career setbacks involves a multifaceted approach. First, you need to embrace the emotional aspects of the setback, allowing yourself to acknowledge and process the associated feelings of disappointment, frustration, and uncertainty. This self-awareness is a crucial step in rebuilding confidence and resilience.

Next, it requires a strategic evaluation of the setback, under-standing the contributing factors and identifying areas for personal and professional development. Seeking feedback, whether from mentors, colleagues, or coaches, can provide valuable insights and guidance for future career decisions. The ultimate goal is to process, deal with the setback and move on.

A lack of ambition or aspiration in your career can be a significant challenge during the tenth stage. This challenge is characterised by a pervasive sense of dissatisfaction and unhappiness with your career journey, often accompanied by a lack of clarity regarding the underlying causes and potential paths for improvement.

Individuals experiencing this challenge may find themselves in a professional rut, feeling stuck and unfulfilled without a clear understanding of how to reignite their sense of ambition. The absence of clear career goals and aspirations can lead to a lack of direction, making it difficult to identify meaningful steps for career advancement.

Overcoming this challenge requires a deliberate process of self-reflection and exploration. Taking the time to assess your values, interests, and passions, considering how these elements align with your current career trajectory. Seeking guidance from mentors, career coaches, or trusted colleagues can provide valuable insights and external perspectives.

Developing a renewed sense of ambition involves setting clear, achievable goals that resonate with your personal and professional aspirations. This may involve acquiring new skills, pursuing further education, or exploring different career paths that better align with your personal values and passions.

Success Strategies of the Stage of Ambition and Career Legacy

Successfully navigating the tenth stage of your career journey requires cultivating three critical mindsets that contribute to personal growth, resilience, and a meaningful professional legacy.

Reflective mindset: this refers to embracing a mindset that encourages introspection and self-awareness. This involves acknowledging the lessons learned from both successes and challenges. Regular self-assessment fosters continuous improvement, helping you make informed decisions and refine your career journey.

Reflective practices, such as journaling or seeking feedback, enable a deeper understanding of your values, strengths, and areas for development. The intention is not to stew on your regrets but to recognise and appreciate your success and areas where you need to course correct.

Adopting a legacy-oriented mindset: cultivate a legacy-oriented mindset focused on the impact you want to leave on your professional domain and the broader community. The trick is to start thinking about this in the early years of your career. Consider the contributions you aim to make to future generations and the values you wish to instil.

This mindset encourages intentional actions aligned with a broader purpose, emphasising the long-term significance of your career. Whether through mentorship, knowledge sharing, or philanthropy, envisioning your career as a legacy-building endeavour adds depth and meaning to your professional pursuits.

Adaptive resilience mindset: develop an adaptive resilience mindset that embraces change and responds effectively to setbacks. The ability to bounce back from challenges, adapt to evolving circumstances, and remain resilient in the face of adversity is crucial during the tenth stage.

Recognise that setbacks are inherent in any career journey and view them as opportunities for growth. This mindset involves building coping mechanisms, maintaining a positive outlook, and leveraging challenges as stepping stones toward greater achievements. Adaptive resilience empowers you to navigate uncertainties, make strategic adjustments, and sustain a thriving professional journey.

By cultivating these mindsets, you can enhance your capacity for self-reflection, legacy-building, and adaptive resilience, contributing to a fulfilling and purpose-driven experience. This, coupled with effective deliberate career practices, can unlock success during this stage.

Strategic personal branding: personal branding is a high-impact practice during this stage involving strategically shaping the way you want to be perceived in your professional sphere. Develop and curate a personal brand that aligns with your values, achievements, and aspirations.

Use digital platforms, thought leadership, and networking to create a positive and authentic online presence. A well-crafted personal brand not only enhances your professional reputation but also leaves a lasting impression on how others perceive your career offerings and contributions.

This is not a once-off exercise; it's a continuous process of clarifying your brand, delivering on your brand, and refining your brand. It involves continuously asking yourself the following questions: How does this enable my brand? How does involvement in this activity deliver on my brand? How can I use my involvement in this activity to leverage my brand? How do I want this group to think, feel and say about me when I'm not in the room?

For example, consider how marketing consultant Neil Patel built his brand by consistently sharing valuable insights on SEO through blog posts, YouTube tutorials, and podcasts. Patel's thought leadership, paired with his ability to deliver on his brand promise, helped establish him as a trusted expert in his field. Another case is Mel Robbins, who built her personal brand through consistent social media engagement, motivational speeches, and her viral TED Talk, "How to Stop Screwing Yourself Over."[114] These efforts amplified her brand as a leading voice in personal development.

Platforms like LinkedIn, Twitter, and Medium are highly popular for career positioning, as they allow professionals to connect, share insights, and establish themselves as thought leaders. LinkedIn, in particular, is widely regarded as the top platform for career growth, with 98 percent of recruiters using it to vet candidates before hiring.

To showcase thought leadership, you can write articles, share industry insights, or create YouTube videos, offering unique perspectives on topics relevant to your field. These efforts enhance visibility and build credibility as an expert in your field.

Mentorship and knowledge transfer: engage in mentorship to pass on your knowledge, experiences, and insights to the next generation of professionals. Actively mentor individuals entering your industry, organisation, or field of expertise. Share practical advice, offer guidance on career, and provide a supportive network.

Mentorship not only contributes to the development of others but also establishes a legacy of positive influence. By investing in the growth of future generations, you ensure that your knowledge and expertise continue to shape the professional landscape even beyond your active career phase.

Aspirations aligned with impactful work: align your personal aspirations with impactful work that contributes to meaningful outcomes that are important to you. Reflect on the legacy you want to leave and the impact you aim to have through your career endeavours. Setting personal aspirations that go beyond traditional personal success metrics and focus on creating positive change or advancing causes that matter to you.

By integrating your personal aspirations with a commitment to meaningful work, you not only find fulfilment in your career but also leave a legacy that reflects your values and contributions.

Embracing these high-impact practices during Stage Ten positions you to shape a positive and enduring legacy, influence future professionals, and find personal satisfaction in the meaningful impact you create.

In conclusion, Stage Ten, the stage of ambition and legacy, is like the grand finale of a theatre production, where all the work you've done throughout your career culminates in a powerful, lasting performance. Just as the actors in a play step into the spotlight to deliver their final lines with conviction, this stage of your career is about owning your accomplishments, embracing your ambitions, and shaping the legacy you want to leave behind.

The positive of this stage is offering an opportunity to align your personal brand with the legacy you aspire to create. It's the moment when all your skills, experiences, and achievements come together, much like the dramatic climax of a stage play, showcasing the full arc of your professional journey.

Stage Ten allows you to take pride in the roles you've played throughout your career and ensure that you leave a lasting impact on your industry, colleagues, and future generations.

However, much like in a theatre production, potential derailers can arise if you become too focused on the applause—seeking external validation over authenticity. If your ambition drives you to compromise your values or if you focus too much on maintaining a "perfect" image, you might risk creating a hollow legacy. Another challenge is the risk of stagnation, where professionals might cling to past accomplishments, much like an actor stuck in an old role, instead of continuing to evolve and adapt to new opportunities.

Navigating this stage requires a clear vision of your legacy, as well as a reflective mindset. Just like in a theatre performance where each scene builds on the next, your career story should be crafted with intention, ensuring that each decision and action contributes to the larger narrative you want to leave behind.

You must also be adaptable—willing to make changes in your script if necessary—while staying true to the core values that define your professional life.

Adopting resilience is another critical mindset for this stage. Just as an actor must deal with criticism and setbacks, you too must remain proactive, focused, and adaptive. By continuously refining your personal brand and actively shaping the legacy you want to leave, you can ensure that this stage of your career ends on a high note—much like a standing ovation after a powerful performance.

Stage Ten is your time to shine. By adopting a thoughtful, reflective, and ambitious approach, you can ensure that your career legacy is both meaningful and lasting, allowing you to leave the stage with pride and purpose.

Stage Ten Coaching Question

What career legacy are you building throughout your career?

Stage Eleven – The Stage of Self-actualisation

Atticus Finch from Harper Lee's novel, *To Kill a Mockingbird*, which was adapted into a film in 1962, is a lawyer in the racially segregated American South during the 1930s who exemplifies the traits of someone at the Stage of Self-actualisation.

In the film, *To Kill a Mockingbird*, Atticus Finch is tasked with defending Tom Robinson, an African American man falsely accused of raping a white woman. Despite knowing the societal backlash he will face, Atticus takes on the case, driven by a deep sense of moral duty and a desire to contribute positively to society. His actions are not motivated by personal gain or recognition but by a genuine concern for fairness and equality.

As Atticus prepares for the trial, he reflects critically on his role in a society that is deeply divided and prejudiced. He understands that his efforts go beyond winning a case; they represent a stand against systemic injustice and an opportunity to challenge entrenched racial norms.

Atticus's role in the story is not merely as a defender of Tom Robinson but as a beacon of integrity and social responsibility. His dedication to his principles, even when faced with significant personal risk and societal opposition, showcases his drive to impact the world positively.

Atticus Finch's character illustrates how self-actualisation involves aligning one's actions with a greater purpose, contributing to societal change, and embodying social consciousness. His commitment to justice, despite the personal and professional costs, demonstrates a profound alignment with the eleventh stage, where individual efforts are geared toward empowering society and challenging the status quo.[115]

Overview of the Stage of Self-actualisation

Stage Eleven is where the intricate dynamics of large groups, future aspirations, and the shared visions that bind us play out. This is the stage linked to friendships, community, teams, and collectives. Central to this stage is the act of envisioning future possibilities, often in collaboration with like-minded individuals, sparking creativity and innovation.

Blake Mycoskie, founder of TOMS Shoes, and Yvon Chouinard, founder of Patagonia, used the power of like-minded individuals to achieve their self-actualised visions, building businesses that were not only successful but also socially impactful.

Mycoskie, after witnessing children in Argentina suffering due to a lack of shoes, developed the One for One model and enlisted customers, employees, and partners who shared his passion for social good. By involving others in his mission, TOMS grew into a movement where people were not just buying shoes, but actively contributing to a larger cause of helping underprivileged children worldwide.

Similarly, Chouinard used Patagonia to rally employees, customers, and environmental activists who believed in his vision of sustainability and ethical business practices. His commitment to minimising environmental impact resonated with like-minded individuals who helped him drive initiatives like using organic cotton, recycling materials, and launching environmental campaigns. Both leaders surrounded themselves with people who shared their values, leveraging their collective strength to build businesses that made a positive impact on society and the environment.

These examples illustrate how, during this stage, we engage with societal structures to harness the power of the groups we belong to through active participation and meaningful contributions. As we establish ourselves as valued participants in society, we use this stage to contribute creatively within our social environment.

In essence, Stage Eleven invites us to actively participate in the stage of broader society, fostering collaboration, igniting change, and collectively shaping a future that transcends individual aspirations. It involves the *connection between personal growth and societal progress*, where friendships and alliances weave the intricate fabric of our shared journey.

Key ideas:

- Your career evolves in a stage with others; you manage your career within a broader societal context; you enter the stage where the broader society plays. In all the other stages, you have been a lone actor, while in this stage, you are in a cast with others.

- This stage challenges us to look at our career aspirations and goals beyond just personal career success such as more money or promotional aspects. It pushes us to look at career success from the perspective of how society will benefit from our work; or put differently, what I am contributing to society.

- It's more about social consciousness; our career choices are elevated to social consciousness. We start accepting or refusing jobs because of our social consciousness. We start getting involved in projects aligned to our social aspirations.

- The concept of "Ubuntu Careers" basically says that my career is nothing without considering others. I build my career through others, and they build theirs through me. It could also mean that I deliberately contribute to others' career success as I build my career.

- Focus on self-actualising through our career; our focus should be on how our individual careers contribute to society. The focus is no longer about pleasing others as it is about giving back or sharing this part of who they are.

- This stage assumes that all your basic needs have been met in the previous stages, and now you can direct your focus on your true calling. This is why the Stage Eleven is sometimes referred to as "the Stage of Being" in that all previous stages are focused on what Maslow calls the deficit need—meaning they are all about fulfilling a deficit you feel you might have. The eleventh stage is all about dealing with who you are in your community, what you bring as a unique individual, and therefore self-actualising.

Positives of the Stage of Self-actualisation

One of the great characteristics of this stage is the yearning to be part of something much larger than yourself. It's a unique opportunity to contribute to the collective efforts of your community or society, emphasising the importance of creating as part of a broader society.

In his writing, "Self-Actualisation and the Hierarchy of Needs," Abraham Maslow highlights the significance of self-actualisation and the need to go beyond personal interests to contribute to the greater good.[116] He argues that self-actualisation encompasses not only personal growth but also the desire to connect with broader social goals and values.

This drive to self-actualise is often fuelled by an intrinsic motivation to achieve one's full potential, a sense of purpose, and the need for meaningful connections with others. At this eleventh stage, individuals aim to fulfil their potential by serving others and engaging with their communities.

This stage prompts you to move beyond your ego identity and strive for integrating to something greater, aligning personal goals with the universal needs of the larger system. I first heard of this yearning while coaching a highly-skilled finance executive who could have worked for any international company, but they chose to work for an entity belonging to their government. The reason was their yearning to contribute to the greater social good.

This can be attributed to our increased levels of *social consciousness* that motivates us to participate in a group—whether political, religious, or social—providing a sense of belonging. Social consciousness refers to the level of explicit awareness a person has of being part of a larger whole. It includes the level at which one is aware of how he or she is influenced by others, as well as how his or her actions may affect others.[117]

At the narrowest level of social consciousness, we lack explicit awareness of our relatedness to others or the *extent to which we are impacted by or impact others*. At the most expanded level, we become more explicitly aware of our interdependence with others, and our ability to influence and be influenced by them. During the Stage of Self-actualisation our worldview shifts from a primarily self-centred mode to one in which the self is experienced as an integral part of a larger whole, we become more compassionate and service-oriented and inspired to act as agents for positive change in our immediate communities and beyond.

This stage cultivates our life energy's to move forward towards greater association, communication, cooperation, and awareness. Unlike the previous stage, where our actions are primarily for personal benefit, the eleventh stage involves *relinquishing personal urges for the collective decisions of the group*. Social consciousness becomes the driving force, leading to involvement in projects with a significant impact on humanitarian issues.

Due to our focus on activities beyond our personal egos and involvement in social or group activities we get to explore our individual social roles we tend to undertake. Our social roles become intricate threads woven into collective efforts. Whether it's being a proactive member of a professional association, contributing to humanitarian projects, or actively engaging in community activities, each role assumed reflects our commitment to something beyond ourselves.

This yearning to have an impact in larger society makes us seek to be in *Responsible Careers*. *Responsible Careers* are defined as careers in which people seek to have an impact on societal challenges such as environmental sustainability and social justice through their employment and role choices, strategic approaches to work and other actions.[118]

The journey to responsible careers goes through multiple stages of self-discovery practices. These may include:

Expressing self: it describes career practices directed at crafting work that is consistent with your personal values, such as concerns about sustainability or social justice, and articulates your unique voice. Work is thus seen as making a statement, with the potential to have an impact in the world. For example, one of my coaching clients (we will call her Sabina) left a well-paying job in one of the global big-four tax consulting firms. Her passion since growing up has been to add value and make an impact in the public sector. The job at the government auditing department helps her express her values of adding value and giving back to the public sector.

Connecting to others is one of the good characteristics offered by socially responsible careers. This involved contacts with like-minded people, helping confirm your vision, purposes and practices. It also involves networking—making contacts that would help develop career opportunities or specific ventures. An example is Vusi, who chose to leave his prestigious executive job. One of his justifications for leaving his executive role and pursuing a job in the socially responsible investment company was the contacts and networks he had built in a short space of time and how these networks were helping him to even be more socially involved which is what mattered the most to him.

Defining personal contribution describes efforts to define how your expertise can be applied to responsible business fields. It's about determining what part of your skills you can use when transitioning from a normal traditional career to a responsible career. For Candice, my previous coaching client, who was a marketing executive for a well-known tech company, transitioning to a responsible career, meant using more of her lobbying skills. Her intention was to use her influence from the board roles she had held in the past to be more influential in lobbying for legislative changes that support social entrepreneurs.

Bringing socially responsible business where you are is when you focus on activities directed at introducing, legitimising and embedding responsible practices within your current organisations. People in such situations explain their career choice of working within mainstream businesses to their responsible career communities in terms of the impacts that can be achieved. Karen was working as a Brand Manager with a liquor company when she felt the urge to transition to a responsible career. With luck she did not have to leave her current employer; rather, she managed to convince her current employer to have a department that will look after the environmental and social impact of their business.

Exploration is one of this stage's important characteristics; exploring happens as you pursue training and qualification, attend networking events, volunteer, and approach other people in the field of responsible careers to test out ideas. Exploration combines an attitude of openness with purposeful creation of opportunities.[119]

It's a transformative stage where we navigate the intricate *dance between personal identity and communal responsibility*, shaping the narrative of our social roles with each collaborative step. It becomes a journey of self-discovery within the larger framework of collective endeavours. As we actively participate in group dynamics and societal initiatives, the roles we assume reveal not only our individual contributions but also our interconnectedness with the broader community.

In the introduction, Atticus Finch shows how personal identity and community responsibility are connected. As he defends Tom Robinson, a Black man wrongly accused of rape, Atticus stands by his belief in justice, even though most people in the town disagree with him. His role as a lawyer and father reveals how his personal values shape his actions within the community. By participating in the trial and standing up for what's right, Atticus discovers more about himself while influencing those around him.

All these great characteristics of the eleventh stage guide us on a transformative journey, steering us towards the pursuit of integration and a profound connection to a higher sense of self. It's a voyage that transcends our individual boundaries, urging us to become an integral part of the expansive universe that extends far beyond the confines of our personal existence.

The collective endeavours, social roles, and conscious choices made during this stage propel us towards a holistic integration—both within ourselves and as an integral element of the vast universe. It's a harmonious dance with the universe, where our actions and contributions become threads intricately woven into the fabric of a reality larger and more interconnected than ourselves.

Potential Derailers of the Stage of Self-actualisation

One crucial pitfall to be cautious of during this stage is the tendency to consistently move in and out of humanitarian or political groups without tangible outcomes to show for it. Individuals who excessively engage in various groups, unions, or political affiliations, often allow their decisions to be heavily influenced by these associations; they might find that their career growth becomes closely tied to their ideological beliefs. Overindulging in this behaviour could limit personal and professional development as your career becomes overshadowed by short-term affiliations.

Imagine someone who is actively involved in various humanitarian and political groups. They will be vocal about their affiliations, often participating in discussions and events aligned with these groups. However, despite this continuous involvement, when assessing their career, there's a lack of substantial achievements or advancements. The constant shift in affiliations and overemphasis on ideological beliefs could lead to a career more associated with group memberships than tangible accomplishments.

A common challenge in Stage of Self-actualisation is failing to recognise its spiritual dimensions. This eleventh stage often involves intangible and elusive elements that are crucial for a holistic understanding and personal growth. Ignoring these spiritual aspects can prevent you from fully experiencing and benefiting from this stage.

For example, someone might focus only on the tangible, visible aspects of this stage, similar to earlier stages, and miss out on its deeper, spiritual insights. This can lead to a shallow understanding of how personal and collective growth are interconnected. As a result, they might approach social projects with a self-centred mindset rather than a genuine desire to make a positive impact on others or the environment.

Individuals may face challenges of excessively focusing on activities associated with this stage while neglecting other crucial aspects of personal and professional development. This unbalanced approach could lead to an extreme concentration on social and community activities, potentially leaving little to show for on a personal level.

For instance, someone who dedicates an extensive amount of time to social and community activities associated with the eleventh stage. They will be actively involved in charity events, community projects, and political movements. However, amidst this high level of social engagement, they might neglect personal and professional development in other crucial areas.

As a result, despite the extensive community involvement, their career lacks the individual achievements and growth that should ideally complement the societal contributions. To successfully navigate Stage Eleven, there are specific tasks that help you achieve this balance.

Key Challenges of the Stage of Self-actualisation

To successfully navigate Stage Eleven, we face a core task involving a shift from an ego-focused, "what's in it for me?" mindset to a broader societal or community-focused perspective. This integration requires us to move beyond personal interests and consider the greater good of the collective we are part of. This transition signifies a deepening commitment to societal well-being and a departure from self-centred motivations.

We face the significant task of striking a delicate balance between our involvement in collective social endeavours and its influence on our professional life and career. This challenge is particularly relevant for individuals whose work is not inherently tied to unions, political parties, or associations. For most of us, participation in these collective structures serves a specific purpose, and it's crucial to be clear about the shared ideals pursued by being part of a particular collective. Being clear about how it aligns or enables your personal vision and goals.

The ability to articulate the impact of collective involvement on one's career is essential. Whether you're contributing to the collective or benefiting from it, being intentional about ensuring a positive impact on your personal brand and long-term career is vital. This involves a thoughtful consideration of how your participation aligns with your values, personal and professional goals and aspirations.

Where possible, avoid situations where involvement in certain community initiatives could sabotage your career. For example, when my friend chose to join the "Stop the War" campaign, he didn't fully consider how this decision would impact his personal brand and the company he worked for. The investors and board of directors at his company were concerned about the company's association with controversial topics. They worried that by supporting the campaign, the company might appear to be taking sides in a polarising issue, which could alienate clients and stakeholders.

Unfortunately, my friend's involvement led to significant tension within the company. The management felt that his public stance could damage the company's reputation and create conflict with their partners. As a result, he was asked to leave.

Another challenge is the continuous effort to balance personal interests, beliefs, and values with those of the community groups to which one belongs. It's imperative to avoid a situation where individual convictions overpower the collective goals or vice versa. Striking this equilibrium ensures a harmonious coexistence where personal values align with the shared objectives of the community groups, preventing any detrimental impact on either side.

Success Strategies for the Stage of Self-actualisation

Stage Eleven's foundation is transformation of mindset and worldview, from egocentric—everything is about me, I have to amass as much money and resources as possible to social consciousness mindset—to understanding the interconnectedness of our world.

Embracing the Ubuntu mindset, an African value which emphasises the interconnectedness of individuals and the understanding that "I am because of others, and they are because of me," can be a transformative approach as you navigate Stage Eleven. This mindset encourages a shift from individualistic and selfish perspectives to recognising the collective impact we have on one another.

It means acknowledging the influence of others on your professional journey and understanding your reciprocal impact on the broader social and professional community. The trick is to align personal growth with the betterment of society, fostering a sense of responsibility, while contributing to a collective success that goes beyond individual achievements.

This mindset coupled with the following practices can help you navigates this stage with success:

1. Expressing self through crafting work consistent with personal values

One of the key practices in socially responsible careers is shaping your work around personal values. This involves aligning your career choices with the causes you deeply care about, such as environmental sustainability, social justice, or ethical business practices. For example, Maria, a graphic designer, decided to focus her work exclusively on helping non-profits and eco-friendly brands, ensuring that her professional output supports causes she believes in. By crafting her career around her values, she became able to express her authentic self while making a meaningful contribution to society.

2. Connecting with like-minded others

Another practice is actively seeking out and building connections with individuals and communities who share similar values and goals. These networks provide emotional support, collaboration opportunities, and a collective force for driving change. Take John, a marketing professional who began attending local sustainability meetups, which eventually led to partnerships on projects aimed at reducing plastic waste. Through these connections, John found a network of allies who inspired and empowered him to pursue more meaningful, socially responsible work.

3. Constructing the contribution of expertise to responsible fields

You can also contribute by applying your expertise to socially responsible fields. This means using your skills to solve problems or create opportunities in areas that positively impact society. For instance, Anita, an engineer, shifted her focus from working in the oil industry to designing renewable energy systems. By reapplying her technical knowledge, she found fulfilment in knowing that her expertise now contributes to a more sustainable future.

4. Institutionalising responsible management practices

Some people take on the challenge of driving change from within established organisations by embedding responsible management practices. This involves advocating for ethical policies, sustainability initiatives, or employee well-being within conventional business structures. An example is David, a finance director at a large corporation, who spearheaded efforts to integrate environmental impact assessments into the company's financial reporting. By institutionalising these practices, David helped shift the organisation's focus toward long-term sustainability, setting a new standard for responsible business behaviour

5. Building emergent fields of responsible management practice

Others take a pioneering approach by building entirely new organisational fields that focus on responsible management. These are the individuals who create new organisations, networks, or industries to address emerging social and environmental issues. For example, Priya, a tech entrepreneur, founded a start-up dedicated to creating software that tracks and reduces carbon footprints for businesses. Her initiative not only introduced a new tool to combat climate change but also sparked a conversation about responsible technology use across her industry.

6. Engaging systematically across diverse actors

Finally, some individuals work systemically by engaging with diverse actors—businesses, governments, non-profits, and consumers—to transform profit-driven practices into more socially conscious ones. Rachel, a consultant, works with companies across various sectors to help them adopt fair trade practices, ensuring that their supply chains are ethical and sustainable. By collaborating with multiple stakeholders, she facilitates a more holistic approach to responsible business, making an impact on a much broader scale than any one organisation could on its own.

Each of these practices helps you move closer to self-actualisation by aligning your career with a deeper purpose that goes beyond personal success. By expressing your values, connecting with others who share your vision, and contributing your expertise to socially responsible fields, you achieve personal fulfilment and make a positive difference in the world. Whether you are driving change from within established organisations, pioneering new fields, or engaging systemically with various actors, these practices enable you to live out your values and realise your full potential, ultimately leading to a more meaningful and socially impactful career.[120]

In summary, the Stage of Self-actualisation marks a profound shift in one's career journey, where the focus expands beyond personal achievement to a deep desire to be part of something bigger. It is the stage where individuals feel a strong calling to make a positive impact on the world, to contribute to causes that benefit others, and to align their work with a sense of higher purpose.

It is characterised by an intense urge for people to go beyond personal goals and accomplishments, striving to align their careers with causes that uplift others and address pressing social or environmental issues. It's as though they are no longer satisfied with merely playing a part in the corporate machine; they yearn to take the stage in a way that contributes to the greater good.

However, navigating this stage isn't without its pitfalls. One of the temptations individuals may face is the risk of using socially responsible careers as a means for personal gain rather than genuine social impact. This can result in people treating socially impactful work as a stepping stone rather than a true calling, which ultimately undermines both their authenticity and the impact they hope to make. The challenge here is maintaining integrity and ensuring that the desire to be part of something larger is driven by authentic passion and a real commitment to social good, rather than the pursuit of personal glory.

A significant challenge during this stage is finding balance. Being deeply involved in collective social endeavours can be incredibly fulfilling, but it can also have a profound influence on one's professional life. Striking a balance between dedicating oneself to causes that benefit society and managing personal or professional obligations can feel like walking a tightrope.

Over-involvement in social projects may lead to professional burnout or a neglect of personal needs, while too much focus on personal advancement could cause one to stray from the deeper purpose they now seek. It requires a delicate dance. To thrive in this stage, individuals must master the art of integrating their social consciousness with their professional commitments, so neither is sacrificed.

To successfully navigate this stage, there are several career practices that one can adopt. Expressing oneself through work that aligns with personal values, building networks with like-minded individuals, and applying expertise to responsible business fields are just a few of the ways to find fulfilment. Additionally, advocating for change within established organisations or even creating new, socially responsible fields can further allow individuals to make meaningful contributions. It's about finding roles in which one can play both the individual and ensemble parts with equal dedication, contributing to the world in a way that's both personally satisfying and socially impactful.

In the grand theatre of life, the eleventh stage invites individuals to step onto the stage not just as performers chasing applause, but as changemakers working behind the scenes to influence the very script society follows. By adopting the right practices, overcoming temptations, and staying true to the deeper purpose of self-actualisation, one can find harmony in this pivotal stage of personal and career development. Ultimately, the goal is not to bask in the spotlight but to ensure that the world is better because you played your part.

Stage Eleven Coaching Questions

In reflecting on your career journey, how do you see your current work contributing to the broader society, and in what ways does this impact help you reach a sense of self-actualisation—where your skills, passions, and values align with the greater good?

Stage Twelve – Transcendence: Surrendering to Collective Service

Welcome to Stage Twelve, where the career journey takes its final bow—the curtain call. It's the concluding act, the epilogue, the moment when everything comes together on the professional stage. Similar to a captivating play, this stage offers a resolution to your career narrative. However, much like a dramatic twist, not every career story concludes neatly; some might end with a cliffhanger, leaving you with anticipation for what comes next.

Take *The Producers*, the play referenced in Stage Ten.[121] In the final act, Max and Leo are caught in a whirlwind of unpredictable events. Although things seem to be wrapping up, a cliffhanger emerges when, instead of facing a tragic downfall, they find themselves back on top, planning another potentially disastrous scheme.

This twist leaves audiences both surprised and eager to see what their next move will be. Similarly, Stage Twelve leaves you reflecting on your career's highs and lows, anticipating the next chapter of your life's journey, even as the curtain closes.

This stage is the grand finale, the culmination of your career performance, and the stage where you take your well-deserved bow after navigating the complexities of the previous acts. It is linked to the themes of endings, final stages of projects, retirement, and the act of surrender. Drawing on the realms of the subconscious and imagination, Stage Twelve offers a reflective space, where success and failures come to the forefront.

This stage represents a period of reflection and deep contemplation. It is a time when we look back on our careers, seeing the cumulative effects of our choices, actions, successes, and failures. It is about gaining a holistic understanding of the professional journey we've created. As we review our pasts, we become more aware of how every decision has contributed to shaping our career.

As Dane Rudyhar explains, this stage can be seen as an encounter with our "karma", the natural consequences of the paths we've chosen. This chapter will explore the key characteristics that define Stage Twelve and how they influence this reflective phase of your career journey.[122] It delves into the characteristics that define the twelfth stage, unravelling the mysteries of endings and the transformative potential embedded within this stage.

Overview of the Stage of Surrendering to the Collective

Stage Twelve of the career journey marks the dissolution of individual career identity, paving the way for an experience of merging into something greater than the self. It becomes easy for the singular sense of "I" to give way to a collective identity, initiating a profound *transformation in how we perceive ourselves within our broader professional context.*

In the twelfth stage, the characteristic of *losing a sense of oneself unfolds in a motion of sacrifice driven by the desire for higher service to others*. This sacrificial motive is rooted in the growing sense of merging with a collective being, indicating a transition from individual aspirations to a broader, altruistic orientation in one's career pursuits.

Characterised by destruction, inflation, and the blurring of boundaries between the self and others, Stage Twelve involves a conflict between the "me-in here" and the "you-out there" phenomena. *Individuals in this stage may find it challenging to form a clearly defined career identity*, often swayed by external influences and experiences encountered along the way.

Stage Twelve delves even deeper into the subconscious and unconscious drivers of our behaviour, transcending the material world and connecting with the higher self. It represents the house of self-undoing and the revelation of spiritual purpose on earth, making it a mystical and transformative stage.

With a theme centred on letting go of limitations and outdated patterns, the twelfth stage encourages us to release exterior shackles hindering our spiritual path. It embraces mysticism and higher knowledge, focusing on spiritual and mental health. This stage acts as a catalyst for transformative changes, inspiring inner reflection and paving the way for us to find our path forward in the career journey.

Positives of the Stage of Surrendering to the Collective

The undoing of self: At the heart of Stage Twelve lies the profound concept of self-undoing. The motivation to pass on acquired skills and experiences to others is deeply rooted in the desire to be of service, transcending the conventional boundaries of self-service. The realisation that our skills and experiences are a result of the grace extended by others fosters a deep sense of gratitude. This gratitude, in turn, fuels the desire to create opportunities for those younger, creating a legacy of empowerment and support. The twelfth stage becomes a transformative phase where we are driven not by personal accolades but by the profound impact we can have on the lives of others. *The dissolution of our career identity that revolves around work* during this stage becomes about formulation of a new identity, one that is not connected to our individual careers

Sense making: the process through which individuals create explanations for experiences". As your career comes to an end, you develop a new narrative depending on how you make sense of your experiences during this stage. As an actor, you create a narrative that can be dominated by either of the following experience:[123]

- *Following a script:* These individuals used their age or length of employment as triggers to the retirement decision.

- *Identifying windows:* A new project is coming up, and you feel it is a good time to leave.

- *Cashing out:* The retiree is offered as an incentive or you wanted to get out before the company reorganised.

- *Being discarded:* You feel you are no longer needed or may be actually laid off.

- *Becoming disillusioned:* Feeling that the company's values are going downhill, you decide it is time to leave.

- *Having an epiphany:* Through illness, the death of a close family member, or other major life event, you may feel that there were other things in life more important than a job.

Your chosen narrative will determine the next path you take during this stage. What is common in all these narratives is *thriving to be of higher service*: During the Stage Twelve, we embark on a journey of profound transformation, where the dissolution of individual career identity paves the way for an extraordinary commitment to higher service. This is marked by a blurring of lines between self and others, fostering a deep sense of empathy and compassion.

The archetypes of the Helper, Martyr, and Saviour become prevalent as we feel an innate calling to alleviate the pain of others. We are more inclined towards care work and a focus on compassion become prominent manifestations of our desire to be of higher service.

As the boundaries between self-identity and the collective blur, the twelfth stage requires us to shift our focus towards the universal and the collective. *The surrender of self* leads to an enhanced capacity for empathy, compassion, and selfless service. This stage becomes a culmination of the positive contributions we amassed throughout our career, consolidating them into seeds of inspiration and support for others.

We are more inclined to become mentors, passing on a wealth of career lessons to younger generations. It becomes a time of sharing accumulated wisdom, nurturing the growth of others, and contributing to the collective well-being.

Focus on universal and collective: Stage Twelve is where we become an inspiration to others, radiating the lessons learned and the wisdom acquired throughout our career. The blurring of self and collective identity propels us towards universal empathy, fostering a *collective consciousness* that goes beyond our personal achievements. This is a stage marked by selfless service, mentorship, and the desire to leave a lasting legacy that echoes the values of compassion, empowerment, and the interconnectedness of all individuals in the grand scheme of collective existence.

Potential Derailers of the Stage of Surrendering to the Collective

In the complex journey of Stage Twelve, while there are transformative and positive characteristics, there are potential pitfalls that individuals may encounter as they navigate this profound stage of their careers. One significant challenge is the *risk of becoming overly sacrificial and losing a sense of personal identity*. The dissolution of individual career identity may lead some to sacrifice too much of themselves, succumbing to a self-sacrifice and a fervent wish to serve others at the expense of their own well-being.

This overemphasis on selflessness can result in burnout, neglect of personal needs, and a blurred sense of self. In the movie *Invictus* you will note Nelson Mandela's secretary always reminding him to delegate some of his commitments to others and focus on himself. You can see her reminding Mr. Mandela to rest or to take some time off when he is not well. This is a classic case of being overly sacrificial and unduly invested in helping others and ignoring self needs.

A second potential challenge in the twelfth stage is the *tendency to become engulfed in the collective, leading to a loss of individual autonomy*. The conflict between personal and collective focus can become overwhelming, causing the boundaries between yourself and others to blur excessively. You may find yourself swayed by external influences, unable to form a clearly defined identity, and susceptible to the whims of the collective.

This lack of personal grounding can impede decision making, career direction, and the ability to set boundaries. Think of someone who is forever coming up with ideas about where their career is going. Such ideas are overly dependent on who they have in their lives, what other people are doing and have nothing to do with what they want to achieve in their career journey. Oftentimes, these ideas never come to fruition because the person changes to something new and fleshy as they come across new career ideas. So, they are forever stuck in an ever-evolving wheel of exploring new and "exciting" career ideas.

Another potential pitfall in Stage Twelve is an *overemphasis on the spiritual and unconscious aspects, neglecting practical considerations*. While this stage delves into the depths of spirituality and hidden potential, an excessive focus on the intangible and elusive aspects of the unconscious may lead to a disconnect from practical realities. Individuals may become so absorbed in spiritual pursuits that they neglect tangible responsibilities, both in their careers and personal lives, resulting in a lack of practical grounding.

Furthermore, the twelfth stage may bring about challenges related to the temptation of escapism. The intense introspection, dreams, and exploration of higher truths may lead some individuals to seek refuge from the practical real world. Engaging in excessive escapism, whether through addictive behaviours or disengagement from reality, can hinder personal and professional growth. It may manifest as a reluctance to face challenges or make necessary changes, ultimately hindering career development.

You have seen people who all of a sudden embrace the idea that they have been chosen to be spiritual healers. This removes them from reality and takes them on a separate (at times costly) journey of becoming spiritual healers (in South Africa, this is called Ubungoma). If this is not their true calling, they will often come back to deal with reality after undergoing the training.

Finally, in Stage Twelve, there's the danger of being overly fixated on endings and closures, overlooking the present and the chance for new beginnings. The strong focus on transcendence and self-undoing might cause us to close chapters in our careers prematurely, without fully considering new possibilities. Being resistant to change and hesitant to embrace fresh starts can hinder flexibility and limit the exploration of new professional opportunities.

It is essential for individuals navigating the twelfth stage to strike a balance between the transformative aspects of spirituality and selflessness and the practicalities of maintaining a grounded and balanced approach to their careers. Awareness of these potential pitfalls can empower individuals to navigate this stage with mindfulness while remaining intentional, ensuring a harmonious integration of the profound lessons it offers.

Key Challenges of the Stage of Surrendering to the Collective

Mastering the challenges of Stage Twelve requires navigating a delicate balance between the yearning for unity and the inherent fear and resistance to the dissolution of the ego. We see this illustrated perfectly in both *Hamlet* by William Shakespeare and *Death of a Salesman* by Arthur Miller, the tension between the yearning for unity and the fear of losing one's individual identity is central to the characters' struggles with ego.

In *Hamlet,* Hamlet wrestles with his desire to restore order in Denmark by avenging his father's death, but his fear of losing control over his personal fate and identity paralyses him. Hamlet's internal conflict reflects the fear of dissolving his ego in the pursuit of a greater purpose, caught between action for the collective good and his personal fears.[124]

Similarly, in *Death of a Salesman*, Willy Loman's ego battles with his longing for connection and significance within the larger social and familial framework. Willy's relentless pursuit of success and individual recognition isolates him, and his inability to relinquish his ego-driven ideals leads to his downfall. Both plays highlight the paradox of seeking unity or purpose within a larger framework— whether family or society—while fearing the loss of one's personal identity. These struggles mirror the challenge of the twelfth stage, where one must learn to embrace unity without losing the self.[125]

The primary challenge lies in managing the paradox of desiring to be part of the whole while simultaneously fearing and resisting the loss of individual identity. This intricate dance is reflected in various aspects of life, including relationships, spirituality, and, notably, in the world of work and careers.

Within the professional sphere, individuals may grapple with the challenge of striking a balance between the yearning to be part of a collective and actions taken to fulfil that yearning. Instead of succumbing to the fear of dissolution, a focus on positive and impactful activities can provide a sense of value and connection to the collective. The temptation to wield power as a means of extending influence over various aspects of life may arise, with the belief that such influence connects you to the broader tapestry of existence.

Another prevalent challenge during Stage Twelve is the *potential immersion in self-destructive behaviours, such as drugs and alcohol,* as a misguided attempt to break through perceived boundaries. This coping mechanism reflects the struggle to reconcile the desire for transcendence with the fear of losing oneself. The dissolution of boundaries between the self and others may lead to confusion about individual identity, resulting in being overly invested in others. Despite good intentions, this intense involvement may not always be positively received by others, emphasising the need for self-awareness and boundaries.

A significant hurdle in mastering the twelfth stage is the experience of a *lack of direction in both life and career*. The pressure from societal expectations regarding career choices and the conflicting yearning for more impactful work can create internal conflict. Individuals may find themselves questioning the meaning of their careers, expressing sentiments such as "Is this all there is to my career?" This internal struggle requires navigating the tension between societal expectations and the inner calling for purposeful and impactful work.

The overarching challenge involves testing one's ability to separate from others and lead oneself back to the spiritual self. This introspective journey requires us to learn to live quietly within ourselves, finding solace and direction in the depths of our spiritual identity. Mastering Stage Twelve involves transcending external pressures, self-destructive tendencies, and the fear of losing oneself, ultimately leading to a harmonious integration of the profound lessons offered by this transformative platform of your career journey.

Success Strategies for the Stage of Surrendering to the Collective

As you enter the twelfth stage, there are specific mindsets and practices crucial for navigating this phase effectively. These encompass:

- *Embracing change and new beginnings*: This crucial mindset shift requires us to embrace change and welcome new beginnings. Instead of being solely focused on endings and closures, we must cultivate an openness to explore uncharted professional territories. Understand that the dissolution of the ego and transcendence don't mean the end but rather a transformation, creating opportunities for fresh starts and continuous growth.

- *Value the present moment*: managing Stage Twelve also requires us to shift our mindset from an exclusive focus on the past or future to appreciating the present moment. The twelfth stage may tempt us to become preoccupied with endings and the afterlife, potentially neglecting the opportunities and challenges of the current stage. Recognise the importance of being present, making the most of our current career situation, and staying open to new possibilities that may arise.

- *Embracing the transformative nature of the stage of surrendering to the collective*: embrace the transformative nature of Stage Twelve. Recognise that it signifies a shift from traditional career perspectives to a more spiritual and holistic understanding. Accept the dissolution of your individual career identity as an opportunity for profound personal and professional transformation.

- *Cultivate a service-oriented mindset*: cultivate a service-oriented mindset focuses on higher service and contribution. Understand that blurring the lines between self and others leads to greater empathy and compassion. Embrace the archetypes of the Helper, Martyr, or Saviour, reflecting a commitment to alleviating the pain of others.

Cultivating the right mindset is crucial during the twelfth stage, and it's equally important to complement this mindset with practical tools and effective practices. These tools and practices serve as a guide to help you not only understand but also actively manage and thrive in this transformative stage of your career. Some *practices* are:

- *Balance transcendence with practicality*: while the twelfth stage encourages transcendence and self-undoing, it's crucial to balance these spiritual aspirations with practical considerations. Avoid prematurely closing career chapters without fully exploring new opportunities. Develop a mindset that appreciates both the spiritual and practical aspects of your professional journey, ensuring that your decisions are grounded in a comprehensive understanding of your goals. Building mentoring relationships with those that can learn and value your experience. Being open to being mentored and learning from others who are already playing in this stage.

- *Identifying volunteer projects* of interests that help you feel you are making an impact in reducing some of the world suffering that you are passionate about. This addresses the need to reduce world suffering and your need to be valued as well as feeling that you are making a positive impact on the collective whole.

- *Celebrating career successes:* identifying some successes that you are proud of from your career journey and celebrating them, no matter how small. Adopting a mindset of gratitude and celebrating, rewarding yourself for all the sacrifices you have made in your career journey, your contributions and your impact.

- *Adopting a practice that helps you feel connected to the spiritual whole.* This speaks to your spiritual journey. There are no prescriptions here, it's up to you to use the channels and practices that work best for you. Some use prayer, some may use meditation, and some use physical body activities such as going for walks in a tranquil peaceful environment. This is supported by various psychological and spiritual theories.

  Carl Jung's Theory of Individuation, for instance, emphasises the importance of spiritual integration in achieving personal wholeness. Jung believed that connecting with the collective unconscious through practices like meditation or contemplation fosters a sense of unity with the greater whole, which is vital for personal growth.

  This is also mentioned by Brene Brown; in her work on spirituality and well-being, she underscores the significance of engaging in practices that nurture the soul, explaining how connecting to something greater than oneself, whether through nature, meditation, or prayer, cultivates resilience and inner peace.

- *Keep the passion burning:* it may sound like this is the end of your career and that can be depressing. What if it was not the end? What if we could look at this stage as an opportunity to connect more with your passions and do what you have always wished you had chosen as your career? What if this was your final opportunity to go off script?

In conclusion, Stage Twelve, the stage of surrendering to the collective, represents the final act of your career journey—much like the closing moments of a stage play where the lead actor steps back, allowing the collective themes of the story to come full circle. It is about finding balance between your individual ambitions and contributions, and how you serve and belong to the larger group.

This stage invites you to reflect on your legacy while opening up space to explore new possibilities that might lie outside the traditional career paths you've followed.

The positive aspects of this stage are abundant. It's an opportunity to step back and evaluate the collective impact of your work, seeing how your contributions have woven into the broader tapestry of your community or industry. It can also be a period of rediscovery and renewal, where you embrace passions that might have been sidelined during your more structured career phases. It's a chance to redefine your purpose, aligning it more closely with personal fulfilment and service to others, which can bring a sense of joy and completeness.

However, potential derailers may arise if this stage is viewed through a lens of fear, particularly related to ageing, changing social roles, or losing professional relevance. If you focus on external perceptions—such as rejection based on age or diminishing status—it may lead to frustration or self-doubt. The challenge lies in adjusting to a less structured and more fluid career landscape, which can feel destabilising if you are used to rigid professional identities and roles.

Key challenges in this stage also include letting go of the past identity tied to a particular role or status and fully embracing a new narrative. As careers evolve, the fear of the unknown and uncertainty about the future can loom large. Balancing self-undoing, where you release your past ego-driven ambitions with the desire to continue adding value in new ways, can be a difficult tightrope to walk.

To navigate this stage successfully, the right mindset plays a pivotal role. Adopting a narrative that sees this stage as an exciting new chapter rather than a closing act will help shift your perspective. Staying present and focused on your well-being through self-care practices can keep you grounded and reduce the anxiety that often comes with transitions. Additionally, continuing to explore new opportunities that align with your long-held passions will keep you engaged and motivated, allowing you to add value in ways that feel personally meaningful.

Ultimately, this stage encourages you to embrace the unknown, craft a narrative that allows you to transition with grace and find meaning beyond the traditional career trajectory. By stepping into this new phase with confidence and resilience, you are writing a powerful final act that speaks to the legacy and values you have cultivated throughout your career.

Stage Twelve Coaching Questions

What bold steps will you take to cement your legacy and ensure that your work leaves a lasting impact? How will you leverage your talents, achievements, and experiences to inspire and shape the next generation?

SECTION TWO
CAREER ARCHETYPES

Career Archetypes That Can Boost or Block Your Career

We have seen in the previous chapters that your career is much like a grand theatrical production, unfolding across the twelve stages. Each stage is like a new act, bringing new scenes to your professional story. At every turn, whether you're just starting out or you're decades in, you're playing a specific role—whether that's as the "Ambitious Newcomer," the "Determined Leader," or even the "Wise Mentor."

Just like actors transform themselves into characters on stage, you unconsciously adopt personas that help you deal with both the triumphs and challenges that come with each of the twelve stages of your career. Just like actors who step into different roles, you may find yourself embodying various archetypes along the way

In the early stages of your career, you might find yourself playing the role of the "Rising Star"—full of energy, eager to prove your potential, and open to learning from every opportunity. But as the curtain rises on the later stages of your career, you might become the "Guide"—no longer the one seeking the spotlight, but instead helping others find their way. Each persona serves its purpose, just as an actor knows when to take centre stage or when to support others from behind the scenes.

The key difference between you and the actors in a play is awareness. Many employees don't realise they are the main character in their career story, nor do they recognise the archetypes they adopt and how these roles can either propel them forward or hold them back.

This chapter seeks to highlight this important but often neglected aspect of career management, helping you become more conscious of the archetypes at play in your career story. By understanding these roles, you can intentionally choose career archetypes that will enhance your success and help you overcome potential obstacles.

However, many of us move through our professional lives without realising the roles we habitually take on. These personas, although adopted unconsciously, significantly shape how we deal with career transitions, how we manage career shocks, and how we make important career decisions. Just as a play's success relies on an actor's performance, your career's trajectory can often depend on the roles you choose to embody.

This chapter will guide you through the various career archetypes that tend to emerge throughout the twelve stages of your professional journey. By understanding these personas, you'll be empowered to consciously select the roles you play in your career, helping you take the lead role in crafting your career story—rather than letting it be shaped by circumstance or old habits.

Archetypes are universal patterns of behaviour, symbols, and themes that exist in the collective unconscious of human beings.

They are innate and inherent in human nature, and they influence our thoughts, emotions, and actions.[126]

Carl Jung, a Swiss psychiatrist and psychoanalyst, first introduced the concept of archetypes in his work. He believed that archetypes are symbols and images that reflect the deepest parts of our psyche, and that they have a powerful effect on our lives. Jung identified several archetypes, including the hero, the shadow, the anima/animus, the mother, the father, and the trickster.

Identifying archetypes (a pattern of behaviours) that are influential in our careers can lead us to be self-aware of how our behaviours have shaped our career journeys in the past and can also help us predict how they will continue to shape our future journey. This awareness and the accompanying insights can help you be deliberate about the transformation you want in your career and therefore change your behavioural patterns in order to achieve the career goals you aspire.}

Archetypes are used in different fields for different purposes; in marketing theory, archetypes are used to create brand personalities and appeal to consumers on a deeper level. Marketers use archetypes to create a narrative or story around a brand that taps into the collective unconscious of their target audience.

For example, a brand that wants to appeal to customers who value tradition and stability may use the archetype of the Caregiver, while a brand that wants to appeal to customers who value independence and adventure may use the archetype of the Explorer.

In addition to psychology and marketing, archetypes are used in various other fields and disciplines, including:

- Literature and storytelling: archetypes are commonly used in literature and storytelling to create characters that readers can identify with and relate to. For example, the Hero archetype is a common character type in many adventure stories, while the Villain archetype is often used to create a sense of conflict and tension.

- Spirituality and religion: archetypes are also used in many spiritual and religious traditions as symbols and representations of various aspects of the divine or cosmic order. For example, the archetype of the Mother is often associated with nurturing and fertility in many goddess traditions.

- Art and design: archetypes are frequently used in art and design to create visual images and symbols that evoke specific emotions or ideas. For example, the Sun and Moon archetypes are often used in graphic design to represent opposites such as light and dark or male and female.

- Personal development and coaching: archetypes are also used in personal development and coaching to help individuals identify their strengths, weaknesses, and life purpose. By understanding their personal archetypes, individuals will gain insight into their motivations and behaviours and make positive changes in their lives.

- Overall, archetypes are a powerful versatile concept that can be applied in many different contexts, from psychology to marketing, to help us understand ourselves and the world around us on a deeper level.

In this book, we use archetype to depict the common roles we tend to adopt in managing our careers. I have created career archetypes based on this universal understanding of the role they play in all our lives. Understanding your career archetypes will help you be aware of the pattern of roles you tend to assume as you navigate different challenges you encounter at different stages of your career.

Your archetypes exert a major influence on the direction your career will take. This is why it is important to spend time understanding your common career archetypes. In work life, just as in theatre, success depends on honing the craft and understanding the roles we play.

Picture an actor stepping into the shoes of the Hero, the Mentor, or the Caregiver—each role carries distinct motivations, behaviours, and influence on the overall story. Similarly, in our careers, we unconsciously adopt archetypes that shape our professional paths. Just as actors must understand their characters to deliver a compelling performance, you must recognise and refine your career archetypes.

Whether you find yourself as the Strategist, guiding the team through challenges, or the Creator, bringing innovation to the table, these roles steer the direction of your career. Mastering your archetypes, like an actor perfecting their role, helps you navigate the challenges and opportunities at each stage of your career journey, shaping both your personal growth and career success.

Each archetype can show up at different stages of your career in different ways, depending on your dominant archetypes. For example, if you have a dominant Victim archetype, you seek sympathy or pity, by assuming a Victim archetype believing that others will either give you the jobs you want because they feel pity for you or believing that you deserve a promotion because of a bad experience that you have been through.

Your career narrative which is evolving continuously building throughout your career journey involves others or circumstances that constantly block your way to career success. You have heard someone complaining, "I have worked so hard my whole life but no one seems to notice."

This archetype is similar to a career slave or puppet archetype. This archetype represents a complete absence of the power of choice and self-authority in your career. Circumstances or others are always making decisions that drive your career. This often shows up when you are asked, "Why did you choose this career?" or "Why did you leave your previous job?".

The opposite to these archetypes is a career shape-shifter archetype which brings the ability to constantly change jobs and careers for a variety of reasons. This archetype comes with a flexible personality that is less tied to a specific career goal. Think of someone who is able to navigate different career changes, be it changing jobs, changing industries, changing geographic location or changing work levels. Alternatively, think of someone who reinvents their careers at different stages of their lives.

I have provided a summary of common career archetypes that most of us assume as we navigate different stages of our career.

1. The Rebel

The Rebel archetype represents an individual who defies norms, challenges injustice, and refuses to conform to societal expectations. Rebels are driven by the belief that no one should dictate their actions or control their choices. Caroline Myss observed that the rebels have defined their sense of personal power as "no one is going to tell me what to do"; typically every idea is a suggestion, no matter how well meaning it is and interpreted as an attempt to control them.[127]

They are the trailblazers, breaking away from conventional paths and paving new ones. This archetype plays a vital role in personal growth and development, helping individuals see beyond preconceptions and championing change. In professional fields, rebels are renowned as change agents, constantly introducing new ideas and challenging the status quo.

In the realm of work and careers, rebels manage their professional lives differently. They are driven by a need to break free from convention and redefine the way things are done. Rebels are not limited by their educational background or past experiences; they have the ability to transition into any profession they desire. However, their career journey is often marked by challenges related to obedience to policies and workplace rules. Insubordination and non-compliance may be persistent issues for rebels, as they resist conforming to established norms.

While rebels are valued for their ideas and creativity, their career progression may be hindered due to their tendency to challenge convention. They often experience challenges in progressing to senior and influential roles, as their nonconventional ways of doing things may be seen as a threat by senior stakeholders. This fear of disruption can limit their advancement and make organisations hesitant to place them in positions of authority where they have to deal with important stakeholders.

The lesson for individuals embodying the Rebel archetype is not to rebel merely for the sake of making noise. It is crucial to understand that every action creates a cycle of change. Rebels need to be clear about the changes they seek, the purpose behind those changes, and whether the sacrifices they make are truly worth it. Balancing their rebellious nature with an understanding of strategic impact can help rebels channel their energy in a way that brings positive and meaningful transformation.

Characteristic Checklist of the Rebel Archetype

- ✓ You have rebellious characteristics since a young age.
- ✓ You speak out against discrimination, injustices, and societal norms.
- ✓ You resist taking orders and prefer to follow your own thinking.
- ✓ You thrive on making changes and upsetting the status quo.
- ✓ You always approach tasks and challenges in non-traditional ways.
- ✓ You are an agent of change, constantly introducing new ideas at work.
- ✓ You are drawn to less known alternatives and are willing to take risks in pursuing their goals.
- ✓ You are attached to the idea of being a shop steward or leading a Works council that represents the interest of fellow colleagues.
- ✓ You have a strong sense of personal power and autonomy.

Amani, a Customer Experience Manager, embodied the Rebel archetype. From a young age, Amani had a strong sense of justice and a rebellious spirit that questioned the status quo. In her role, Amani constantly challenged conventional customer service practices, seeking to revolutionise the way the company interacted with its customers.

She quickly became known for challenging the status quo, questioning outdated practices, and pushing back against authority when she believed things could be done better. She wasn't afraid to speak her mind in meetings, often suggesting bold, unconventional ideas that shook up the norm. Her rebellious nature earned her the reputation of being the "disruptor" in his organisation—a double-edged sword.

However, Amani's career had consistently faced challenges in Stage Six of his career: "Bringing Your Whole Self to Work." She struggled to integrate her authentic self into a work environment that valued conformity, and this difficulty had cost her previous job. Her previous employer saw his relentless pushback as a refusal to collaborate, and after several clashes with management, Amani ultimately chose to leave. Despite these setbacks, she held onto the belief that her bold, rebellious nature was a strength that could drive real change.

One day, her new company announced a traditional top-down management system, which Amani saw as outdated and restrictive. True to her rebellious nature, Amani openly opposed the change during a company-wide meeting, questioning the decision and urging management to explore a more agile, flexible structure.

Her defiance struck a chord with several team members who admired her courage. Some even saw her as a voice of reason, advocating for innovation and forward-thinking. Amani's ideas were fresh and bold, earning her recognition as someone who wasn't afraid to challenge the system. This helped accelerate her career in the short term; she gained visibility, and leaders began to see her as a creative force in the organisation.

However, Amani's tendency to always push back had a downside. Over time, her rebellious streak began to alienate some of her colleagues. She was so focused on challenging authority that she neglected to see the value in compromise or collaboration. Her boss, who had initially admired Amani's drive, became frustrated with her unwillingness to listen to others' perspectives or work within the team dynamic.

Amani's overuse of the Rebel archetype, without self-awareness, eventually started to derail her career. While her boldness had helped her stand out in the early stages, she failed to realise that the ability to work cohesively with others was equally important at this point along her journey. Instead of bringing her whole self to work in a balanced way, she leaned too heavily on her rebellious persona, ignoring the need for growth in emotional intelligence and teamwork.

One particularly heated meeting became a turning point. After publicly clashing with a senior executive over a strategic decision Amani found herself being sidelined from important projects. Her once-celebrated courage was now viewed as reckless stubbornness, and her inability to adapt to the evolving needs of his role cost her opportunities for advancement. It was at this point that Amani sought coaching . She did not want to lose the Rebel in her but wanted to learn to use it to her advantage without derailing her career.

2. The Queen/ Executive

The Queen archetype embodies a natural confidence and a desire to marry and remain loyal to her husband. Her larger-than-life qualities make her stand out, and she is often attracted to powerful men who fit the Kingly archetype. In the modern corporate world, this archetype is seen in women who believe they can achieve their professional goals without compromising their feminine power. There is a sense of entitlement and privilege associated with the executive archetype, from wanting beautiful clothes and a prestigious office to the status symbols that come with a high-ranking position. This archetype can be bestowed by corporations, associations, personal businesses, or one's charismatic character.

However, the Queen archetype faces several challenges. The misuse of power and the temptation to use it for personal gain is a significant challenge. Vanity and a sense of entitlement can also derail this archetype, and in extreme cases, narcissism may emerge. The lesson for the Queen archetype is to use personal power in ways that do not bring suffering to others through self-serving choices.

It is essential to understand the source of power, differentiate between authentic and illusionary power, and manage it effectively. Failure to manage these challenges can lead to a continuous search for a corporate home and difficulties in negotiating power in the presence of other executives.

In the world of work, the Queen archetype manifests as a charismatic and respected leader in positions of authority. They possess strong leadership skills and are capable of organising and determining the pattern of social discourse. They rule with kindness, firmness, and strength, and their people respond with loyalty and respect.

However, the unapproachable nature of this archetype may lead to feelings of loneliness at the top. The positive impact of the Queen archetype is the ability to be a change agent in others' lives, opening doors and providing opportunities. Generosity and intuition play a significant role in making a difference for others. It is important for the Queen archetype to navigate power dynamics and maintain a balance between personal and authentic power.

Characteristic Checklist of the Queen/ Executive Archetype

- ✓ You are charismatic with a personality that commands respect.
- ✓ You are often in position of authority at work, in the community and in business.
- ✓ You are a capable leader, whether in the home environment or at work.
- ✓ In your networks / friendship group you are likely to be the leader of the group, organising social gatherings and determining the pattern of social discourse.
- ✓ As a leader you are benevolent, compassionate and inclusive, keen to be receptive to the needs of your "subjects".
- ✓ You rule with kindness but also with firmness and strength, not tolerating those who act against you and seeking retribution against those who invoke your wrath.
- ✓ Your people understand your strengths and respond to them with loyalty and respect.
- ✓ Because of the unapproachable character, you sometimes find yourself lonely at the top.

Lindiwe embodied the Queen archetype, possessing natural leadership qualities and a commanding presence that captured the attention of her colleagues. A Marketing Director in an FMCG company, she had always known that she was a natural leader. Whether in her workplace, among friends, or within her community, people naturally gravitated toward her, recognising her charisma and the strength of her personality. She had earned her position as the head of a prestigious marketing firm through hard work, sharp instincts, and the kind of authority that inspired loyalty from those around her. She was the queen in every sense of the word—revered, respected, and at times, feared.

At work, her leadership style was both her greatest strength and her silent curse. Lindiwe had built a close-knit team that admired her ability to make tough decisions with compassion. She was known for her fairness, always considering her team's well-being before making company-wide changes. When new projects arose, she ensured that everyone had a voice at the table, fostering an environment of inclusivity and creativity. Her team members were fiercely loyal to her, and she had earned their respect through consistent acts of generosity and strength.

It was her need for control and perfection, the darker side of her queenly nature, that started to undermine her reign. As the company began to expand, Lindiwe felt the pressure of having to oversee every detail. She found herself unable to delegate, worrying that others might not execute her vision with the precision she demanded. Her firm hand, once a symbol of stability, began to feel oppressive to those around her. She expected nothing less than excellence, but the weight of her expectations stifled innovation and demoralised her team.

Soon, the benevolent leader who once led with compassion began to isolate herself. She ruled with a sense of entitlement, assuming that those who disagreed with her were undermining her authority. A whisper of dissent was enough to stir her wrath, and she grew quick to punish any perceived betrayal. Her closest advisor, Thabo, once a trusted confidant, had gently suggested a new direction for a major campaign—one that went against Lindiwe's original idea. Feeling threatened, she publicly dismissed his proposal and began freezing him out of important meetings.

The fallout was immediate. Thabo, hurt and disillusioned, resigned a few months later, leaving a gaping hole in the team's morale. Lindiwe's inner circle grew smaller as others became fearful of challenging her ideas. The more isolated she became, the more defensive she grew. And though she never realised it, her unapproachable demeanour had made her lonely at the top.

Lindiwe's career shocks in Stage Seven came from the cracks in the team she had worked hard to form. She realised she was losing her grip, both professionally and personally, as the bad traits of her Queen archetype began to overshadow the good.

But Lindiwe was nothing if not self-aware. One late evening, after reading yet another resignation letter from a valued team member, she realised that her leadership had become more about her need to maintain power than about the well-being of her team. She saw how her insistence on control had pushed away the very people who had once been her greatest supporters. The thought hit her like a wave: A true queen does not rule alone.

Determined to change, Lindiwe began to step back. She re-learned how to listen—truly listen—to her team without feeling the need to assert her authority at every turn. She brought in a coach to help her navigate the delicate balance of leadership, learning to trust her team and delegate responsibilities. She apologised to those she had wronged, including Thabo, whose departure still weighed heavily on her. Slowly, the tides began to turn.

Once afraid of her wrath, her team began to open up again, offering ideas and creativity without fear of judgement. Lindiwe, now more inclusive than ever, rebuilt her circle of trust. She embraced the strength that came from collaboration, realising that her role as a leader wasn't to control everything but to empower those around her.

In the end, Lindiwe found balance. Her Queen archetype remained dominant—strong, charismatic, and respected—but now tempered by the wisdom of experience. She had learned that leadership was about more than ruling; it was about building, nurturing, and, sometimes, letting go.

And so, her kingdom was restored, but it was no longer a solitary throne. It was a shared space, one where her power came not from dominance, but from the respect, loyalty, and trust of those she led.

3. The Visionary

Visionaries possess a unique ability to imagine and think ahead, setting the stage for innovation and transformative change. Whether they are entrepreneurs, innovators, or pioneers, Visionaries have a knack for perceiving the world in a radically different way than others and charting a roadmap towards their vision. They give birth to ideas that shape the future of humanity and inspire others with their imagination, motivation, and hope.

However, Visionaries often feel constrained by traditional systems, rules, and familiar ways of doing things. They see hidden potential in life and may struggle to understand that not everyone thinks the way they do. One of the *challenges* they face is being overwhelmed by multiple ideas simultaneously. This can lead to a lack of focus, as they quickly lose interest in one idea and become distracted by a new one. Visionaries may abandon great ideas before fully exploring their true potential.

Imagine a person who delights in sharing new ideas but fails to take action or bring those ideas to fruition. They find themselves trapped in a cycle of ideation without execution.

An inherent ability of Visionaries is their tendency to poke holes in their own ideas. While they generate creative ideas, they also excel at generating excuses or reasons why those ideas won't work. This self-critical tendency can hinder their progress and prevent them from taking action.

In terms of their career, Visionaries may struggle to find the right job because they are constantly seeking to create their own occupation rather than stepping into an existing one. This can lead to a perception of professional unreliability from others.

One of the key *lessons* for Visionaries is to believe in their ideas and potential to impact the lives of others. By embracing this belief, they can overcome the hurdles that prevent their ideas from materialising. To succeed in the world of work, Visionaries need to learn how to bring others along on their journey of idea development. They must recognise that not everyone possesses their visionary perspective and may struggle to see the future potential they envision. The art of storytelling, communicating their ideas in simple language that others can understand, becomes a valuable skill for their career advancement.

Having a visionary partner who can understand their ideas and provide support throughout the process of turning visions into actions is essential for Visionaries in the workplace. This partner serves as a sounding board, challenging them and helping them think of practical ways to bring their ideas to life.

Characteristic Checklist of the Visionary Archetype

- ✓ You receive and rely on intuitive guidance.
- ✓ You have the ability to envision yourself as something out of the ordinary.
- ✓ You see many opportunities out of life and can't wait to give them form.
- ✓ You are strongly dependent on intuition and rely on intuition as a source of creative ideas.
- ✓ You have the ability to balance possibilities and probabilities.
- ✓ You are continuously coming up with ideas.
- ✓ You do not worry about taking risks.
- ✓ You are seen as an agent of change.
- ✓ You sense transformation in the outer world before it happens.
- ✓ You look for ways to free yourself from traditional rules and ways of doing things.
- ✓ You approach careers, work and jobs in a nonconventional way.
- ✓ You can be seen as eccentric and free spirited.
- ✓ You see problems and immediately think of solutions.

Jonathan had always embodied the Visionary archetype, a natural forward-thinker who was never content with just managing his current responsibilities. From the moment he joined the tech company as a junior developer, he was driven by a bigger purpose — to shape the future of the industry. While others focused on daily tasks, Jonathan was always thinking ahead, spotting trends and anticipating shifts in the market. His ideas were bold and innovative, and his ability to envision future possibilities propelled him into leadership, where he was entrusted with shaping the company's long-term strategy.

Jonathan's Visionary archetype not only helped him excel in his career but also allowed him to proactively manage it. He always had a clear vision of where he wanted to go, constantly adapting his role to align with emerging opportunities. His forward-thinking approach meant he wasn't just reacting to industry changes — he was driving them.

This proactive stance kept him ahead of competitors, allowing him to spearhead projects that positioned the company as a market leader. By focusing on the future, Jonathan always had a path to follow, guiding both his career and the company's strategic direction.

When the company announced restructuring, and Jonathan's role was made redundant, it was a major career disruption. For many, this would have been a devastating setback, but Jonathan's visionary mindset allowed him to pivot and navigate the transition with ease.

Rather than seeing the loss as the end of his career, Jonathan immediately began thinking about the next chapter. His ability to anticipate trends helped him spot new opportunities in emerging industries like sustainability and tech, areas that aligned with his personal values and long-term goals.

Jonathan didn't just wait for opportunities to come to him; he proactively sought out new connections, networking with thought leaders and positioning himself for future roles. His visionary nature also led him to reframe his job search, focusing not on traditional roles but on how he could create value in these emerging fields. He built a portfolio of projects that showcased his visionary thinking and shared his ideas through thought leadership, reinforcing his brand as a forward-thinking leader.

Because he always had a vision for his career, Jonathan was able to manage the transition of Stage Seven with confidence. His Visionary archetype allowed him to see redundancy not as an end but as a new beginning—an opportunity to realign his career with his evolving vision. In the end, Jonathan landed a role as Chief Innovation Officer at a sustainability tech start-up, perfectly aligned with his career vision.

4. The Intellectual/ Professional / Student

The Intellectual archetype embodies individuals who are deeply engrossed in the realm of the mind. They prioritise intellectual pursuits over emotional impulses and physical pleasures, finding great fulfilment in the life of the mind. Scientists, scholars, students, philosophers, and geeks are part of this family of archetypes. They are characterised by their relentless quest for knowledge and their insatiable desire to understand the "why" of things. Intellectuals are driven by a genuine love of learning and a thirst for uncovering the truth.

On their career journey, Intellectuals thrive on the pursuit of knowledge across various domains. They revel in the world of data, analytics, and cyberspace, constantly seeking to expand their understanding and discover the underlying truths. Their industry-specific knowledge gives them a competitive edge, and they take pride in being well-informed and highly educated.

However, Intellectuals can face certain challenges in the work environment. Their intense focus on knowledge can make it difficult for them to be open to new ideas from external sources. They may come across as know-it-alls, dismissing alternative perspectives that do not align with their own sources of information. Overthinking and analysis paralysis can also hinder their decision-making process. Learning to strike a balance between gathering enough facts and making timely decisions is a crucial lesson for Intellectuals.

Additionally, Intellectuals may struggle to recognise and appreciate different forms of intelligence in others. This can lead to unhealthy competition and intellectual one-upmanship in the workplace. To thrive, Intellectuals need to cultivate open-mindedness and embrace the notion that not everything in life has a rational or logical explanation. They must learn to balance their logical thinking with heart-centred understanding when interacting with people. Incorporating intuition alongside factual data is also a valuable lesson for this archetype, enabling them to become a formidable force in their professional endeavours.

Characteristic Checklist of the Intellectual Archetype

- ✓ You learn for the sake of learning and love of pure knowledge.
- ✓ You are intrigued by spending time online feeding your curiosity.
- ✓ You are on a search for a deep understanding of the secrets of this universe and common laws that explain how the world works.
- ✓ You continuously challenge and grow your thinking through reading, lectures and studying.

- ✓ You approach life like a scientist testing hypotheses, proving and disproving them.
- ✓ You are drawn to people with active minds who like stimulating conversations.
- ✓ You respond to people with your head not your heart.
- ✓ You view the world as a web of interconnectedness.

Emma was a young and talented Social Media Manager working for a prestigious blue-chip company. Her intellect and analytical prowess had propelled her into this role, where she was responsible for driving the company's online presence and digital marketing strategies. Emma's days were filled with data analysis, content creation, and strategic planning.

As an intellectual, Emma revelled in the world of social media and digital marketing. She spent hours researching the latest trends, analysing user behaviour, and delving into the depths of algorithms and analytics. Her inquisitive mind sought to understand the underlying mechanisms that governed online platforms and their impact on consumer behaviour.

However, Emma's intellectual nature also posed challenges in her career. She was often reluctant to consider ideas or perspectives that contradicted her own extensive research. When her colleagues suggested alternative strategies or approaches, Emma would dismiss them, firmly believing that her data-driven insights were superior. This tendency to be rigid in her thinking created tension and limited collaboration within her team.

Moreover, Emma's overthinking and analysis paralysis hindered her decision-making process. She would delve so deeply into data analysis and research that she struggled to make timely decisions, causing delays and missed opportunities. Her colleagues began to perceive her as slow and indecisive, which impacted her effectiveness as a manager.

Recognising the need for change, Emma embarked on a journey of self-reflection and growth. She realised that her intellectual strengths needed to be balanced with openness and humility. Emma began actively seeking out different perspectives, engaging in discussions with colleagues and industry experts to broaden her horizons.

Furthermore, Emma learned the importance of integrating intuition with factual data. She started trusting her instincts and combining them with her analytical skills to make more confident decisions. This newfound balance allowed her to tap into her intellectual strengths while embracing the wisdom of other perspectives.

As Emma continued to evolve, her career trajectory shifted. Her willingness to listen and consider diverse viewpoints fostered a more collaborative work environment. She became known for her ability to meld the analytical rigour of an intellectual with an open-minded and inclusive approach.

The lessons Emma learned as an intellectual were invaluable. She discovered that true intellectual growth involved not only accumulating knowledge but also remaining receptive to new ideas. Emma realised that her career success depended not only on her analytical prowess but also on her ability to connect with and inspire her team. By finding the delicate balance between the mind and the heart, Emma forged a fulfilling career journey as a Social Media Manager, leaving a lasting impact on the company and those she worked with.

Lessons learned from Emma's experiences:

- Balance intellect with open-mindedness: embrace diverse perspectives and be receptive to ideas that challenge your own.

- Combine intuition with factual data: trust your instincts and integrate them with analytical thinking for more confident decision making.

- Cultivate collaboration and humility: recognise the value of teamwork and foster a collaborative work environment by embracing the wisdom of others.

- Strive for continuous growth: intellectual pursuits should be accompanied by personal and professional development, evolving not only intellectually but also emotionally and socially.

- Embrace the mystery: acknowledge that not everything can be explained by rationality alone. Leave room for wonder and acceptance of the unexplainable.

5. The Advocates

The Advocates archetype is a force dedicated to advancing humanitarian matters for the benefit of society. They possess an unwavering commitment to championing the human rights of those who cannot speak for themselves. Their noble goal lies in the realm of social, political, economic, and environmental transformation. Advocates firmly believe they were born to make a difference.

In various professions such as lawyers, social workers, environmentalists, philanthropists, community organisers, writers, and media professionals, you will find the presence of the Advocates archetype. They possess exceptional public speaking skills and are known for their ability to rally support and drive positive social change.

As a devoted advocate, you willingly commit to projects that strive for social, environmental, humanitarian, or economic change. You understand the personal and financial risks involved in such endeavours, yet you wholeheartedly embrace them. Advocacy becomes not just a profession but a calling, a way to contribute to long-term transformation.

Some Advocates take up causes as a hobby, seeking to make a meaningful difference while staying connected to their regular lives. Others become compulsive Advocates, driven by personal emotional needs fulfilled through social activism. However, for compulsive Advocates, the allure of social camaraderie sometimes overshadows the cause itself. Eventually, the investment of time and energy starts to feel confining rather than fulfilling, leading them to seek excuses to withdraw and move on to the next adrenaline thrill. Thus, the cycle continues.

Advocates face various challenges, one of which is setting realistic expectations for the social change they seek to drive. Often, Advocates hold utopian ideals that are challenging to achieve. As a result, they may exhaust their resources, leaving them feeling frustrated and unfulfilled. While it is important not to abandon utopian ideals altogether, it is crucial to be realistic in their pursuit, understanding one's strengths and weaknesses, and making informed decisions about where to invest time and resources in the near term.

Another common challenge faced by Advocates is being drawn to social causes due to personal or family experiences. For example, being personally affected by crime may inspire someone to join a crime-fighting cause. However, it becomes essential to manage personal issues and set them aside for the greater purpose of focusing on the group's agenda. Failure to do so may result in personal issues manifesting through anger and passive-aggressive behaviour, ultimately derailing the cause itself.

The main lesson for Advocates is the ability to choose which causes to get involved in. The workplace, with its myriad social ills, may tempt Advocates to participate in numerous projects or drive multiple initiatives simultaneously. However, spreading oneself too thin may diminish their impact, leaving them frustrated and feeling ineffective. It is crucial to remember that while advocating for fairness and change in the workplace is important, maintaining good relations and balancing the need to work and earn a living is equally vital.

The shadow side of the Advocates archetype involves being judgemental of others who do not share the same level of passion or commitment to the causes they champion. It is important to avoid alienating and name-calling those who do not align with their ideals. Similarly, developing a superiority complex towards those who have not embraced the same lifestyle changes or workplace objectives may hinder the ability to influence others effectively.

Fresh out of university and full of passion, Maya embodied the Advocate archetype. She possessed an unwavering belief that she could make a positive impact in the workplace and create a more humane environment for her colleagues.

Maya's advocacy journey began with small actions. She would speak up for colleagues who were mistreated, raising their concerns to higher management. She tirelessly researched and proposed initiatives to improve work-life balance and promote diversity and inclusion within the organisation. Maya dedicated herself to fostering a culture of respect and empowerment.

However, Maya's idealism sometimes clouded her judgement. She took on numerous projects simultaneously, believing she could single-handedly drive change across the entire organisation. Her passion was commendable, but her lack of experience and understanding of organisational dynamics led her to spread herself too thin.

As Maya became consumed by her advocacy work, she neglected her core managerial responsibilities. Her team noticed a decline in leadership presence and guidance. Maya's career decisions were driven solely by her desire to create a positive impact, often without considering the implications for her own growth and development. She volunteered for projects that aligned with her advocacy goals but did not necessarily contribute to her professional advancement.

The impact on Maya's career journey was twofold. Firstly, she became overwhelmed and burnt out, unable to sustain her enthusiasm and energy. Secondly, her neglect of core managerial responsibilities resulted in strained relationships with her team and superiors, who felt she was neglecting her primary role.

Recognising the need for change, Maya had to reassess her approach. She realised that being an effective advocate required balance and strategic decision making. She needed to prioritise her own growth and development to enhance her ability to make a meaningful impact. She sought guidance from mentors within the organisation who helped her understand the importance of aligning her advocacy work with her career goals.

Maya learned valuable lessons through her experiences. She discovered that being an advocate was not just about championing causes but also about being an effective leader. She also understood the significance of managing her time and resources wisely, focusing on projects that aligned with her career trajectory. She learned to strike a balance between her advocacy work and her managerial responsibilities, understanding that she needed to lead by example to effect real change.

Moreover, Maya discovered the importance of building coalitions and working collaboratively with other like-minded individuals within the organisation. She realised that sustainable change required collective effort and strategic alliances. Maya harnessed her exceptional communication skills to inspire and influence others, building strong networks and fostering a sense of shared purpose.

As Maya made these changes and re-evaluated her approach, she gradually regained her momentum and reconnected with her true potential as an advocate and manager. Her career trajectory shifted as she focused on projects that allowed her to grow professionally while still driving positive change in the workplace. Maya's dedication and newfound strategic mindset propelled her career forward, earning her the respect of her colleagues and superiors.

Maya's journey serves as a valuable lesson for aspiring Advocates. While passion and advocacy are important, it is crucial to strike a balance between driving change and fulfilling core professional responsibilities. Building alliances, managing time effectively, and aligning advocacy work with career goals are essential for long-term success.

Maya's transformation highlights the importance of self-awareness, adaptability, and a willingness to learn and grow. By embracing these lessons, aspiring Advocates can navigate their career journeys more effectively, making a lasting impact while also nurturing their own professional development.

Characteristic Checklist of the Advocates Archetype

- ✓ You possess an innate drive to identify what needs to be changed in the world.
- ✓ Your passion compels you to address societal wrongs.
- ✓ Your purpose in life revolves around making the workplace a better and more humane environment.
- ✓ You are naturally drawn to social, political, or environmental concerns.
- ✓ Making a difference in the world of work is an integral part of your being.
- ✓ You are dedicated to fixing what is not working in the workplace.
- ✓ You speak out for those colleagues who have no voice.
- ✓ You are committed to advancing the idea of a humane workplace.

6. The Sell-Out

The Sell-Out archetype, often referred to as just the Sell-Out, is a fundamental aspect of human nature that arises when we feel compelled to compromise a part of ourselves in exchange for something we desire. This archetype thrives on fears related to survival and security, prompting us to trade our integrity, talents, and ideas in compromising ways for financial gain, social acceptance, or recognition. It extends beyond the literal concept of selling one's body and encompasses situations where we compromise our values to advance in life.

We have all faced challenges that required us to play the role of the Sell-Out in some way or another. It involves compromising who we are and what we truly value to navigate the world around us. Examples include:

- Working weekends to maintain a secure job, sacrificing precious time with loved ones.
- Accepting the authority of a dictatorial boss due to fear of the risks associated with searching for a new job.
- Putting in extra hours to befriend influential individuals, compromising personal boundaries.
- Writing uninspiring pieces instead of pursuing one's true passion, succumbing to external opinions.

If you believe you have not experienced the Sell-Out archetype in your life, reflect on a time when you found yourself torn between two options, feeling nervous about the risks on one hand and resentful of the security on the other. The Sell-Out archetype is present in those moments. It can manifest as making a deal with the devil, such as working for someone you despise because you love the company or accepting a pay raise at the expense of sacrificing family time.

The primary lesson associated with this archetype is cultivating integrity when faced with either/or situations that challenge our spirit or values due to fears of physical or financial survival. It speaks to the unconscious parts of ourselves that are susceptible to seduction and control, reminding us that we are all capable of buying a controlling interest in another person just as much as we are capable of selling our own power for security.

Furthermore, the Sell-Out archetype calls for the cultivation and refinement of self-esteem. It is about understanding that while everyone has a price, we have a choice not to compromise the core of who we are. In our careers, we trade our skills and talents, but there comes a point where we may trade them in ways that compromise our well-being, family life, and overall health. Often driven by financial benefits, we neglect the detrimental impact our careers may have on our lives, only realising it when it's too late.

The journey of working with the Sell-Out archetype begins with recognising what holds value for us and cultivating self-worth. It requires aligning our actions with our true convictions and not allowing external factors to compromise our core identity.

Characteristic Checklist of the Sell-Out Archetype

- ✓ You compromise your beliefs by associating with people or organisations you did not truly believe in.
- ✓ You remain in an uncomfortable job or work environment solely for financial protection, sacrificing your own well-being.
- ✓ You manipulate or coerce another person into compromising themselves for your personal gain.
- ✓ You buy someone's loyalty, support, or silence to manipulate outcomes in your favour.
- ✓ You disregard your values to seek approval from colleagues.
- ✓ You let go of your dreams in exchange for comfort and security.
- ✓ You prioritise financial gain over pursuing your passions or convictions.
- ✓ You remain in a toxic work environment and relationships for social or financial benefits.

✓ You engage in actions that contradict your values, beliefs, and ethics for personal benefit, regardless of how small.

✓ You find yourself being insincere or falsely nice to others in order to gain something from them.

By honestly examining these aspects, we can begin to understand the presence of the Sell-Out archetype in our lives and take steps towards reclaiming our integrity and self-worth.

Robert's story demonstrates this archetype very well. Robert had worked his way up the corporate ladder as a Sales Manager over the years, fuelled by ambition and a relentless drive for success. He was known for his exceptional strategic thinking and strong business acumen, which had earned him the respect and admiration of his peers and superiors alike. However, beneath his polished exterior, Robert grappled with the presence of the Sell-Out archetype.

As Robert's career progressed, he found himself facing increasingly difficult choices. The pressure to meet financial targets, secure lucrative deals, and maintain his position at the top began to weigh heavily on him. Slowly but surely, the Sell-Out archetype started to influence his decision making, nudging him toward compromising his values for short-term gains.

One pivotal moment occurred when Robert's team proposed a project that aligned with his personal values and would make a positive impact on society. However, it required a significant investment of time and resources, with uncertain financial returns. Fearing the potential risk to his reputation and the financial security of the company, Robert hesitated. The Sell-Out archetype whispered in his ear, reminding him of the importance of maintaining financial stability and security, urging him to prioritise short-term profitability over long-term social impact.

Reluctantly, Robert made the decision to forgo the project, instead opting for a more conventional initiative that promised immediate financial gains. While the company thrived financially in the short term, Robert's inner conflict intensified. He couldn't shake off the feeling that he had compromised his integrity and betrayed his own values.

As time went on, Robert found himself overlooking ethical concerns, cutting corners to achieve results, and compromising the well-being of his team members for personal gain. His reputation suffered, and whispers of his questionable practices began to circulate within the organisation.

One day, Robert received a wake-up call in the form of a failed merger negotiation. The other party had become aware of the unethical practices and lack of integrity within Robert's division, resulting in the collapse of the deal. It was a sobering moment for him, a realisation that his pursuit of short-term gains had led him astray and cost him significant opportunities for professional growth.

Ultimately, Robert's story serves as a cautionary tale about the influence of the Sell-Out archetype in the workplace. It highlights the importance of maintaining integrity, staying true to one's values, and considering the long-term consequences of career decisions. Through self-awareness, self-reflection, and a commitment to ethical leadership, one can navigate the complex landscape of the corporate world while staying aligned with their authentic self.

7. The Saboteur

The name of this archetype suggests that it is something bad that is a sabotage. However the most surprising thing you will learn about this archetype is that just like all the other archetypes it has its good and bad side. Most of us connect and experience the bad side. The side that is made up of fears and issues related to self-esteem that cause us to make choices in life that block our own empowerment and success.

The shadow shows us the parts that are buried deep within, occupy our subconscious mind, and often emerge unexpectedly, in destructive ways. It is mostly fearful of change, as a result it will normally show up in situations that require you to change, especially if that change is going to rearrange your whole reality. It is no surprise then that the Saboteur will often become evident during Stage Seven when you experience career shock and in Stage Eight when navigating career transitions.

However, it is important to recognise that like all archetypes, the Saboteur has both a shadow side and a light side. The shadow side represents our fears and self-esteem issues, which often lead us to make choices that block our own success. On the other hand, the light side of this archetype offers opportunities for personal growth and empowerment.

To experience the positive aspects of the Saboteur, we must confront and understand it, making it an ally rather than an enemy. By connecting with our Saboteur, we become aware of situations where self-sabotage is at play, saving ourselves from repeating the same mistakes. This connection also enhances our intuition and ability to discern between fear, excitement, desire, and true gut instinct.

A significant *lesson* is recognising the shadow side of the Saboteur, which manifests as guarding our hearts and pushing away people or opportunities that bring us joy. The Saboteur is skilled at creating dramatic stories that are detached from reality, causing us to doubt our instincts and leading us to give up or postpone our dreams due to fear of failure or inadequacy.

In a career context, the role of the Saboteur is to protect us. However, it fails to realise that by shielding us from pain, it perpetuates it. The Saboteur may show up in self-destructive behaviours resulting in unintended consequences that damages your career.

Characteristic Checklist of the Saboteur Archetype

- ✓ Whenever you try to get too close to people, the Saboteur will help you to subconsciously create situations that cause conflict and pain, and leave you feeling disappointed, hopeless, or lonely.
- ✓ You judge, criticise, and put yourself down, telling yourself that you are unworthy of good things.
- ✓ You have stopped trusting the wisdom of your heart and instincts.
- ✓ Self-doubt Saboteur: this Saboteur archetype manifests when you constantly undermine your own abilities and potential. You may hesitate to take on new challenges or opportunities due to fear of failure or lack of confidence. As a result, you may sabotage your career progression by holding yourself back from reaching your full potential.
- ✓ Procrastination Saboteur: this Saboteur archetype appears when you consistently delay or put off important tasks or projects. You may struggle with time management and prioritisation, leading to missed deadlines and decreased

productivity. Procrastination can hinder career growth and success by preventing you from making progress in your professional endeavours.

✓ Imposter Saboteur: the Imposter Saboteur manifests when you constantly doubt your own competence and feel like a fraud. You may believe that you don't deserve your achievements or recognition, leading to a fear of being exposed as inadequate. This self-doubt can hold you back from taking on new responsibilities or seeking advancement in your career.

✓ Fear of change Saboteur: this Saboteur emerges when you resist change and clings to familiarity. You may feel anxious or uncomfortable with new ideas, technologies, or processes, preventing you from adapting to evolving work environments. Your resistance to change can hinder career growth, as you may miss out on opportunities that require embracing innovation.

✓ Conflict Saboteur: the Conflict Saboteur arises when you consistently engage in conflicts or create a hostile work environment. You may struggle with managing relationships and resolving disagreements, leading to strained professional connections. The constant turmoil and discord can sabotage your career progression and limit your potential for collaboration and growth.

David's story is a good example of different ways the Saboteur can show up at work impacting your career. David was a talented and experienced Finance Manager in a reputable company in London. He had all the necessary skills and expertise to excel in his role. However, unbeknownst to him, his Saboteur archetype had a firm grip on his career aspirations.

Whenever David had the opportunity to move up the corporate ladder or take on new leadership roles, his Saboteur kicked in, planting seeds of doubt in his mind. He constantly questioned his abilities and worthiness, feeling like a fraud despite his achievements. The Imposter Saboteur within him prevented him from pursuing advancement opportunities, fearing exposure and failure.

Moreover, David's Saboteur manifested as a fear of change. As the company introduced new strategies, technologies, and processes, David resisted, clinging to the familiar. He felt anxious and uncomfortable with the idea of adapting to the evolving work environment. This resistance hindered his growth, as he missed out on opportunities that required embracing innovation and change.

Additionally, the Saboteur within David led him to procrastinate. Important projects and tasks were often delayed, impacting his productivity and credibility. His struggle with time management and prioritisation caused missed deadlines and decreased efficiency, tarnishing his reputation.

As David's career progressed, his Saboteur fuelled negative self-talk and self-criticism. He constantly judged himself, believing he was unworthy of success and that his achievements were merely a stroke of luck. These self-sabotaging thoughts further eroded his confidence and hindered his ability to make bold career moves.

Over time, David's self-sabotage became a pattern that held him back from reaching his full potential. Despite his talent and experience, he remained stuck in middle management, unable to break free from the grip of his Saboteur.

This story of David serves as a cautionary tale of how the Saboteur archetype can undermine your career success. Fear, self-doubt, and low self-esteem stemming from this archetype can lead individuals to make choices that hinder their professional growth and limit their advancement. Confronting and understanding the Saboteur's influence is crucial for breaking free from self-sabotaging patterns and creating a path toward career fulfilment and empowerment.

8. The King / Boss

The King archetype, or what some may refer to as the Boss archetype, represents the epitome of masculine energy and power. This archetype is characterised by a commanding presence, self-control, and a deep sense of authority. The King exudes confidence and earns the respect of those around him through his calm and controlled demeanour.

The King archetype provides order and protection, bringing stability to the chaotic world. He possesses the ability to manifest his desires and influence those in his realm. His decisions are carefully considered, weighing risks and rewards, enabling him to make calculated choices that benefit both himself and his subjects. This requires him to be studious, deliberate, and thoughtful in his actions.

The King archetype typically possesses a strong sense of direction and self-assuredness, allowing him to navigate his career without relying on or concerning himself with the opinions of others. However, this archetype may also face challenges, such as a sense of entitlement or resistance to criticism and questioning regarding his authority and control over his kingdom. These challenges arise from a deep-rooted need to exert control and maintain his dominion.

Another negative aspect of the King archetype is his potential to appear aloof and detached, perceiving others as beneath him. This detachment may stem from a lack of meaningful interaction with those around him, resulting in an imbalance in self-esteem.

The key lesson for the King archetype is learning vulnerability by becoming less judgemental and more emotionally available. It is crucial for the King to connect with others, especially those he deeply cares about, by allowing himself to be open and receptive of feedback especially in leadership positions.

Characteristic Checklist of the King Archetype

- ✓ You are a critical thinker, reflecting inwardly on the best course of action before making your moves rather than reacting in haste or temper.
- ✓ You have a need to hone these skills which means that you are usually a mature rather than young individual, having taken years to learn to control your temper and desires.
- ✓ Age has taught you how to act with wisdom, grace and maturity in any given situation to ensure the best outcome for all involved.
- ✓ You are self-aware, understanding your own weaknesses and failings as well as how best to overcome these.
- ✓ Your job is centred around helping others.

James typifies the King archetype very well, known for carefully considering his actions before making any moves, always striving to act with wisdom and grace. His job as a Human Resources Manager centred around helping others, providing guidance and leadership.

In his career, James was naturally drawn to leadership positions where he could exert control and influence over his "subjects." At his best, James was admired and respected as a leader, appreciated for his calm and calculated decision making. However, his tendency to be aloof and detached sometimes hindered his ability to earn the respect he desired from his colleagues and subordinates.

James' career challenges always centred around Stage Seven which requires him to manage career shock. This time, James He was assigned a diverse team that required strong interpersonal connections and collaboration. His usual approach of maintaining control and distance seemed inadequate in this situation. James realised that in order to lead effectively, he needed to connect with his team members on a deeper level.

Recognising the lesson he needed to learn, James shared this concern with his mentor who guided him through a difficult journey to becoming more emotionally available and less judgemental. Learning from his mentor began engaging in open and honest conversations with his team, expressing his vulnerabilities and acknowledging their contributions. By creating an atmosphere of trust and understanding, James saw a remarkable transformation within his team dynamics. They became more motivated, productive, and supportive of each other.

Through this experience, James learned two valuable lessons. First, he discovered that true leadership goes beyond exerting control and authority. It requires emotional intelligence, vulnerability, and the ability to connect with others on a personal level. Second, James realised that his career success was not solely dependent on his individual achievements but also on the collective efforts and contributions of his team.

In embracing these lessons, James's career took a positive turn. He became a respected leader who not only provided direction but also nurtured and empowered his team members.

9. The Career Damsel

The Career Damsel archetype, as described by Caroline Myss, is rooted in the oldest female archetype of a beautiful and vulnerable woman in need of rescue. In a career context, individuals embodying this archetype may possess excellent qualifications, experience, and produce outstanding results.[128] However, they struggle to talk about their achievements and wait for others to recognise their hard work and advocate for their deserved raise or promotion. They may shy away from self-promotion, believing it to be political or uncomfortable.

The positive aspect of the Career Damsel is the potential for self-empowerment and learning to overcome challenges through their own strength. This archetype often emerges in work environments that reinforce patriarchal views, promoting the perception of women as weak and reliant on protection. The Career Damsel may expect someone else to fight their battles while they remain concealed and physically attractive in the background.

One significant challenge for this archetype is stepping out of the shadows and being comfortable with self-promotion. They must overcome the expectation that someone else will take care of their career, understanding that they have the power to shape their own professional destiny. Another challenge is letting go of the belief that recognition and career growth will automatically come solely from hard work without actively advocating for oneself.

Characteristic Checklist of the Career Damsel Archetype

- ✓ You are a hardworking person, you go all out to get things done and are hoping everyone can see that and you wait for your recognition.

✓ You have been disappointed before when you did not get the recognition you felt you deserve because of your hard work.

✓ You are shy about talking openly about your accomplishments and capabilities.

✓ You expect that if you put all the hard work, your career will automatically progress to where you want it to go.

✓ You have felt used as a pawn by others to move their career forward.

The story of Emma, a Human Resources officer at a manufacturing facility in Cape Town, is a typical demonstration of the Career Damsel archetype. A talented professional with impressive qualifications and a track record of success. However, she embodied this archetype, always waiting for someone to recognise her hard work and move her career forward. Emma was extremely shy about discussing her accomplishments and capabilities, believing that her efforts would automatically lead to recognition and progression.

The breaking point came during a critical moment in her career. Emma had been working tirelessly on a new HR initiative to improve employee retention. She quietly contributed her ideas to the project, assuming her work would be recognised when the initiative succeeded. However, during a company-wide presentation, her manager took full credit for the project, praising Emma only as part of the team without acknowledging her significant role. As she sat in the audience, stunned and hurt, Emma realised how invisible she had become. This was the incident that shook her.

Devastated, Emma couldn't understand why this kept happening. She had always believed that hard work would naturally lead to recognition, yet she felt like a pawn in other people's success stories. Her quiet dedication was consistently overlooked. It was at this point that Emma realised something had to change. She couldn't keep waiting for others to notice her contributions.

Seeking help, Emma decided to seek help from her friend. In their discussion, they explored the reasons behind her reluctance to advocate for herself and worked on strategies to boost her confidence. Her friend helped her understand that her Career Damsel mindset—waiting for someone to "rescue" her—was holding her back. She learned that self-promotion was not about boasting but about making her value visible.

Armed with this new perspective, Emma gradually began to change her approach. The first step was difficult—she had to learn to speak up in meetings, even when she felt unsure. She started scheduling one-on-one discussions with her manager, not just to talk about projects but to share her career aspirations. Emma also began building her personal brand by speaking more openly about her accomplishments and contributions.

The transformation didn't happen overnight, but over time, Emma's confidence grew. She started receiving the recognition she had long hoped for because she was no longer waiting for others to acknowledge her worth—she was showing it to them. Her career began to progress, and she no longer felt like a pawn in someone else's game.

10. The Child Archetype

The Child archetype, as viewed through the lens of Carl Jung and Caroline Myss's theoretical framework, represents various aspects of our inner child that can influence our career decisions. It encompasses different forms, such as the wounded child, the innocent child, the magical child, the eternal child, and more. Each of these variations impacts our approach to work in distinct ways.

One aspect of the Child archetype is the wounded child. This archetype often inspires a deep desire to help others avoid experiencing the same wounds that we have endured. However, the shadow side of the wounded child manifests as consistent self-pity and a tendency to blame others, including family or colleagues, for negative career experiences. This can hinder personal growth and prevent individuals from taking charge of creating positive career experiences.

On the other hand, the magical child brings qualities of wonder, beauty, and the ability to inspire others to see the wondrous side of life even in challenging circumstances. This aspect of the Child archetype can instil wisdom and courage in the face of difficulties, fostering resilience and creative problem-solving.

The eternal child archetype embodies the determination to remain forever young in body, mind, and spirit. Individuals with this archetype radiate positive energy and a zest for life. However, the shadow side of the eternal child is the resistance to stepping up and assuming more senior responsibilities. This can lead to being overlooked for career growth opportunities due to the perception of immaturity or an inability to handle greater levels of responsibility.

The key lessons for individuals with the Child archetype are to harness its positive qualities while also recognising the need for personal growth. It's important to understand that certain childlike behaviours may not be conducive to the professional world. Balancing the childlike wonder and enthusiasm with mature decision making and professionalism is crucial.

Another essential *lesson* is learning to embrace adulthood when necessary. This involves recognising when to exhibit mature behaviour and professionalism, especially in work-related situations. It can be challenging to shift from a childlike response pattern to an adult one, but the goal is not to completely relinquish the child archetype. Instead, it's about being conscious of when to tap into that energy and when to exhibit maturity.

Characteristic Checklist of the Child Archetype

- ✓ You always come across as needy and not comfortable to independently make your own career decisions.
- ✓ You feel that you are not part of your team or the company as a whole.
- ✓ You are holding on to memories of ill treatment and abuse at work.
- ✓ You credit these early painful career experiences with having a substantial influence on your later career.
- ✓ You have a tendency to blame your wounded career child for all the dysfunctional work relationships, be it with your boss or colleagues.
- ✓ You have a tendency to be more comfortable dealing with minor tasks at work, shying away from and being scared of or doubting your abilities to take on more responsibilities.
- ✓ You are always being perceived as the youngest one or the junior one in the team even when the situation is not so.

Take Mia Thompson as an example, an ambitious professional in her mid-thirties, possessed a dominant Child archetype in her approach to work. She constantly found herself waiting for others, her superiors or the organisation, to take care of her career. She would raise her hand only when she wanted a specific job, a raise, or a promotion. If her desires were not met, Mia would become upset and consider leaving for another employer.

This pattern had hindered Mia's career growth and left her feeling unfulfilled. She realised that she was trapped in a cycle of dependence, relying on others to steer her professional journey. Mia's childlike behaviour, although not uncommon, prevented her from taking ownership of her career and making proactive decisions.

Fortunately, a mentor entered Mia's life and recognised her potential. This mentor, a seasoned professional named Sarah Johnson, observed Mia's talent, enthusiasm, and innate ability to connect with people. Sarah understood that Mia's Child archetype had kept her from fully realising her potential.

Over time, Sarah took Mia under her wing, acting as both a guide and a supporter. She helped Mia recognise some of her behaviours that showed the Child archetype. From her personal experience she taught Mia of embracing this archetype in her career. Sarah encouraged Mia to take charge of her professional development, set goals, and seek opportunities to expand her skillset. She empowered Mia to become an active participant in shaping her own career, rather than waiting for others to do it for her.

Through Sarah's guidance and mentorship, Mia began to exhibit more mature behaviour, taking initiative, and demonstrating leadership.

11. The Networker

The Networker archetype, as described by Sally Hogshead in her book *Fascinate: How to Make Your Brand Impossible to Resist*.[129] Hogshead explores various archetypes in branding and personal influence, including the Networker, which she refers to as the "Connector" archetype. According to Hogshead, the Connector thrives on building relationships and leveraging their network to create opportunities.

This archetype excels in environments where collaboration, communication, and social engagement are crucial. The Connector is driven by a genuine interest in people and possesses an intuitive understanding of how to bridge gaps between individuals, teams, or organisations. They build trust and foster partnerships by being approachable, resourceful, and adept at managing social dynamics, making them invaluable in roles where networking and relationship management are essential.

One of the positive aspects of the Networker archetype is the development of social fluidity and empathy. Networkers have the ability to find common ground with people who may not initially seem like potential allies. They possess excellent communication skills, share valuable information, and inspire different groups of people. Their natural aptitude for connecting with others enables them to expand their sphere of influence and build strong networks.

However, there are also challenges associated with the Networker archetype. One such challenge is the tendency to engage in gossip and rumour spreading. This can lead to a reputation for being untrustworthy and may result in the Networker feeling isolated and experiencing a sense of loneliness. Building deeper, more meaningful relationships beyond surface-level networking can be a struggle for some Networkers, as they interact with numerous individuals and may find it daunting or overwhelming to invest in more profound connections.

Key lessons for the Networker archetype are learning to be sincere in interactions with others and developing the ability to build deeper relationships beyond superficial networking. Networkers should strive to demonstrate genuine interest and care for others rather than appearing insincere or transactional. Building trust and nurturing meaningful connections will enhance the Networker's ability to leverage their networks effectively.

Characteristic Checklist of the Networker Archetype

- ✓ You enjoy connecting with different people sharing information.
- ✓ You enjoy discussing secret information about others.
- ✓ You are able to build connections with different people no matter their position or level.
- ✓ You are a good listener.
- ✓ You always have a positive attitude.
- ✓ You are helpful to others.
- ✓ You excel at building relationships and connecting people.
- ✓ You enjoy being the centre of attention.
- ✓ You have a strong need for approval by others.
- ✓ You enjoy attending social events, networking and meeting new people.
- ✓ You are optimistic, energetic and enthusiastic by nature.
- ✓ You are approachable, people find it easy to talk to you.

Nandi Mbatha is a typical example of someone with a dominant Networker archetype, a charismatic accountant with a natural knack for networking. Nandi possessed an outgoing personality and a strong desire to connect with people from all walks of life. From her early career days, she attended industry events, conferences, and social gatherings, making it a point to meet new individuals and build relationships.

Nandi's ability to connect with different people, regardless of their position or level, set her apart. She had a genuine curiosity about others, actively listened to their stories, and provided support whenever she could. Her positive attitude and helpful nature made her approachable and easy to talk to, drawing others to her naturally.

As Nandi advanced in her career, her expansive network became her greatest asset. She had access to decision-makers, industry experts, and a wide range of professionals across various fields. Recognising the value of her network, Nandi strategically used her connections to accelerate her career. She leveraged her relationships to secure new business opportunities, gain insights into market trends, and collaborate on innovative projects.

However, Nandi also learned the importance of sincerity and building deeper relationships beyond the surface level. She realised that her success as a Networker relied not only on the quantity of her connections but also on the quality of her relationships. Nandi made a conscious effort to foster genuine connections with key individuals in her network, investing time and energy in understanding their goals, challenges, and aspirations. This approach allowed her to form meaningful partnerships and establish a reputation as someone who genuinely cared about others' success.

Over time, Nandi's career flourished as her extensive network provided a continuous stream of opportunities. She became a trusted advisor to many, known for her ability to connect people, share valuable information, and facilitate collaborations. Nandi's outgoing nature and strong network positioned her as a respected figure in her industry, opening doors to new ventures and career advancements.

Nandi's story exemplifies how the Networker archetype, when harnessed effectively, can lead to career success. By utilising her networking skills, fostering genuine connections, and leveraging her relationships, Nandi created a robust professional network that propelled her forward and provided valuable resources and opportunities along the way.

12. The Mentor

The Mentor archetype is a wise and experienced individual who has undergone various life and career transitions and now seeks to help others in their own journeys. They possess extensive knowledge and expertise in a particular field, gained through years of experience, making them valuable resources for young individuals seeking guidance and growth.

Mentors go beyond simply teaching technical skills; they also pass on wisdom and shape the character of their students. They understand the challenges and obstacles that arise during different career stages and offer support and advice to navigate those transitions. Their role is to not only provide knowledge but also refine the character and abilities of their proteges.

However, one of the challenges faced by the Mentor archetype is the tendency to hold onto control over their students' development. They may struggle with allowing their proteges to move on and become masters in their own right. This can result in an overbearing attitude, where the mentor imposes their beliefs and ways of doing things instead of allowing their students to find their own path.

A key lesson for the Mentor archetype is to know when to let go and empower their proteges to explore their own unique approaches once the critical skills and knowledge have been imparted. It is essential for mentors to recognise when their work is done and when it is time to gracefully step back and allow their students to flourish independently.

Characteristic Checklist of the Mentor Archetype

- ✓ Being helpful, outgoing, and generous.
- ✓ They possess valuable experience and offer advice based on their own journeys. Mentors excel in one-on-one or small group settings, where they can provide personalised guidance.
- ✓ They exhibit optimism and persuasive skills, inspiring and motivating others to achieve their goals.
- ✓ Mentors enjoy the fulfilment of helping others and are recognised by their peers for the knowledge and counsel they have to offer.
- ✓ Their mission is to pass on their knowledge and skills to young "students" seeking growth and success.

In the context of career development, the Mentor archetype can shape one's professional journey in intriguing ways. As a mentor, you excel at assisting and supporting others in navigating their careers, offering them valuable advice and guidance. However, it's crucial to be mindful of neglecting your own career needs while focusing on the growth of others.

There might be a tendency to live vicariously through the successes of your proteges, deriving fulfilment from their achievements without giving due attention to your own career aspirations. It's essential to strike a balance, ensuring that while you help others take care of their careers, you also invest in your own development and pursue your own goals and dreams.

Take for example, Sandra Harris, an accomplished marketing executive, who had spent years honing her skills and establishing herself as a respected leader in her field. Recognised for her expertise and achievements, Sandra embraced her role as a mentor to young marketing professionals entering the industry. She dedicated herself to guiding them and helping them grow in their careers.

One of her proteges was Lisa, a recent college graduate with a passion for digital marketing. Lisa admired Sandra's knowledge and looked up to her as a role model. Under Sandra's guidance, Lisa developed a solid foundation of marketing strategies and learned the intricacies of client management.

Sandra's mentorship went beyond teaching technical skills. She took the time to understand Lisa's aspirations, strengths, and areas for improvement. Sandra provided invaluable advice, sharing her experiences and lessons learned throughout her career. She pushed Lisa to step outside her comfort zone, encouraging her to take on challenging projects and nurturing her confidence.

As months passed, Lisa's skills flourished, and she started receiving recognition for her work. However, Sandra faced a significant challenge: the fear of letting go. Seeing Lisa's growth and potential, Sandra struggled to loosen her grip on the mentor-student relationship. She had grown accustomed to being the guiding force, and the thought of Lisa branching out and becoming a master in her own right filled her with mixed emotions.

Sandra recognised that her role as a mentor was to empower Lisa and allow her to flourish independently. It was time for her to trust in the knowledge and guidance she had imparted. With a heavy heart, Sandra stepped back, giving Lisa the space to take charge of her career and make her own decisions.

To Sandra's delight, Lisa's career continued to soar. She developed her unique style and approach, combining the lessons learned from Sandra with her own creativity and passion. Sandra watched with pride as Lisa became a respected marketer in her own right, leading successful campaigns and mentoring others.

Through this experience, Sandra learned the importance of knowing when to let go and allow her proteges to find their own paths. She discovered that true fulfilment as a mentor came from seeing her students thrive independently, rather than maintaining control over their development. Sandra's role had been to pass on her knowledge and refine the character of her proteges, and she had succeeded.

Sandra's story illustrates the transformative power of the Mentor archetype in a professional setting. By nurturing and empowering others, mentors like Sandra contribute to the growth and success of the next generation, leaving a lasting impact on the industry as they pass on their knowledge and wisdom.

13. The Servant

The Servant archetype engages aspects of our psyche that call us to make ourselves available to others for the benefit and enhancement of their lives. A servant is commonly understood as the one who serves others to the exclusion of self. The Servant archetype wants to be acknowledged and recognised. The servant often attends to others' needs and neglects their own needs. When the acknowledgement and recognition does not come, that is when the shadow side of this archetype comes out.

The main challenge of this archetype is making choices that serve their own inner highest potential. This archetype gives up personal power and emotional needs in order to win approval and acknowledgement from others. Other challenges have to do with being consumed by the needs of those around them and losing focus of all the value of their own lives.

The main lessons for this archetype is balancing serving others while also taking care of self and looking after personal needs, so that they do not lose themselves in the process of serving others. They need to learn to empower themselves and give acknowledgement to themselves for jobs well done.

They also need to learn to always prioritise serving their spiritual or higher purpose needs. Other lessons for this archetype is to not give out their personal power and emotional needs in order to win approval and acknowledgements from others. This archetype projects its power to others and makes them more powerful than they are, investing them with qualities it would like to express but wouldn't dare.

Characteristic Checklist of the Servant Archetype

- ✓ You find joy in serving the needs of others.
- ✓ You find it exciting to please others by helping them.
- ✓ You enjoy serving others in hopes that they will praise and acknowledge you.
- ✓ You believe that your existence is to serve others.
- ✓ You take on more activities than you can complete.
- ✓ You are often working in the background waiting for your opportunity to serve other's needs.

How this shows up in your career decisions can be in the way you will rather give up pursuing a career you have always dreamt of just because someone else deserves it more. Compromising your career ambitions is your way of serving others. For example you compromise your career because it is not the right time to leave the team, or to leave your boss.

Rachel, a business analyst in a bank based in Nairobi had a natural aptitude for numbers and an innate desire to be of service to others. However, hidden within her was an archetype that deeply influenced her career—the Servant archetype.

The Servant archetype manifested in Rachel's career as a deep sense of responsibility and a strong desire to support and assist others. She thrived on providing exceptional service to her clients and colleagues, often going above and beyond to ensure their reporting needs were met. Rachel's dedication and reliability earned her a reputation as a dependable and trustworthy analyst .

One example of how the Servant archetype affected Rachel's career was her tendency to prioritise the needs of others over her own. She would often sacrifice her own professional development opportunities to ensure the success of her clients and the smooth operation of her team. Rachel would willingly take on extra tasks and responsibilities, often working late into the night to meet deadlines or assist her colleagues with their challenges.

Rachel's inclination to serve others also impacted her ability to advocate for herself. She found it challenging to ask for promotions or negotiate salary increases, as she believed that her primary role was to serve others rather than prioritise her own advancement. Consequently, Rachel remained in the same position for an extended period, receiving incremental raises but failing to achieve the career progression she desired.

Moreover, Rachel took on an excessive workload, as she felt compelled to help anyone who sought her assistance. She became the go-to person for financial analysis within her organisation, often juggling multiple projects simultaneously. The weight of this responsibility caused her stress and overwhelmed her at times, but she persisted, believing it was her duty to provide unwavering support.

As the years passed, Rachel's dedication and selflessness were both admired and taken advantage of by her colleagues. She had become an indispensable asset to the company, known for her self-sacrifice and willingness to put others' needs before her own. However, Rachel began to realise that her career had plateaued, and she yearned for growth and personal fulfilment.

Rachel's moment of realisation came when she found herself once again buried under tasks that weren't hers to do. Late one evening, after finishing yet another project for a colleague who had passed the responsibility onto her, she sat at her desk exhausted and frustrated. It dawned on her—no one was coming to save her.

The pattern was clear: she was always helping others move forward while her own career remained stagnant. The weight of this realisation hit her hard, creating a sense of urgency. She knew something had to change or she would stay stuck, forever waiting for someone to recognise her efforts.

Driven by this tension, Rachel embarked on a path of self-discovery and empowerment. She sought out a mentor who helped her see the importance of valuing herself and setting boundaries. It was uncomfortable at first, but with each small step, Rachel started to shift her focus toward her own growth. She attended workshops, networked with industry leaders, and invested in developing her skills.

Gradually, her confidence grew, and she began taking on assignments that challenged her and aligned with her career goals. Balancing her instinct to serve with her newfound ambition, Rachel learned that her career success required her active participation—not just in helping others, but in advocating for herself.

As Rachel's career evolved, she discovered that true service came from a place of empowerment rather than self-sacrifice. She continued to excel in her role, but now with a renewed sense of purpose and a balanced approach to serving both others and herself. Her dedication, combined with her newfound assertiveness, propelled her into positions of leadership and opened doors to new opportunities.

Rachel's transformation showcased the potential for the Servant archetype to positively impact one's career. Through self-awareness, personal growth, and setting healthy boundaries, she was able to harness the innate qualities of service and apply them in a way that supported her own professional development.

Rachel's journey served as an inspiration to others, illustrating the power of embracing the Servant archetype while maintaining a focus on personal fulfilment and growth.

14. The Slave

This archetype represents absence of power of choice and self-authority. It aligns well with careers where you may be expected to carry out orders unconditionally without any personal agency or no questions asked. Some of these orders may be in conflict with your personal values. It often occurs if you have to give up your will power to those with financial authority. In the world of work this happens a lot when we have to succumb our power to those with hierarchical power.

The ability of the slave to go on in the face of inhumane levels of agony and exhaustion is one good character about this archetype. However the question is always how long before the slave snaps in quest for freedom and what will the snap involve.

The **challenge** of this archetype is finding self, Understanding their personal power and their power of choice. Claiming the self back and knowing what to do with the self once you have claimed it back. It has a lot to do with understanding your personal purpose. If your personal purpose and your reason for being is not clear you run a risk of being a slave to others' purpose and vision.

Some key lessons for this archetype are self-awareness, self-determination and the value of personal choice. These are the important elements that will open up the quest to understand your personal purpose, what you want to do with your career and the value you bring to this world. It will also open up your exploration of what choices you have in life and the choices you have for your career.

Characteristic Checklist of the Slave Archetype

- ✓ You feel powerless and have given your personal choice to those who have authority over you.
- ✓ You are not clear what your values are and how they relate to the work that you do.
- ✓ You do not like the work that you do but you are doing it because you feel forced or you feel you have no choice.
- ✓ You struggle about who you are outside of your work or those that have authority over you.
- ✓ You do not believe you have a way to leave the work you do and do something else or work for someone else.
- ✓ You feel you are in the shadow of someone else with no concept of personal identity at all.

The typical manner in which the Slave archetype shows up in our careers is the tendency to stay very long in a job or working for a company or a boss that you do not like, that treats you horribly and that has no respect for you and who you are. This is often coupled with some rationalising. The source of this rationalising is not believing in yourself and your abilities. You keep complaining about how unbearable the situation at work is. Everyone else is surprised you are tolerating the situation, and your reasoning never seems to make sense, yet you remain committed to it, despite constantly describing it as unbearable.

James, a talented engineer working for MineralX, a mining start-up company, had a brilliant mind and a deep passion for his work. However, hidden within him was an archetype that affected his career—the Slave archetype.

The Slave archetype manifested in James' career in a way that made him feel bound to his work and unable to break free from the demands and expectations placed upon him. James was known for his exceptional technical skills and dedication, which led to him being assigned challenging projects and tight deadlines. While his colleagues admired his work ethic, James felt trapped in a cycle of constant pressure and unrelenting demands.

One example of how the Slave archetype affected James' career was his inability to set boundaries. He would consistently take on additional tasks and responsibilities, even if it meant sacrificing his personal time and well-being. James believed that saying "no" would jeopardise his professional reputation and opportunities for advancement. As a result, he became overwhelmed, working long hours and neglecting his own needs for rest and relaxation.

The Slave archetype also manifested in James' fear of disappointing others. He constantly sought validation and approval from his superiors and colleagues. This fear drove him to work tirelessly, striving for perfection in every project. James believed that any mistake or failure would result in disappointment and criticism. This fear of disappointing others led to excessive self-criticism and anxiety, hindering his ability to take risks and explore innovative ideas.

Furthermore, the Slave archetype limited James' career growth by keeping him confined to a specific role. He felt that he could not explore new opportunities or pursue career transitions, fearing that he would not meet expectations or possess the necessary skills. James became stuck in a repetitive cycle, performing the same tasks year after year, feeling unfulfilled and lacking professional growth.

Over time, the Slave archetype took a toll on James' well-being and satisfaction in his career. He experienced burnout, chronic stress, and a sense of disillusionment. His once-passionate drive for engineering began to fade as he felt trapped and unappreciated in his work.

Fortunately, James recognised the detrimental impact of the Slave archetype on his career and well-being. Through self-reflection and seeking support, he started to challenge his beliefs and behaviour. James began setting boundaries, learning to prioritise his own well-being and communicate his limits to his colleagues and superiors. He also sought opportunities for growth and development, attending workshops and networking events to explore new areas within his field.

As James embraced a more empowered mindset, he discovered that he had more control over his career than he had initially believed. He started to pursue projects aligned with his passions and strengths, fostering a sense of fulfilment and personal growth. James also became a vocal advocate for work-life balance and healthy boundaries, inspiring his colleagues to prioritise their well-being as well.

While on his journey, James transformed his relationship with the Slave archetype. He learned that his worth was not solely defined by his work and that he had the power to shape his own career path. James became an example of resilience and self-empowerment, inspiring others to break free from the chains of the Slave archetype and find true fulfilment in their professional lives.

15. The Thief

Also known as the swindler. This archetype is characterised by the need to silently get into places and take what you want. It can be thieving for your personal satisfaction or on behalf of others just like Robin Hood.

It can take many forms, ranging from sophisticated high-level thieving which might involve, high-level fraud and corruption to street thieving. It can involve stealing assets or plagiarism or theft of others ideas.

The main characteristic of the Thief archetype is lying, stealing or cheating yourself towards achieving your goal. Your goal could be earning more money, achieving a promotion, more regard or respect . Thieves resort to taking whatever is not theirs because they believe they do not have an ability to provide for themselves through their own capabilities. It has to do with self-belief, self-respect, understanding and respecting personal talents and abilities.

The challenge for this archetype is to realise your own personal capabilities and how to use these capabilities to be or to obtain what you want in an acceptable way. It is realising that the same talent you are using to swindle others can be used in a positive way to create and offer value to others.

The lessons for those that tend to be thieves is learning to generate, create or build what you want using inner abilities, personal powers, or personal talents. It has to do with learning to respect your personal talents and finding ways to use your talents in a way that adds value instead of extracting or destroying value for others.

Characteristic Checklist of the Thief Archetype

- ✓ You always see opportunities to take from others without their permission.
- ✓ You rationalise the thieving—be it stealing from the rich to provide to the poor. Or stealing from someone who is also stealing.
- ✓ The impact always is negative on your career, resulting in shame, embarrassment and career derailment.
- ✓ You create career gaps that aren't always easy to explain.
- ✓ Individuals with this archetype always find themselves needing to reinvent or relaunch their careers because one way or the other the thieving has a way of destroying their career and they find themselves having to rebuild from scratch.

This has multiple ways of showing up in the world of work, think of some highly qualified individuals, they have the experience and the networks, but they somehow find themselves fired from work because of some fraudulent activities. The most common is those that tend to steal other colleagues' ideas and present them as their own work, getting the undue credit and recognition.

Tom had worked his way up the corporate ladder in the renowned company, Solar Powered Industries. However, unbeknownst to his colleagues and superiors, Tom harboured a hidden archetype within him—the Thief archetype.

The Thief archetype began to impact Tom's career in various ways, as he succumbed to the temptations of deceit and dishonesty. Tom was known for his persuasive communication skills and ability to present compelling ideas. However, deep down, he lacked confidence in her own creativity. As the Thief archetype took hold,

Tom started stealing ideas from his team members during brainstorming sessions.

He would subtly manipulate the discussions to make the stolen ideas appear as his own, receiving recognition and praise for the work he had not truly contributed to. This behaviour not only undermined the trust within his team but also stifled the innovation and growth potential of his colleagues.

The Thief archetype led Tom to seek personal recognition and advancement at the expense of others. In team meetings or project presentations, he would deliberately take credit for his subordinates' accomplishments, diminishing their contributions. Tom would present their work as his own, using manipulative tactics to convince senior management of his indispensability. This unethical behaviour created a toxic environment, where team members felt undervalued and unmotivated, hindering their professional growth and overall team success.

Tom's Thief archetype pushed him to engage in manipulative practices to further his career ambitions. He would undermine his colleagues, spreading false rumours or planting seeds of doubt to weaken their standing within the company. By creating an atmosphere of uncertainty and competition, Tom hoped to secure his position as the manager. This manipulative behaviour not only eroded trust among his colleagues but also hindered collaboration and teamwork, negatively impacting overall project outcomes and employee morale.

Over time, the consequences of Tom's actions became apparent. The morale within his team plummeted, resulting in increased turnover and decreased productivity. Other managers and team members grew suspicious of his deceitful practices, and his reputation as an untrustworthy individual spread throughout the company. As a result, Tom's upward mobility within Solar Powered Industries came to a halt, and he found herself isolated and mistrusted by his colleagues and superiors.

Tom's deceitful practices, including idea theft, credit stealing, and manipulative tactics, not only damaged his own reputation but also had far-reaching consequences for the team dynamics and overall success of the company.

16. The Victim

The Victim archetype, as outlined by Caroline Myss in Sacred Contracts and informed by Carl Jung's work on archetypes, represents a mindset of powerlessness in which an individual feels perpetually wronged or disadvantaged by external forces. From a career perspective, the Victim archetype can manifest in subtle ways that influence one's professional path, both positively and negatively.

The Victim archetype's shadow side can derail a career. Individuals who lean into this archetype negatively tend to externalise blame, seeing themselves as powerless in their circumstances. They may avoid taking responsibility for their role in career challenges, attributing setbacks to unfair bosses, office politics, or external circumstances beyond their control.

This attitude can lead to stagnation, as these individuals may become passive, waiting for external forces to improve their situation rather than taking proactive steps. Over time, this can damage one's professional reputation, leading to missed opportunities and stunted growth. Colleagues may also perceive them as overly pessimistic or draining, further alienating them from potential sponsors or mentors.

One of the major challenges of the Victim archetype is the self-perpetuating cycle it creates. The more one identifies as a victim, the less likely they are to take ownership of their career, thus reinforcing feelings of helplessness. Another challenge is recognising the fine line between valid grievances and adopting a victim mentality. Individuals with this archetype may struggle to balance standing up for themselves with taking proactive responsibility for their actions and career trajectory.

Key lessons required to break free from this archetype, is learning to shift from externalising blame to recognising their own agency. This includes accepting that while external circumstances can be unfair, they have the power to respond and make changes. Empowerment comes from recognising that setbacks are opportunities for learning and growth rather than evidence of defeat. Building resilience, fostering a growth mindset, and embracing personal responsibility are essential lessons for those with the Victim archetype.

Characteristic Checklist of the Victim Archetype

- ✓ You have a sense of powerlessness, a focus on past wounds or injustices, and a constant search for sympathy or validation from others.
- ✓ You may struggle with taking responsibility for your actions and tend to see yourself as perpetual victims of your circumstances.
- ✓ You may have difficulty asserting yourself, setting boundaries, or advocating for your own needs and desires.
- ✓ You often feel a sense of powerlessness, perceiving yourself as at the mercy of external circumstances. You may believe they have limited control over your life and experience a lack of agency in shaping your own destiny.

- ✓ You have a tendency to attribute responsibility for negative outcomes to external factors or other people. You may also have difficulty taking personal accountability for your choices and actions, often shifting the blame onto others or external circumstances.
- ✓ You may exhibit self-pity in your focus on your past wounds or perceived injustices. You may dwell on your hardships and struggle to move forward, often seeking sympathy or validation from others.
- ✓ You may adopt a martyr-like mentality, sacrificing your own needs and desires for the sake of others. You may consistently put yourself in situations where you feel taken advantage of or mistreated, reinforcing your victimhood.
- ✓ You believe in your helplessness, leading to a lack of initiative or action to change your circumstances. You may struggle to assert yourself, set boundaries, or advocate for your own needs and desires.

The Victim archetype can significantly impact an individual's career choices and professional growth. Those embodying this archetype may shy away from taking risks or pursuing ambitious goals due to a fear of failure or a belief that external forces will always impede their success. They may settle for less fulfilling or lower-level positions, feeling trapped and unable to break free from perceived limitations.

Furthermore, individuals influenced by the Victim archetype may struggle with workplace dynamics, such as asserting themselves in negotiations or advocating for promotions and raises. They may find it challenging to handle setbacks or criticism, often perceiving them as personal attacks rather than opportunities for growth. This mindset can hinder professional development and limit the ability to navigate challenges effectively.

To illustrate the long-term impact of the Victim archetype on someone's career, consider the case of Carol. Carol possessed significant talent and potential in her field of marketing. However, due to a series of setbacks early in her career, including a company-wide downsizing, she developed a victim mindset. She began to perceive herself as a victim of a challenging job market, believing that external factors were responsible for her stalled career.

As a result, Carol became hesitant to pursue new opportunities or take risks that could advance her career. She avoided applying for higher-level positions, fearing rejection, and instead settled for roles beneath her capabilities. Her victim mentality also affected her confidence, leading to self-sabotaging behaviours during interviews and interactions with colleagues.

Over time, Carol's Victim archetype perpetuated a cycle of missed opportunities and stagnation. She became increasingly resentful, blaming her circumstances and others for her lack of progress. The victim mindset eroded her motivation, and she struggled to find fulfilment in her work. As a result, she remained trapped in a professional rut for several years, unable to break free from the limitations imposed by her Victim archetype.

Recognising and addressing the Victim archetype is crucial for personal and professional growth. By cultivating self-awareness, individuals can begin to challenge disempowering beliefs, take ownership of their actions, and seek opportunities for positive change. Through therapy, coaching, or self-reflection, it is possible to overcome the Victim archetype and shift towards a mindset of empowerment and resilience.

In this chapter, we explored the concept of career archetypes and how they influence the way we navigate our career journeys. Archetypes, as recurring patterns or themes, have a significant impact on how we approach career decisions, challenges, and opportunities. Throughout these pages, I've used examples to illustrate how these archetypes manifest in our actions, thoughts, and behaviours, sometimes boosting our progress and other times creating roadblocks.

The Rebel, for instance, resists conformity and questions authority, sometimes leading to innovative breakthroughs but also risking alienation from peers or supervisors. The Victim archetype tends to feel helpless in the face of adversity, always seeking external factors to blame for career stagnation, while the Slave archetype endures situations out of obligation, sacrificing personal growth for the comfort of security.

By examining these archetypes through real-life situations, I've shown the importance of recognising how they play out in your career and how they influence your mindset. In a sense, our career journey is like a grand theatre production, and the archetypes are the roles we unconsciously adopt. Some roles, like the Rebel, can help you innovate and carve new paths, while others, like the Victim or Slave, may prevent you from reaching your full potential. But just like an actor on stage, you have the power to switch roles, to choose the archetype that best serves your goals at any point in time.

The key takeaway from this chapter is the importance of awareness. Understanding the archetypes that you habitually fall into can make a substantial difference in your career. This awareness empowers you to be intentional about which archetypes to embrace—those that will propel your career forward—and which to avoid—those that tend to block your growth. By deliberately choosing to embody archetypes that boost your career, you take control of your narrative, ensuring that your career journey aligns with your ambitions and values.

My call to action for you is this: be mindful of the archetypes you adopt. Don't allow unconscious patterns to dictate the course of your career life. Instead, take an active role in shaping your journey by choosing archetypes that align with your goals, passions, and values. With this awareness and intentionality, you can unlock greater career success and personal fulfilment. Remember, the stage is yours—step into the role that will allow you to shine the brightest.

SECTION THREE
CAREER COMPETENCIES

Career Competencies to Navigate Your Career

When exploring the career management philosophy of various companies online, a common theme emerges: many employers encourage their employees to take ownership of their own career development. This places the responsibility for career growth and advancement in the hands of the employee, with companies providing support and resources. Below are quotes sourced from different employers websites that highlight this philosophy:

Brandon Hall Group: "Employees must have tools to explore career options to take ownership of their career development. Employers must provide these tools, but it's up to employees to take the necessary steps to grow into new roles."[130]

General Electric (GE): "At GE, we believe that employees are responsible for taking ownership of their career development, whether by pursuing learning opportunities or initiating career conversations with their managers."[131]

Facebook (Meta): "Employees should take ownership of their own development, initiating feedback, and exploring opportunities within the company to grow and evolve in their careers."[132]

Microsoft: "We encourage our employees to own their career progression by setting clear goals, seeking feedback, and proactively looking for growth opportunities within Microsoft."[133]

Amazon: "We provide employees with a wide array of resources to foster career development, but it is each individual's responsibility to take ownership of their career trajectory."[134]

Deloitte: "Career ownership at Deloitte means our professionals take control of their personal development, continuously seeking out opportunities for growth while aligning with our organisational goals."[135]

The core message from these statements is clear: as an employer, we are committed to offering resources and opportunities for career growth. However, the responsibility for taking action and driving your career forward rests entirely with you. It's up to you to make the most of these tools and take control of your own development.

This means that as employees, we can no longer rely solely on our employers for career development and security. The onus is now on us to upskill ourselves and become adept at managing our own careers.

Gone are the days of static career paths based solely on accumulating job competencies and tenure in one role. Instead, dynamic careers are emerging, characterised by horizontal shifts across various organisations and industries. This underscores the need for us to proactively manage our employability, adapting to frequent job changes and potential multiple contracts.

In this chapter, we'll delve into the behaviours that empower you to take charge and successfully manage your career. You'll not only gain an understanding of these behaviours but also discover the specific stages where they can be most impactful. My hope is that as you navigate this chapter, you'll recognise those areas in your career journey where these competencies can make a significant difference. By learning and applying career competencies, you'll be able to accelerate your career growth and achieve your professional goals more effectively.

What are career competencies?: career competencies are personal traits and abilities that play a crucial role in managing one's career effectively. They encompass knowledge, skills, and behaviours that are essential for career development and success. These competencies can be influenced and improved by the individual through continuous learning and development. They are instrumental in how you navigate, shape, and progress in your career throughout your working life.

What makes career competencies valuable is that they can be enhanced and refined through continuous learning and development efforts. These competencies are crucial in how individuals navigate, shape, and advance in their careers over time. They empower you to self-manage your work experiences and learning opportunities, facilitating the achievement of career goals and progression in your chosen fields.

In essence, they represent your ability to manage your career journey and make meaningful progress towards your professional aspirations. They serve as a guide for understanding why some individuals excel in managing their careers while others face challenges. Through self-assessment against these competencies, you can identify areas for improvement and embark on a development journey to bridge any existing gaps.

Why Do Career Competencies Matter Now More Than Ever?

Because individuals are more and more responsible for achieving career success, it is crucial to master career-related competencies that can help them navigate their careers. As the world of work continues to evolve and undergo significant changes in ways of work, in career management and responsibilities for personal career development, it has become increasingly crucial for individuals to navigate these shifts effectively and manage their careers amidst transformations. Expecting individuals to successfully navigate their careers without adequate training on essential competencies is like casting an actor in a lead role without providing any acting training.

Just as an actor must master character development, vocal control, movement, and script interpretation to deliver a compelling performance, career management requires its own set of skills. No actor would be expected to excel on stage without learning these foundational techniques; similarly, you need proper guidance and training on career competencies to effectively take ownership and manage your careers.

In the theatre, once you learn the craft of acting, you can step into any role, no matter the character or play. New productions may come along, but the core skills remain the same. In the same way, the world of work is constantly evolving. However, if we are equipped with the right skills to manage our careers, we can continue to navigate these changes and thrive professionally, just like seasoned actors transitioning between different roles.

But how do we learn the competencies needed to take control of our employability? Just as an actor trains for years to perfect their craft, individuals must develop career competencies that allow them to adapt, grow, and continue to perform in an ever-changing job market. By building these "career management skills," we position ourselves to land and retain roles in our professional lives, no matter how much the labour market shifts or changes.

Career competencies are essential for proactively managing your career, a skill that should be required for anyone entering the workforce. These competencies help you assess your strengths and areas for improvement, while identifying gaps in your skills. In understanding them, you can focus your learning and development efforts to ensure continuous growth and success in your career.

Using a competency framework provides a structured approach to preparing ourselves for success in the dynamic world of work. It allows us to identify the specific competencies that we need to be able to manage our careers effectively. The value of focusing on competencies lies in our ability to self-assess, set clear development goals, and take actionable steps to enhance our capabilities.

But can these career competencies really impact our career trajectory? Absolutely, research has indeed shown that career competencies can significantly influence our career trajectory and overall satisfaction. For instance, a study conducted by Haase and colleagues in 2007 revealed a positive correlation between specific career competencies and various aspects that are crucial to career success. These competencies were found to enhance self-knowledge, career skills, networking abilities, and understanding of office politics, ultimately contributing to higher levels of career satisfaction.[136]

Additionally, research conducted by Forrier, Sels, and Steynen has reinforced the importance of career competencies as predictors of career success. Their findings suggest that individuals possessing strong career competencies are more likely to achieve their career goals and experience positive outcomes in their professional endeavours.[137]

Moreover, studies by Kuijpers, Cheyns, and Scheerens demonstrated a clear association between career competencies and objective career success. Objective career success refers to measurable achievements in one's career, such as promotions, salary increases, job titles, or awards, which reflect external recognition of professional progress.[138.]

Another study by Akkermans and colleagues confirms that possessing and developing career competencies may need to be demonstrated in behaviours in order to achieve desired career outcomes such as perceived employability.[139] Perceived employability refers to your perception of possibilities to seek, obtain, and maintain employment. In modern times, employability has replaced job security, in that employers are no longer able to offer secured lifetime employment.

Perceived employability is concerned with employment opportunities both internal the company and outside your employer. It is positively related to self-efficacy, career satisfaction as well as marketability. Based on the multiple research reviewed we can conclude that career competencies will help you become employable which in turn will help you have a successful career.

The competencies discussed in this chapter come from an integrated framework that combines four of the most well-known competency models:

- The boundaryless career perspective
- The protean career perspective
- The career self-management perspective
- The human capital perspective.

This is based on the work by Akkermans, Blonk and Brenninkmeijer in their 2013 thesis. The combination of all these career frameworks resulted in three critical career development competencies. I will explain each one and share relevant studies. I will then discuss in which of the stages is the competency most applicable.[140]

You should bear in mind that each of these competencies will be relevant and applicable in almost all the stages, however there are some stages where the competency is more critical. Let's begin with the reflective competencies.

Reflective Career Competencies – Who You Are

These competencies focus on creating an awareness of your long-term career and on combining personal reflections and your professional career. They are all about understanding who you are and what you want your career to become. Put differently who you are becoming and what you want your career to be. Key to this competency is reviewing one's own desires and values with respect to one's career.[141]

The first one is *personal motivation* (the ability to *reflect on motivation*), this refers to your ability to reflect on your values, your passion, and motivations as it relates to your personal career. It is about clarifying your personal values—all the things that you hold dear and are important to you both at work and outside of work.

It is about clarifying what is important to you at work. Do you value autonomy and independence, do you value camaraderie? What are those work values that are important to you?

It is also about reflecting on your passions and the activities you love and engage in that keep you motivated. Early on in our careers, we get to identify the activities we love doing; when we engage in them, we can lose track of time. It is about being clear on all the things that motivate you such as your personal purpose and vision in life.

This competency is important in the stages where you are shaping your career identity such as *Stage One's career identity*, where you are reflecting on who you are, the unique characteristics that makes you a unique individual, and who you are in your career. What stories do you want to tell about yourself and your career? This reflective competency helps create the meaning that links your motivations, interests, and skills with your acceptable career. This results in your career narrative—the stories you tell yourself and others.

This competency is also important for *Stage Six*, where you are "bringing your whole self to work". As you bring yourself to work, you encounter situations that will either boost or dampen your motivation. Reflecting on the motivations that align with your work environment and the characteristics that temper your motivation is key.

Reflective Career Competency – What You Have

Reflecting on qualities refers to your strengths, shortcomings, skills, as they relate to your career. This is about understanding the personal characteristics you bring to the world of work and knowing how to communicate them. It's about being able to communicate them when responding to that question " Tell us about yourself". This competency helps you define what you have—your strengths and your weaknesses, what's important to you, why is it important, and what are you good at.

This plays out a lot in Stage Two, where you are "building your career foundation", i.e., your career capital, with all the knowledge, experiences, skills, and connections you bring to the process. It has to do with intangible assets such as self-esteem and self-worth.

It also takes centre stage in Stage Five, where you are showcasing your talents, gifts, and skills. An ability to reflect on your talents, strengths, passions, skills, and personality helps you gain a sense of what you are good at. This is an important confidence booster when all the lights and cameras are on you, and you are expected to have your best performance.

If you lack this competency, you will often find yourself in career situations, where you are unhappy and dissatisfied about your job or employer, but you are unable to articulate what is causing the unhappiness. This is because you are not able to reflect on which of your values is not being honoured and which interests are being compromised.

The reflective competencies are demonstrated well by those who are clear about their motivators, such as personal work values, their career anchors, their strengths and talents, and aligning this to those work environments that value who they are and what they bring.

Key indicators of the lack of this competency include the ability to match yourself to suitable roles. It can be pursuing roles that are not aligned to your personality, your skills, and your passions. It entails choosing to be driven and motivated by external factors in making career decisions as well as disregarding your personal values, your career anchors, and your talents and strengths.

In summary, reflective competencies affords you the ability to continuously reflect on your values and key motivators and align them to your career interest. It also allows you to reflect on your personal qualities and the resources—both tangible and intangible—that you bring and being able to make decisions on achieving personal career success.

Communicative and Interactive Career Competency

Communicative competencies are about being able to effectively communicate with important stakeholders to improve your career success. It are about being able to effectively communicate with significant others to improve your chances of career success.[142]

This competency can be reflected by two main behaviours, the first one is *networking*— the awareness of the presence and professional value of an individual network and your ability to expand this network for career-related purposes. It instils the mindset that recognises the important role played by others in any person's career journey. Most of us leave this important factor to chance— meaning we shy away from networking and see it a daunting task and rely on the limited networks that we have.

As you would have seen in the preceding chapters, networking plays a key role as you manage your career throughout some of the stages. From *Stage Three*, we start highlighting the effect of your networks or family on your career. If you come from a family that is well networked and well known in the community, this becomes a positive background effect that will help your career.

In *Stage Seven,* the importance of networks is also highlighted as you navigate career shocks, from making sense of them by connecting with some of the networks that have experienced the change you are dealing with, to seeking other opportunities as a way of responding. Networks play a key role throughout that journey.

In *Stage Eight,* connections and networks play a key role as you undergo transitions. Your networks allow for a soft landing as you transition from one role to another or from one employer to another. They make integrating to a new environment easier, deliberately connecting you to key stakeholders as you learn the ropes.

In *Stage Nine,* as you begin to look at your career beyond personal benefits, seeking to build a career that is bigger than yourself, connections and networks play a key role. Similarly in *Stage Eleven,* you seek to build a purposeful career, connecting with those with similar aspirations plays a key role. This applies *to Stage Twelve* as seeking to be of service to and working with others focused on the causes that drive common interests is helpful.

I have highlighted a few stages where the role played by your networks and connections is prominent; however, you could argue that networks play a key role as you manage all the stages of your career. The same can be said about the second communicative competence: self-profiling.

The second behaviour of communicative competence is self-profiling. It is all about being able to present and communicate personal knowledge and your abilities and skills to the labour market. In simple terms, the second competencies are about your ability to build networks continuously throughout your career, understanding the importance of networks and being able to access your own at the right time in order to grow and develop your career.

It is also about being able to develop your brand and the ability to position and sell who you are—what story you tell yourself and others about your career. The practice of self-profiling directly aligns with the work done in Stage One while developing your career identity.

At this stage, you begin to shape how you perceive your career and the narrative you create around it. Self-profiling helps to consciously define and understand the image you project to yourself and others. By clarifying your strengths, values, and aspirations through self-profiling, you are effectively expanding on the foundation built during the Career Identity Stage.

In Stage Two of building career capital, the competency of self-profiling plays a crucial role. It's not enough to simply develop career capital—skills, talents, values, and experiences—without knowing how to effectively communicate them. Self-profiling enables you to strategically showcase the most relevant aspects of your career capital to your target market, whether potential employers, clients, or industry networks.

This skill helps you position yourself and your capabilities in a way that resonates with the needs and expectations of the market, making it easier to stand out and align your strengths with opportunities. By mastering self-profiling, you ensure that your career capital doesn't just exist but actively works to propel your career forward.

Self-profiling is about continuously creating a story about yourself, who you are, what you have, what you bring, what you do, the change, the impact you make, the track record you build, and why all of this makes you the best person for the job you seek. This is often referred to as personal branding. It is another area of our career that is often left to develop on its own. If you do not focus on your personal brand, it develops on its own or other people create it for you. Oftentimes, it's not the brand you like. This is why taking ownership of creating your personal brand is crucial. Developing the competency of self-profiling will make this task easy and manageable for you.

Self-profiling is important from Stage One of your career as you create your career identity, and it remains relevant up until the last stage. This is because you are continuously shaping your personal brand as you navigate and manage the different stages of your career. The experiences you deal with, how you navigate and manage these experiences in each stage defines who you are and impacts your personal brand. Mastering this competency will help identify personal branding opportunities throughout all the stages and become deliberate in how you show up as you navigate them.

Another aspect of self-profiling is *self-presentation*: self-presentation is a critical competency that directly influences career success across the twelve stages. It's about how you portray yourself to key stakeholders, such as potential employers, colleagues, and clients, during crucial interactions like interviews and important meetings.

Effective self-presentation involves conveying confidence, professionalism, and authenticity in your communication and demeanour. It's about showcasing your strengths, accomplishments, and unique value proposition in a compelling and memorable way. Mastering self-presentation enhances your ability to make positive impressions, build rapport, and leave a lasting impact, ultimately propelling your career progress and opportunities for advancement.

Self-presentation also involves self-nomination: it reflects your confidence and ability to effectively communicate why you are the best candidate for a specific role, promotion, or salary increase. This competency involves articulating your achievements, skills, and contributions in a persuasive manner to key decision-makers. It's about advocating for yourself, showcasing your value proposition, and demonstrating why investing in your growth and development benefits the organisation. Mastering self-nomination empowers you to take ownership of your career trajectory, seize opportunities for advancement, and assertively pursue your professional goals.

When essential competencies like self-presentation and self-nomination are lacking, you often find yourself in situations where you constantly work hard, hoping your efforts will be noticed and rewarded. You may believe that your dedication and diligence will naturally lead to a promotion or salary increase.

However, without the ability to effectively nominate yourself and advocate for your achievements, you risk being overlooked or undervalued. This can lead to significant dissatisfaction and frustration when your hard work goes unrecognised, impacting your fragile morale and motivation.

Interacting or influencing others sits within this competency. It encompasses interpersonal skills such as conflict management, assertiveness, and delegation. These skills are essential for understanding how others contribute to your individual career growth. They enable you to navigate workplace dynamics effectively, manage conflicts, assert your needs, and delegate tasks efficiently.

Environmental knowledge is a component of this competency, focused on your understanding of the broader work environment. This includes factors like organisational culture, industry trends, and market dynamics. By developing environmental knowledge skills, you gain the ability to constantly monitor your surroundings, anticipate changes, and adapt your strategies accordingly. This proactive approach allows you to stay agile in response to evolving circumstances and make informed decisions that positively impact your career progression.

Proactivity / Taking Action

Proactive and taking action competencies are focused on your capability to actively shape your career by taking *proactive steps*. This involves *work exploration,* where you actively seek and explore opportunities related to your work and career in the job market. It encompasses *career control,* where you actively influence learning and work processes to align with your personal career goals by setting goals and planning how to achieve them.

Additionally, it includes career-related planning and influencing learning and work processes to attain desired career objectives. Moreover, it's about proactively matching and aligning your identity and competencies with the necessary values and behaviours required in a specific work setting.

These competencies play a crucial role in managing all career stages, but they become particularly significant in Stage Three. During this stage, you are actively analysing the effects of your background on your career. It's essential to be proactive and deliberate in identifying which background effects can be advantageous and which ones can potentially disadvantage your career. With proactive action, you can strategically use positive effects to your advantage while simultaneously working to limit the impact of negative effects on your career progression. This requires a proactive and intentional approach to managing your career path and making informed decisions based on a thorough analysis of your background influences.

In Stage Four of your career journey, proactive and action-oriented competency is equally vital. This stage necessitates a proactive understanding of your career anchors, which are the overriding concerns or needs that guide your career decisions. By possessing this competency, you can actively identify your career anchors and leverage them to match yourself with jobs that align closely with these anchors. This proactive approach allows you to make informed decisions about your career path, ensuring that you pursue opportunities that resonate with your core values, motivations, and aspirations.

Stage Five, known as the stage of expressing your talents, places a high emphasis on the proactive and action-oriented competency. This competency is crucial during this stage as it enables you to focus on deliberate actions that showcase your strengths, talents, and passions. By leveraging this competency, you become intentional in seeking experiences that propel you towards achieving your career goals. Whether it's pursuing projects that align with your passions or actively showcasing your strengths in various work settings, this competency empowers you to take meaningful steps forward in your career journey during Stage Five.

During Stage Seven, which involves managing career shocks, proactive competency plays a vital role in guiding your actions. This competency assists you in being proactive as soon as you sense that something might not be heading in the right direction or when you foresee potential risks. By utilising this competency, you take proactive steps to address and avoid potential career shocks or to mitigate their impact. Whether it involves identifying potential challenges early on, implementing pre-emptive strategies, or adapting quickly to unexpected situations, this competency empowers you to navigate Stage Seven with resilience and foresight.

During Stage Eight, this competency proves invaluable especially when undergoing a career transition. Career transitions demand a proactive approach, requiring us to take control of our career trajectories and drive action as we deliberately navigate a new job, career path, or industry. By leveraging this competency, you empower yourself to actively seek out opportunities aligned with your transition goals, whether it involves acquiring new skills, networking strategically, or adapting your mindset to embrace change. This stance ensures that you remain proactive and purposeful in your career journey during the transition phase.

Stage Nine, dedicated to pursuing a purposeful career, greatly benefits from this competency. It involves proactively clarifying your personal purpose and aligning it with career opportunities. By leveraging this competency, you actively engage in self-reflection to understand your core values, passions, and aspirations.

This clarity empowers you to seek out career paths, roles, and organisations that resonate with your purpose, ensuring that your professional endeavours are meaningful and fulfilling. Proactive action in this stage involves deliberate efforts to identify and pursue opportunities that align with your purpose, enabling you to build a career that is not only successful but also deeply meaningful to you.

Summary of Career Competencies

Theme	Career Competency	Competency Description
Reflective career competencies	• Reflection on motivation • Reflection on qualities	• Reflecting on your values, passion and motivations with regards to your career • Reflecting on strengths, shortcomings and skills with regards to your personal career
Communicative career competencies	• Networking • Self-profiling	• Your awareness of the presence and professional value of an individual network and ability to expand this network for career-related purposes • Presenting and communicating personal knowledge, abilities and skills to the internal and external labour market
Proactivity/ Taking action	• Work exploration • Career control	• Actively exploring and searching for work-related and career-related opportunities on the internal and external labour market • Actively influencing learning processes and work processes related to one's personal career by setting goals and planning how to fulfil them

In conclusion, the journey through the twelve stages of your career is akin to an actor preparing for a performance; without the necessary training and competencies, the path can be fraught with challenges and uncertainties. Just as an actor must hone their craft to successfully embody various roles, you must develop key career competencies to effectively navigate the complexities of your professional journey.

These competencies, much like the tools and techniques actors use to embody their roles on stage, provide the foundation for navigating the twelve stages of your career. Without mastering these competencies, the career journey can feel like stepping onto a stage unprepared, unsure of how to respond to the complex demands of the roles you must play. But with the right tools, you become the actor who has not only memorised the lines but can also embody the character fully, adapting to any surprise the script throws your way

One of the most significant challenges highlighted in this chapter is the gap in formal training provided by employers to help develop these crucial skills. Many employers today expect individuals to take ownership of their careers while providing resources and tools for growth, yet they seldom offer direct guidance on how to manage one's career effectively.

This lack of structured support can leave employees feeling uncertain, unsure of how to utilise available resources or how to navigate their career journeys independently. However, through the development of career competencies, you can bridge this gap, taking full advantage of the tools and resources offered and ensuring you remain in control of your career paths.

These competencies provide the essential tools for taking ownership of your career, empowering you to make informed decisions and adapt to evolving circumstances. They enhance your ability to identify opportunities, leverage your strengths, and articulate your personal brand, all of which are vital for progression through each stage. By investing time in developing these skills, you will equip yourself to respond to the demands of each phase, fostering resilience and adaptability along the way.

In the early stages of your career, reflective competencies—akin to the actor studying their script—are fundamental. This is where self-awareness and goal-setting come into play, enabling you to develop your career identity, building your career capital to support the direction you're heading. As you progress through the stages, communicative and interactive competencies become increasingly prominent. Effectively articulating what sets you apart as the ideal candidate for a role, showcasing your personal brand, and demonstrating your abilities during critical moments hinge on your mastery of these competencies. Mastering these skills enhances your ability to engage while it also empowers you to convey your value confidently, making a significant impact when it matters most.

Proactive competencies come into focus, driving the narrative of your career as you continuously anticipate what's coming next, much like an actor who steps beyond their lines, improvising when necessary to keep the show going smoothly. These competencies push you to seek new growth opportunities, manage transitions, and take control of the evolving storyline of your career.

Mastering career competencies is the key to taking ownership of your career journey, allowing you to write your own script and navigate the various stages of your career with confidence. By honing these essential skills, you position yourself as the leading character in your career story, enabling you to choose the archetypes that best align with your ambitions and aspirations. Just as an actor selects the right character to bring their narrative to life, you can match the right competencies to your career script, ensuring that you embody the qualities necessary for success.

This is what it truly means to take charge of your career. Developing these competencies accelerates your journey, empowering you to transition smoothly between stages and seize opportunities as they arise. Embrace this transformative process and let your career narrative unfold with intention and purpose. The stage is set, and it's your time to shine!

Conclusion

As the curtain falls on the final chapter, we arrive at the denouement—the moment when all the threads of your career journey are tied together, much like the resolution of a great play. You have navigated the twelve stages of your career, each revealing a new act filled with unique challenges and opportunities. Some stages were easy to traverse, while others required resilience and adaptability. This journey is akin to an actor preparing for a performance, where every experience contributes to a more nuanced portrayal of oneself.

In the theatre of your career, the denouement represents the realisation of your power to take charge of your own narrative. The dynamic landscape of the workplace calls for you to become the director of your professional life, guiding each scene with intention and purpose. You have explored how your career unfolds across twelve distinct stages, each with its own lessons and insights. With this knowledge, you are better equipped to navigate the highs and lows of your journey, understanding when to embrace change, when to reflect, and when to take decisive action.

However, it's not just about understanding the stages; it's also about the roles you play within them. Throughout your career, you may have adopted various archetypes. Perhaps you started as the "Victim," feeling overwhelmed by circumstances, or transformed into the "Rebel," challenging the status quo in pursuit of your goals. These personas are the characters you embody while on your career stage, shaping the narratives you share with yourself and others. Some roles propel your career forward, while others may hinder your progress. The key to mastering your career lies in being intentional about the roles you choose, ensuring that you actively craft your own story.

As you reflect on the journey you've taken through this book, consider these questions: What stories have I been telling about my career? What roles have I inhabited? More importantly, how can I consciously control my future roles to ensure they support my career?

On a personal level, my journey through various career transitions has imparted invaluable lessons. Each position I have embraced has served as a crucial stepping stone, setting the stage for the next opportunity. I've become intentional about the experiences I accumulate in each role, consistently asking myself, "What chapter does this add to my career narrative?"

Finally, no actor steps onto a stage without training and practice; the same principle applies to your career. A common misconception is that we can navigate our careers instinctively, without learning the necessary skills. In this book, I have emphasised the importance of developing career competencies—the skills and behaviours that empower you to thrive in an ever-evolving work environment. By cultivating these competencies, you can take charge of your employability and professional development, transforming uncertainty into opportunity.

The good news? These skills are not innate; they can be learned and refined. In mastering them, you enhance your chances of achieving your career aspirations.

Now that you have gained valuable knowledge, it is time to return to your career stage with greater awareness, intention, and ownership. The spotlight is now on you: what role will you choose to take on next? Seize this opportunity to take charge of your career and allow your unique story to unfold.

Acknowledgements

The journey of writing *Master Your Career* has been both exhilarating and challenging, and it would not have been possible without the support of many remarkable individuals.

To my family—especially my mother, sister, nieces, and nephews—thank you for your unwavering love, patience, and belief in me. Your constant encouragement has been the bedrock of my strength, keeping me grounded and motivated throughout this process.

I owe a special debt of gratitude to my editors, Leila Summers and Chelsea Friday. Your keen insights, thoughtful feedback, and commitment to excellence have been instrumental in transforming this manuscript into the book it is today. I'm also deeply grateful to the team at Talent Intel Publishing for guiding me through the complexities of the publishing journey with professionalism and care.

To my dear friends and colleagues, thank you for your thought-provoking conversations and creative ideas which have enriched this work in countless ways. My heartfelt gratitude extends especially to my mentors—Garth Towell, Peggy Ament, Maggie Mojapelo, and my mentor coach, Stephanie Martinis—whose guidance and wisdom I have long cherished and drawn upon in my journey as a coach.

This book is also a testament to the wisdom and expertise of many professionals in the field. I would be remiss not to acknowledge the thought leaders and researchers whose work has significantly informed my own. To the experts who generously shared their insights and to my coaching clients whose experiences have shaped many of the ideas in this book—**I'm deeply thankful!**

Lastly, to you, the reader: thank you for picking up *Master Your Career*. It is my sincerest hope that these pages inspire you to navigate your career journey with confidence and purpose.

With deep gratitude,
Gugu Khazi

About the Author

Gugu Khazi is a talent consultant, career coach, and international speaker specialising in personal career management and leadership development. She is passionate about coaching others to find jobs they love and be successful in their chosen careers. Gugu holds a Master's in Business Management, an MSc in Trade Industry & Development, and is a qualified and accredited coach by the International Coaches Federation.

Having grown up in South Africa, she started her career as a social worker before transitioning to work in recruitment and growing her career as a well-respected HR executive holding senior HR leadership roles across international organisations, including Kimberly-Clark and The Coca-Cola Company, in Europe, the Middle East, and Africa.

Gugu uses her extensive experience to coach, write, and speak about how to build a fulfilling career from your passion, talents, interests, and strengths. Her journey in finding a career she loves and helping others manage their careers inspired her to write her two books, *Passion to Careers* and *Master Your Career*.

References

[1] Howard Sasportas, (1985). *The Twelve Houses: Exploring The Houses Of The Horoscope*. Flare Publications.

[2] Sharpe, A. (2024). The psychological contract in a changing work environment. The Work Institute.

[3] De Smet, A., Dowling B., Hancock, B. "The Great Attrition is making hiring harder. Are you searching the right talent pools?" July 13, 2022. https://www.mckinsey.com/capabilities/people-and-organizational-performance/our-insights/the-great-attrition-is-making-hiring-harder-are-you-searching-the-right-talent-pools.

[4] Gallup (2024) Employee Engagement. Accessed 11 October,2024. https://www.gallup.com/394373/indicator-employee-engagement.aspx.

[5] World Economic Forum. "The Future of Jobs Report." 30 April, 2023. https://www.weforum.org/publications/the-future-of-jobs-report-2023/.

[6] McKinsey Global Institute. (2017). *Jobs Lost, Jobs Gained: Workforce Transitions in a Time of Automation*. McKinsey & Company.

[7] Frey, C. B., & Osborne, M. A. (2017). *The Future of Employment: How Susceptible Are Jobs to Computerisation?* Technological Forecasting and Social Change, 114, 254–280

[8] Ferrara B, Pansini M, De Vincenzi C, Buonomo I, Benevene P. (2022, September,28) "Investigating the Role of Remote Working on Employees' Performance and Well-Being: An Evidence-Based Systematic Review." Int J Environ Res Public Health. 19(19):12373. doi: 10.3390/ijerph191912373. PMID: 36231675; PMCID: PMC9566387.

[9] Bloom, N. (2023). "7 Key Findings About Working From Home." *Stanford Report*. Retrieved from https://news.stanford.edu.

[10] Herzberg, Frederick. (1968). "One More Time: How Do You Motivate Employees?" Harvard Business Review, Vol. 81, No. 1, 1968, pp. 87-96. https://hbr.org/2003/01/one-more-time-how-do-you-motivate-employees.

[11] Bersin, J. Bersin J, O'Connor J. and Trougakos, J.P. (2023) Companies and work time reduction centre of Excellence, "Four-Day Work Week: Learnings from Companies at the Forefront of Work-Time Reduction." https://joshbersin.com/the-four-day-work-week/.

[12] Shakespeare, W. & Gaston, C. R. (1902) Shakespeare's As you like it . New York, The Macmillan Company; London, Macmillan & Co., ltd.

[13] Jung, C. G. (1969). *The archetypes and the collective unconscious* (R. F. C. Hull, Trans.). In H. Read, M. Fordham, G. Adler, & W. McGuire (Eds.), *The collected works of C.G. Jung* (Vol. 9, Part 1, 2nd ed.). Princeton University Press. (Original work published 1954).

[14] Myss, C. (2001). *Sacred contracts: Awakening your divine potential.* Harmony Books.

[15] Hillman, James. (1996). The Soul's Code: In Search of Character and Calling. Random House.

[16] Schein, E. H. (1978) Career Dynamics: Matching Individual and Organisational Needs. Reading, MA.: Addison-Wesley.

[17] Sullivan, S.E. and Crocitto, M. (2007), The developmental theories: a critical examination of their continuing impact on careers research, in Peiperl, M. and Gunz, H. (Eds), Handbook of Career Studies, Sage Publications, Thousand Oaks, CA, pp. 283-309.

[18] Meijers, F. 1998. The development of a career identity. International Journal for the Advancement of Counselling, 20: 191-207.

[19] Cochran, L. (1997). Career counselling: A narrative approach. Thousand Oaks, CA: Sage.

[20] Linde, C. (1993). Life stories. The creation of coherence. New York: Oxford University Press.

[21] Savickas, M. (2005). The theory and practice of career construction. In S.D. Brown & R.W. Lent (Eds.), Career development and counselling: Putting theory and research to work. (pp. 42 70). Hoboken, NJ: John Wiley & Sons.

[22] Wijers, G., & Meijers, F. (1996). Career guidance in the knowledge society. British Journal of Guidance and Counselling, 24, 185, 198.

[23] Tang, Yi-Yuan. (2017). The Neuroscience of Mindfulness Meditation. 10.1007/978-3-319-46322-3.

[24] Pennebaker, J. W., & Chung, C. K. (2007). Expressive Writing, Emotional Upheavals, and Health. In H. S. Friedman & R. C. Silver (Eds.), Foundations of health psychology (pp. 263–284). Oxford University Press.

[25] Atwater, L.E and Yammarino, F.J. (1997) Self-other rating agreement: A review and model. Research in Personnel and Human Resources Management 15, 1997, pp. 141-164.

[26] Clark, T. Osterwalder, A. & Pigneaur, Y. (2012). Business Model You: A One-Page Method For Reinventing Your Career. New Jersey: John Wiley & Sons.

[27] DeFillippi and Arthur, 1994. *The Boundaryless Career: A Competency-Based Perspective.* Vol. 15, No. 4, Special Issue: The Boundaryless Career (Jul., 1994), pp. 307-324 (18 pages). Accessed 21/03/2024. https://www.jstor.org/stable/i342677.

[28] Lamb, M & Sutherland, M (2010) The components of career capital for knowledge workers in the global economy, The International Journal of Human Resource Management, 21:3, 295-312, DOI: 10.1080/09585190903546839.

[29] Michael R. Meyer, (2010). *Dane Rudhyar's The 12 Astrological houses: the way of creative accomplishment.*

[30] Hornstra, Maaike & Maas, Ineke. (2021). Does the impact of the family increase or decrease over the life course? Sibling similarities in occupational status across different career points. Research in Social Stratification and Mobility. 75. 100643. 10.1016/j.rssm.2021.100643.

[31] DiPrete, T.A. and Eirich, G.M. (2006) 'Cumulative Advantage as a Mechanism for Inequality: A Review of Theoretical and Empirical Developments', Annual Review of Sociology 32(1): 271–97.

[32] Bourdieu, P. (1986) 'The Forms of Capital', in J.G. Richardson (ed.) Handbook for Theory and Research for the Sociology of Education, New York: Greenwood Press.

[33] Ferrer, A. M. (2005). Signalling, inequality and the social structure. Economica, 72(287), 515–529.

[34] Bourdieu, P. (1984). Distinction. A social critique of the judgement of taste [1979]. Cambridge, MA: Harvard University Press.

[35] Fossati F., Wilson, A. & Bonoli G., What Signals Do Employers Use When Hiring? Evidence from a Survey Experiment in the Apprenticeship Market, European Sociological Review, Volume 36, Issue 5, October 2020, Pages 760–779, https://doi.org/10.1093/esr/jcaa020.

36 Ferrer, A. M. (2005). Signalling, inequality and the social structure. Economica, 72(287), 515–529.

37 Bills, D. B. (1988). Educational credentials and hiring decisions: What employers look for in new employees. Research in Social Stratification and Mobility, 7, 71–97.

38 Solon, G., Page, M. E., & Duncan, G. J. (2000). Correlations between neighbouring children in their subsequent educational attainment. Review of Economics and Statistics, 82(3), 383–392.

39 Nicoletti, C., & Rabe, B. (2019). Sibling spillover effects in school achievement. Journal of Applied Econometrics, 34(4), 482–501.

40 Ballarino, G., Cantalini, S., & Panichella, N. (2020). Social origin and compensation patterns over the occupational career in Italy. Acta Sociologica, 64(2), 166–183.

41 Bandura, A. Autobiography. M. G. Lindzey & W. M. Runyan (Eds.), A History of Psychology in Autobiography (Vol. IX). Washington, D.C.: American Psychological Association; 2006.

42 Schein, E. H. (1980). Career anchors: Models for understanding a person's career decisions. In D. O. Mitchell, V. L. M. Orpen, & E. H. Schein (Eds.), Career development: A human resource development perspective* (pp. 38-44). New York, NY: John Wiley & Sons.

43 Schein, E. H. (1990). *Career anchors and job/role planning: The links between career pathing and career development*(Working Paper No. 3192-90). Massachusetts Institute of Technology (MIT), Sloan School of Management.

44 Wrzesniewski, A., LoBuglio, N., Dutton, J. E., & Berg, J. M. (2013). Job crafting and cultivating positive meaning and identity in work. In A. B. Bakker (Ed.), *Advances in positive organizational psychology* (pp. 281–302). Emerald Group Publishing. https://doi.org/10.1108/S2046-410X(2013)0000001015.

45 Schein, E. H. (1978). *Career dynamics: Matching individual and organizational needs.* http://ci.nii.ac.jp/ncid/BA01260066.

46 Schein, E. H. (1978). *Career dynamics: Matching individual and organizational needs.* http://ci.nii.ac.jp/ncid/BA01260066.

47 Freese, C., & Schalk, R. (1996). Implications of differences in psychological contracts for human resource management. *European Journal of Work and Organisational Psychology, 5*(4), 501-509.

48 Feldman, D. C., & Bolino, M., C. (2000). Career patterns of the self-employed: career motivations and career outcomes. Journal of Small Business Management, July 2000, 53-67.

49 Robert Green (2012) Mastery. London. Profile books.

50 Robert Green (2012) *Mastery*. London. Profile books.

51 Howard Sasportas (2007). *The twelve houses: exploring the houses of the horoscope.* London: Flare publications.

52 Marcus Buckingham. (2004). Now Discover Your Strengths: how to develop your talents and those of people you manage. London, Pocket Books.

53 Buckingham, M., & Clifton, D. O. (2001). Now, discover your strengths. New York, Free Press.

54 Gagne, F (2000) *Understanding the Complex Choreography of Talent Development Through DMGT-Based Analysis.* https://bit.ly/3xuZ28y: *accessed on 29/02/2024.*

55 Thorne, K. and Pellant, A. (2006), The Essential Guide to Managing Talent: How Top Companies Recruit, Train and Retain the Best Employees, Kogan Page, London.

56 Marcus Buckingham (2004) Now discover your strengths: how to develop the talents and those of the people you manage

[57] Marcus Buckingham, (2015). *Standout 2.0: assess your strengths, find your edge, win at work.*

[58] Erikson, E. H. (1959). *Identity and the Life Cycle.* New York: International Universities Press.

[59] Chamarro-Premuzic T. (2017). The Talent Delusion, why data not intuition is the key to unlocking Human Potential. St Yves: Clays Ltd.

[60] Cartwright, S., and C. L. Cooper (1997). Managing Workplace Stress Thousand Oaks, CA: Sage.

[61] Duchon, D., & Plowman, D.A. (2005). Nurturing the spirit at work: Impact on work unit performance. *The Leadership Quarterly*, 16(5), 807–833. https://doi.org/10.1016/j.leaqua.2005.07.008.

[62] Vaill, 1998. P. Vaill, Spirited leading and learning, Jossey-Bass, San Francisco (1998).

[63] Shamir, 1991. B. Shamir, Meaning, self and motivation in organisations, Organization Studies 12 (1991) (3), pp. 405–424.

[64] Wrzesniewski, 2003 • A. Wrzesniewski, Finding positive meaning in work. In: K. S. Cameron, J. E. Dutton and R. E. Quinn, Editors, Positive organizational scholarship, Berrett-Koehler, San Francisco (2003), pp. 296–308.

[65] Lerner, M., . (1997). The politics of meaning. Reading: Addison-Wesley.

[66] J. Pfeffer, Business and the spirit: Management practices that sustain values. In: R. A. Giacalone and C. L. Jurkiewics, Editors, The handbook of workplace spirituality and organizational performance, M. E. Sharpe, New York (2003), pp. 29–45.

[67] L. W. Fry, Toward a theory of spiritual leadership, *The Leadership Quarterly* 14 (2003), pp. 693–727.

[68] Ashmos D. and D. Duchon (2000), Spirituality at work: A conceptualization and measure, *Journal of Management Inquiry* **9** (2000) (2), pp. 134–145.

[69] Dutton & Heaphy, 2003. Dutton, J. E. and Heaphy E. D. (2003), The power of high-quality connections. In: K. S. Cameron, J. E. Dutton and R. E. Quinn, Editors, Positive organizational scholarship, Berrett-Koehler Publishers, Inc., San Francisco (2003), pp. 263–278.

[70] Weisbord, M. R. (1991). *Productive workplaces: Organizing and managing for dignity, meaning, and community.* Jossey-Bass.

[71] Pfeffer, J. (2003). Business and the spirit: Management practices that sustain values. In R. A. Giacalone & C. L. Jurkiewicz (Eds.), Handbook of workplace spirituality and organisational performance (pp. 29-45). M. E. Sharpe.

[72] Ryff, C. D., Boylan, J. M., & Kirsch, J. A. (2021). *Eudaimonic and hedonic well-being: An integrative perspective with linkages to sociodemographic factors and health.* In M. T. Lee, L. D. Kubzansky, & T. J. VanderWeele (Eds.), *Measuring well-being: Interdisciplinary perspectives from the social sciences and the humanities* (pp. 92–135). Oxford University Press. https://doi.org/10.1093/oso/9780197512531.003.0005.

[73] American Psychological Association. (2020). *Stress in America™ 2020: A national mental health crisis.* https://www.apa.org/news/press/releases/stress/2020/report.

[74] Wooll, M. (2022) Workplace stress: Think it isn't getting to you? Think again. Betterup.com. https://www.betterup.com/blog/effects-of-workplace-stress.

[75] Sonnentag, Sabine; Tay, Louis; Nesher Shoshan, Hadar (2023): A review on health and well-being at work: More than stressors and strains, Personnel Psychology, ISSN 1744-6570, Wiley, Hoboken, NJ, Vol. 76, Iss. 2, pp. 473-510, https://doi.org/10.1111/peps.12572

76 Seibert, Scott & Kraimer, Maria & Heslin, Peter. (2016). Developing career resilience and adaptability. Organizational Dynamics. 45. 10.1016/j.orgdyn.2016.07.009.

77 Coleman, James S. (1988) "Social Capital in the Creation of Human Capital." American Journal of Sociology, vol. 94, no. 1, pp. S95–120. JSTOR, http://www.jstor.org/stable/2780243. Accessed 7 Sept. 2024.

78 Porter, C. M., Woo, S. E., Alonso, N. A., & Snyder, G. P. (2023). Why do people network? Professional networking motives and their implications for networking behavior and career success. Journal of Vocational Behavior.

79 Wolff, Hans-Georg & Moser, Klaus. (2009). Effects of Networking on Career Success: A Longitudinal Study. The Journal of applied psychology. 94. 196-206. 10.1037/a0013350.

80 Michael/Yukl 1993; Forret/ Dougherty 2001, 2004; Wolff/Moser 2009, 2010; Macintosh/Krush 2017.

81 Michael/Yukl 1993; Forret/ Dougherty 2001, 2004; Wolff/Moser 2009, 2010; Macintosh/Krush 2017.

82 Scott E. Seibert, Maria L. Kraimer, Peter A. Heslin. (2016). *Developing Career resilience and adaptability. Organizational Dynamics (2016) 45, 245 – 257.*

83 Seibert, S. E., Kraimer, M. L., & Heslin, P. A. (2016). Developing career resilience and adaptability. Organizational Dynamics, 45(3), 245-257.

84 Dweck, C. (2017). Mindset-updated edition: Changing the way you think to fulfil your potential. Hachette UK.

85 Seibert, Scott & Kraimer, Maria & Heslin, Peter. (2016). Developing career resilience and adaptability. Organizational Dynamics. 45. 10.1016/j.orgdyn.2016.07.009.

[86] Arthur,M.B., and Rousseau,D.M. (1996). *The Boundaryless Career: A new Employment Principle for a new Organizational Era,* Oxford University Press,New York, NY.

[87] Hall,D.T.(2002).*Careers in and out of organisations,* Sage Publications,Thousand Oaks, CA.

[88] Super, D. E. (1980). A Life-Span, Life-Space Approach to Career Development. Journal of Vocational Behavior, 16, 282-298.

[89] Sullivan,S.E. and Baruch,Y. (2009)."Advances in Career Theory and Research: A Critical Review and Agenda for Future Exploration",*Journal of Management,* 35(6),1542-1571.

[90] Wanberg, C. R., & Kammeyer-Mueller, J. (2008). A self-regulatory perspective on navigating career transitions. In R. Kanfer, G. Chen, & R. D. Pritchard (Eds.), Work motivation: Past, present, and future (pp. 433–469). Routledge/Taylor & Francis Group.

[91] Savickas, M. L., & Porfeli, E. J. (2012). Career Adapt-Abilities Scale: Construction, reliability, and measurement equivalence across 13 countries. Journal of Vocational Behavior, 80(3), 661–673. https://doi.org/10.1016/j.jvb.2012.01.011.

[92] Savickas, M. L., & Porfeli, E. J. (2012). Career Adapt-Abilities Scale: Construction, reliability, and measurement equivalence across 13 countries. *Journal of Vocational Behavior,* 80(3), 661-673. https://doi.org/10.1016/j.jvb.2012.01.011.

[93] Stoltz, K. B., Wolff, L. A., Monroe, A. E., Farris, H. R., & Mzahreh, L. G. (2013). Adlerian lifestyle, stress coping, and career adaptability: Relationships and dimensions. *Career Development Quarterly, 61,* 194-209. doi:10.1002/j.2161-0045.2013.00049.

[94] Ibarra, H. (2004). *Working identity: Unconventional strategies for reinventing your career.* Harvard Business Press.

95 Hatano, K., Sugimura, K., & Mizokami, S. (2014). Identity development and well-being among adolescents: Trajectories of identity processes and the role of relationships. *Developmental Psychology, 58*(5), 977–989. https://doi.org/10.1037/dev0001326.

96 Mussagulova, A., Chng, S., Goh, Z. A. G., Tang, C. J., & Jayasekara, D. N. (2023). When is a career transition successful? A systematic literature review and outlook (1980–2022). *Frontiers in Psychology, 14*, 1141202.

97 Meca A, Sabet RF, Farrelly CM, Benitez CG, Schwartz SJ, Gonzales-Backen M, Lorenzo-Blanco EI, Unger JB, Zamboanga BL, Baezconde-Garbanati L, Picariello S, Des Rosiers SE, Soto DW, Pattarroyo M, Villamar JA, Lizzi KM. Personal and cultural identity development in recently immigrated Hispanic adolescents: Links with psychosocial functioning. Cultur Divers Ethnic Minor Psychol. 2017 Jul;23(3):348-361. doi: 10.1037/cdp0000129. Epub 2017 Feb 16. PMID: 28206778; PMCID: PMC5491363.

98 Buckingham, M., & Clifton, D. O. (2020). *Now, discover your strengths: The revolutionary Gallup program that shows you how to develop your unique talents and strengths* (2nd ed.). Free Press.

99 Arthur, M. B., & Rousseau, D. M. (Eds.). (1996). *The boundaryless career: A new employment principle for a new organizational era.* Oxford University Press.

100 Hall, Douglas & Yip, Jeffrey & Doiron, Kathryn. (2018). Protean Careers at Work: Self-Direction and Values Orientation in Psychological Success. Annual Review of Organizational Psychology and Organizational Behavior. 5. 10.1146/annurev-orgpsych-032117-104631.

101 Savickas, M. L. (2005). Career Construction Theory and Practice. In Career Development and Counseling: Putting Theory and Research to Work. Wiley.

[102] Steger, M. F. (2017). Creating Meaning and Purpose at Work. In The Wiley Blackwell Handbook of the Psychology of Positivity and Strengths-Based Approaches at Work. Wiley.

[103] Frankl, V. E. (1992). Man's search for meaning: An introduction to logotherapy (4th ed.) (I. Lasch, Trans.). Beacon Press.

[104] Bailey, C., & Madden, A. (2016). "What makes work meaningful—or meaningless." *MIT Sloan Management Review, 57*(4), 52-61.

[105] Bailey, C., & Madden, A. (2016). What makes work meaningful—Or meaningless. *MIT Sloan Management Review, 57*(4), 52-61.

[106] Catherine Bailey and Adrienne Madden (2016), What makes work meaningful or meaningless . downloaded on 3/1/2024. https://sloanreview.mit.edu/article/what-makes-work-meaningful-or-meaningless/.

[107] Adapted from Brooks, Mel, and Thomas Meehan. The Producers: A New Musical. Original Broadway production, April 19, 2001.

[108] A. Hirchi and D Spurk . 2021. Striving for success: Towards a refined understanding and measurement of ambition. Journal of Vocational Behavior 127 (2021) 103577. https://shorturl.at/gis16 downloaded 9 January 2023.

[109] Barrick, M. R., Mount, M. K., & Li, N. (2013). The theory of purposeful work behavior: The role of personality, higher-order goals, and job characteristics. Academy of Management Review, 38(1), 132–153. https://doi.org/10.5465/amr.2010.0479.

[110] Judge, T. A., & Kammeyer-Mueller, J. D. (2012). On the value of aiming high: The causes and consequences of ambition. Journal of Applied Psychology, 97(4), 758–775. https://doi.org/10.1037/A0028084.

[111] Cheng, J.-W., Chiu, W.-L., Chang, Y.-Y., and Johnstone, S. (2014). Do you put your best foot forward? Interactive effects of task performance and impression management tactics on career outcomes. *J. Psychol.* 148, 621–640. doi: 10.1080/00223980.2013.818929.

[112] Gorbatov, S., Khapova, S. N., & Lysova, E. I. (2019). Get noticed to get ahead: The impact of personal branding on career success. *Frontiers in Psychology, 10,* Article 2662. https://doi.org/10.3389/fpsyg.2019.02662.

[113] Hunter, E. G., & Rowles, G. D. (2005). *Leaving a legacy: Toward typology. Journal of Aging Studies,* 19(3), 327-347.

[114] Kelley, J. (2015). *How to stop screwing yourself over* [Video]. TEDx Talks. 12 Jun 2011. https://www.youtube.com/watch?v=Lp7E973zozc.

[115] Lee, Harper. (2006). To kill a mockingbird. New York:Harper Perennial Modern Classics.

[116] Maslow, A. H. (1943). Self-actualization and the hierarchy of needs. In *A theory of human motivation.* Psychological Review, 50(4), 370-396. https://doi.org/10.1037/h0054346.

[117] Schlitz, Marilyn & Vieten, Cassandra & Miller, Elizabeth. (2010). Worldview Transformation and the Development of Social Consciousness. Journal of Consciousness Studies. 17. 18-36.

[118] Tams, S. and Marshall, J.(2011). Responsible careers: Systemic reflexivity in shifting landscapes, Human Relations, 64(1): 109-131.

[119] Tams, S. and Marshall, J.,(2011). Responsible careers: Systemic reflexivity in shifting landscapes. Human Relations, 64 (1), 109131.

[120] Tams, S. & Marshall, J., (2011). Responsible careers: systemic reflexivity in shifting landscapes. Human Relations, 64(1), pp. 109-131.

[121] Weinstein, M. (Producer), & Brooks, M. (Writer). (2001). *The producers: A new musical* [Theatrical play]. Roger Berlind, & Kevin McCollum; Mel Brooks.

122 Ruhyar, D. ((2010) The 12 astrological houses: The way of creative accomplishment. California, Khaldea.com.

123 Vough, H. C., Bataille, C. D., Noh, S. C., & Lee, M. D. (2015). Going off script: How managers make sense of the ending of their careers. Journal Of Management Studies, 52(3), 414-440. doi:10.1111/joms.12126.

124 Shakespeare, William, 1564-1616 author. (1954). The tragedy of Hamlet, Prince of Denmark. [London]:The Folio Society.

125 Miller, A. (2000). *Death of a salesman*. Penguin Classics.

126 Campbell, J. (2008). *The Hero with a Thousand Faces* (3rd ed.). New World Library.

127 Myss, C. (2002). Sacred Contracts: Awakening Your Divine Potential. New York: Harmony Books.

128 Myss, C (2002) Sacred Contract: Awakening your Divine Potential. New York: Harmony Books.

129 Hogshead, Sally. (2010). Fascinate: How to Make Your Brand Impossible to Resist. Harper Business.

130 https://www.brandonhall.com/blogs/empowering-employees-to-take-ownership-of-their-careers/.

131 https://www.ge.com/news/reports/developing-skills-and-careers.

132 https://www.thecareercoach.com/2023/01/own-your-career-at-facebook.

133 https://careers.microsoft.com/us/en/careergrowth.

134 https://www.aboutamazon.com/news/workplace/own-your-career.

135 https://www2.deloitte.com/us/en/pages/careers/articles/career-ownership-at-deloitte.html.

[136] S. Haase. J. Francis-Smythe (2007) . Career competencies - a new approach to successful individual career Development. Eprints.worc.ac.uk.

[137] Frrier, A.', Sels L., & Stynen, D, (2009). Career mobility at the intersection between agent and structure: A conceptual model. Journal of occupational and organisational psychology, 82(4), 739-759.doi:10.1348/096317909X470933.

[138] Kuijpers, MACT, Schyns, B. & Scheerens, J. (2006). Career Competencies for career success, Career Development Quarterly, 55(2), 168.

[139] Akkermans, J., Brenninkmeijer, V., Huibers, M., & Blonk, R. W. B. (2013). Competencies for the contemporary career: Development and preliminary validation of the Career Competencies Questionnaire. Journal of Career Development, 40(3), 245–267. https://doi.org/10.1177/0894845312467501.

[140] Akkermans, J., Brenninkmeijer, V., Huibers, M., & Blonk, R. W. B. (2013). Competencies for the contemporary career: Development and preliminary validation of the Career Competencies Questionnaire. *Journal of Career Development*, 40(3), 245-267. https://doi.org/10.1177/0894845312467501.

[141] Kuijpers, Marinka & Schyns, Birgit & Scheerens, Jaap. (2006). Career Competencies for Career Success. Career Development Quarterly. 55. 10.1002/j.2161-0045.2006.tb00011.x.

[142] Jos Akkermans, Veerle Brenninkmeijer, Marthe Huiber, and Roland W. B. Blonk; Competencies for the Contemporary Career: Development and Preliminary Validation of the Career Competencies Questionnaire.

www.ingramcontent.com/pod-product-compliance
Lightning Source LLC
Chambersburg PA
CBHW051435050726
47593CB00005B/1787